DIE TO LIVE

DIE TO LIVE

Maharaj Charan Singh
Answers Questions on Meditation

RADHA SOAMI SATSANG BEAS
PUNJAB, INDIA

Published by
S.L. Sondhi, Secretary
Radha Soami Satsang Beas
P.O. Dera Baba Jaimal Singh
Dist. Amritsar 143204
Punjab, India

First edition	1979	7,500 copies
Second edition	1980	10,000 copies
Third edition	1983	7,000 copies
Fourth edition	1988	7,000 copies

(Revised as directed by the author)

Phototypeset by Align Graphics, 9E Gopala Tower, Rajendra Place, New Delhi-110008 and printed at Surya Print Process, 9/54 Kirti Nagar, Industrial Area, New Delhi-110015.

The Master answering questions in the International Guest House at Dera.

CONTENTS

PREFACE

"Die to LIVE and LIVE forever," we are told by our Master. Satsangis, his initiates, daily die to this world in their meditation. Daily they rehearse for that inevitable final departure. But now, with their Master always with them, they travel those regions of Light and Sound through the Celestial Spheres of the creation within, back to the level of the Father, back to their Divine Source. Through meditation, and with the grace of the Master, the purpose of human birth is fulfilled, and the soul, liberated for eternity, is taken back to Him for whom it has been yearning since its separation. Hence, the theme for all Saints and Masters is, attend to meditation.

This book, then, has its conception in our Master's exhortation to attend to meditation. Its intent is to explain what meditation is, and to dispel any doubts, questions, and apprehensions a seeker may have regarding meditation. It states clearly the Master's teachings about how we must conduct our lives to make meditation our foremost and primary concern.

The sequence of the book is designed to guide the disciple through all phases of meditation: from managing one's daily activities to creating the right atmosphere for meditation; from actually attending to the practice, to realizing and understanding the effects of meditation.

Then the Master gives us encouragement as we follow the Path. He tells us that controlling the mind, as each disciple quickly becomes aware, is no small task. To withdraw one's consciousness and reach back to the level of the Father is the most difficult and the highest of all goals to achieve. So the Master comforts us by providing insight into our plight. He gives a perspective to our journey as he guides us with His grace at every step on our Path Homeward.

The original manuscript for this much needed and highly appreciated work was brought into being by Arnold Howard of the United States. The immense task of gathering, accurately transcribing, organizing and typing the material taken from the past decade of tapes of the evening meetings held at the International Guest House at the Dera in India was commendably carried out.

The manuscript was then reorganized, additionally edited, and prepared for publication in its present form by Dr. James Said and his wife, Connie, of U.S.A. More recorded material was included by Mr. Virendra Kumar Sethi of Indore and Miss Anthea Guinness of U.S.A. Subsequently, the entire manuscript was thoroughly checked by Professor M.S. Bhatnagar and Miss Louise Hilger at the Dera, and the latter saw the volume through the press.

The format for this book, consisting entirely of questions from disciples regarding meditation, followed by Master's answers, has been designed in an attempt to retain the fresh and spontaneous atmosphere of the meetings, as well as the profoundly and lucidly beautiful truths spoken by the Master.

To all those involved with bringing this work to completion, we are deeply grateful.

Radha Soami Satsang Beas
Punjab, India S.L. Sondhi
August 1, 1978 *Secretary*

1

Teachings of the Saints

Teachings of the Saints

Every Saint has the same message to give, and the same teachings to impart. No Saint, no perfect Master, comes into this world to create a religion, to divide people, to set one nation against another or one religion against another. They come only to show us the Way which leads us back to our original Home. After a Master departs, people generally turn to rites and rituals, and give his lofty teachings the form of an organized religion. Then we become bigoted, we start fighting and quarreling with one another, and the real teachings of the Saint are soon forgotten.

Saints do not come into the world of their own will; they are always appointed and sent by the Father. By themselves, neither do they desire to preach, nor do they want to initiate anybody. Whenever the Lord wishes, He Himself sends a Master to collect His marked souls, the souls which He has allotted to him. Christ speaks of "the Father which hath sent me," and says, "For I came down from heaven, not to do mine own will, but the will of Him that sent me."[1] Guru Arjan, speaking about the coming of Saints to this world, says:

> They are beyond both birth and death.
> They, the compassionate and merciful ones,
> Come to grant new life and kindle devotion,
> And enable the soul to meet the Lord.[2]

Saints may be born in the East or the West, in any country, caste or creed—it makes no difference. They come on a mission of mercy to save us from the sufferings of this world. The purpose of every Mystic in coming to this world is to save His chosen souls, to put them on the Path to God-realization, to give them comfort, to give them rest, and to take them back to their eternal Home, to the level of the Father. For unless we reach the level of the Father, we cannot attain everlasting peace. The Master puts his disciples on the spiritual Path and gives them certain teachings and guidelines regarding their spiritual practice and their conduct in the world.

Worldly Responsibilities

Saints tell us that in order to realize God, we do not need to undertake any external formalities, such as fasts, pilgrimages, and adopting a particular type of dress or hair style; nor do they advocate that we withdraw from society or run away from worldly responsibilities. Namdev says, "By going to forests and becoming a hermit, thou escapest not desire, attachment and delusion."[3]

We have to do our duty as a citizen, as a husband, a wife, a son, a brother, a friend. But we should not be so obsessed by these duties and relationships that we forget the real purpose of our life, our real destination. We have to keep our goal in view and follow the Path which leads us back to our Home. But the Saints say that, along with spiritual practice, we must also continue to fulfill our worldly responsibilities.

Temple of the Living God

Saints do not ask us to go to forests or mountains, churches or synagogues to worship the Lord, because He is not to be found outside. He is within our body. St. Paul explains that the body is the temple of the living God:

> And what agreement hath the temple of God with idols? for ye are the temple of the living God; as God hath said, I will dwell in them, and walk in them; and I will be their God, and they shall be my people.[4]

> Know ye not that ye are the temple of God, and that the Spirit of God dwelleth in you?... for the temple of God is holy, which temple ye are.[5]

Since the Lord is within us, we must seek Him within this "temple" of the body. Guru Amar Das says:

> Within the body He Himself resides,
> Yet He cannot be seen, that Invisible One.
> Under the sway of mind,
> Fools know not the truth,
> And search for Him outside.[6]

Every Saint, every Master, has tried to explain to us that this body is the temple of the living God. Guru Amar Das says,"This body is truly the *Hari mandir.*"[7] *Hari* means Lord, *mandir* means the place where the Lord resides. Indian sages refer to it as *nar Naraini-deh,* meaning the human body, in which the Lord is located, and in which our soul can become the Lord again by merging back into Him.

Each Saint teaches us the simple truth that the Lord is within every one of us; and since He is within every one of us, naturally we have to seek Him within. The human body is a laboratory in which we have to undertake research for reunion with Him, for it is only when we have been given this precious human form that we can realize God within ourselves.

Human Birth is Invaluable

The human form is a great blessing. It has been called the "top of the creation" by Muslim Saints, and Christ describes it as superior to all other forms of creation. In fact, in the Bible we read that man is made in the image of God, and Jesus, when he replies to the accusation that he is blaspheming by claiming to be the Son of God, reminds us that all men are God:

> Jesus answered them, Is it not written in your law, I said, Ye are gods?[8]

This form is granted to us only after many births in the lower species. Soami Ji says, "After drifting through millions of births, at last you've obtained this precious human form."[9] Emphasizing the great privilege of human birth, Guru Arjan says we should make use of this rare chance to meet the Lord:

> Many lives have you had as insects and worms,
> And many lives as elephants, fish and deer;
> In many lives were you born a snake or a bird,
> And countless times, you lived as a tree.
> After aeons you've obtained the glory
> of human birth:
> Now it's your chance—meet the Lord![10]

Kabir also stresses the importance of the human form and the opportunity it offers for returning to the Lord: just as a ripe fruit once fallen from its branch can never go back again, so also, once wasted, the human form is difficult to get again.

This form is bestowed upon us for the sole purpose of attaining God-realization. It is the only exit with which the Lord has provided us to escape from this vast prisonhouse of the phenomenal world. But we get so deeply engrossed in worldly activities and sensual pleasures that we completely ignore the purpose of our incarnation; we chase the shadow, but lose the substance.

The Saints have also compared this body to the top rung of a ladder. If we try hard, we may succeed in stepping onto the "roof," the realm of everlasting peace and bliss within. Otherwise, we shall slip and fall into the turbulent ocean of the world once more. It is only in the human birth, in other words, that we have the possibility of attaining liberation. For it is as a human being alone that we can meet a perfect Master, be told about the Path within, and follow the practice of Shabd or Word, which leads to our ultimate Goal.

The True Name

We all talk of the Lord's Name, but fail to distinguish between the spoken or written word, and the true Word, which can neither be spoken nor written. Names like Ram, Rahim, Allah, Wahiguru, Radhasoami, Jehovah or Khuda can be spoken and written, and their time and history can be traced. But the true Name of the Lord, to which all Saints refer, existed before time began. The whole Universe, including time and space, was created by that Name, out of the Name. Guru Amar Das says, "Everything that we see in this world was created by the Name."[11]

This Creative Power has been referred to by Indian Saints as Shabd (Word), Nam (Name), Dhun (Sound), Akash Bani (Voice from the Heavens), Bani (Sound, Voice); Muslim Saints have called it Kalma (Word), Kun (Command), Bang-i-Ilahi (Voice of God), Nada-i-Asmani (Voice from the Heavens); and in the Bible, the same Power is referred to variously as the Word or Logos, the Holy Ghost, the Spirit, the Comforter, the Living Water.[12]

All the Saints say that God and the Word are one and the same, and that the Word created the entire Universe. In the Bible it says:

> In the beginning was the Word, and the Word was with God, and the Word was God. The same was in the beginning with God. All things were made by Him; and without Him was not anything made that was made.[13]

Guru Nanak expresses the same truth when he says:

> The Word created the earth,
> The Word created the sky,
> Through the Word emanated light.
> The entire world is sustained by the Word;
> The Word dwells in each and every being.

There is no difference between that Word, or Name of the Lord, and the Lord Himself. Talking of this Name, Muinuddin Chishti says, "Between the Name and the Named One, difference there is none." It is this Name which is capable of detaching the mind from the sensual pleasures and giving it spiritual bliss, and of leading the soul to salvation. It is in the form of this Word that the Lord pervades the entire creation.

That Name or Word is not to be found in books or scriptures—they only glorify it. But the Name itself is within us. Saints and sages who, in their time, realized God, have recorded in the scriptural texts their experiences and the particulars of the Path, for our guidance. From them, we come to know the difficulties on the Path and obtain a clear conception of the ideal; but we cannot realize God by merely reading books.

The important point is to realize the difference between the name of a thing and the thing itself: we should not confuse the doctor's prescription with the medicine, nor think that repetition of the word "food" will satisfy hunger. Mere reading of the scriptures or listening to the teachings of Saints is not enough. We must put the teachings into practice and travel the Path ourselves.

The Lord and The Soul

It is only common logic that if the Lord is one and He is within every one of us and we have to seek Him within our body, the Path leading to that destination, to our Home, cannot be but one. It is impossible even to think that for Christians there is one path leading to the Lord's house, and for Hindus or Sikhs or Muslims there is a different path leading to Him. There may be a difference in our interpretation, in our understanding, but there cannot be two paths leading to Him. If we seek Him within, we will find the same Path, the Path of Sound and Light. But if we search for Him outside, we find that everybody has his own path, leading perhaps nowhere.

The soul is the essence of the Lord, a drop of the Divine Ocean. In the beginning, it separated from its Source and descended into this world of misery and suffering. Forgetting its Origin, the soul took the mind as its guide and companion. But the mind itself is under the sway of the senses. Whatever the senses desire, the mind does their bidding and dances to their tune. And whatever deeds the mind commits under their influence, the soul, itself pure and stainless, must reap the fruits and suffer the consequences. Soami Ji, addressing the soul, says:

> O soul, you are miserable, this I know.
> You've been suffering since the day
> You separated from the Word
> And made friends with mind.
> In the company of the reckless mind,
> You remain bound by the body
> And entrapped by sense pleasures.[14]

The Saints well know our pitiful condition. They know that we live in delusion. So they come to reveal the true plight of the world. They tell us this is all the Lord's play, that He has created everything. This play is set on a dream stage where nothing is real. Yet we come into this play and, having forgotten our true heritage, think this is our home, as we weep, cry and laugh with one another. But when our karmic debts for this life have been paid, we depart like the patrons of an inn. We leave one another's company after only a brief stay, having no lasting relationship with anyone at all.

Mind and Senses

The Saints tell us that the mind is the greatest and the only obstacle in the way of God-realization. It is egocentered, pleasure-loving and vain. It forgets that its existence in the world is no more than a bubble that may burst at any minute, and that the body enclosing it will eventually perish. Its outward and downward tendencies keep it tied to the transient, evanescent objects of the world. Its actions, whether good or bad, only result in keeping the soul in the perpetual round of birth and rebirth.

Mind is the deadliest of foes, but the most useful of servants. When it turns wild and gets out of control, it heads for certain destruction. When properly awakened and controlled, there is no limit to what the mind can do. As a step towards liberation, Soami Ji calls upon us to "turn the hostile mind into a friend."[15]

In order to gain mastery over it, we have to study its nature. Relentlessly and restlessly, the mind tries to experience and enjoy everything. But nothing seems to satisfy its ravenous hunger. The acquisition of wealth and power gives rise to endless desires. Our possessions become the master, instead of being our slave. The passions gradually forge heavy chains around us, bind us to the baser things of the world and invariably harden our heart.

Though the mind is fond of pleasures, no single pleasure ever pleases it for all time. It gives up one pleasure as soon as it gets or sees a better one. Unless, therefore, it comes across something vastly superior to the pleasures it already has, it cannot be successfully weaned away from them. Otherwise, if it should become detached and find nothing to attach itself to, it would react and rebound, and go back to its pleasures and enjoyments with redoubled vigor.

There is no end to our desires and cravings, and we have to return to this world in order to fulfill them. Barely do we leave one body before another stands ready for us. We are hardly rid of one fetter when a tighter one is fastened onto us. Ceaselessly are we goaded by the invisible angels of Death. What sufferings do we not go through, what rapids and whirlpools do we not face, what lashings of the mighty waves do we not encounter, what tempestuous storms and raging gales do we not have to struggle against. And every succeeding link of the chain of our lives is stronger than the one that preceded it.

The realization of the deception of this drama comes only when we wake up—at the time of our death. The moment death closes upon us, everything of this world—friends and relations, wealth and possessions, name and fame, caste and creed—is left behind. Only then do we realize that our time has just been wasted in illusion, in trying to make ours that which can never become ours. We nonetheless persist in taking this illusion as the ultimate reality. We continue to feel miserable and unhappy because our soul, being separated from the Father, is perpetually yearning for its own Source.

The Saints constantly tell us that there is no lasting peace and happiness outside in this world. Instead of trying to find it outside, they say we must try to find that peace and happiness within ourself. It is not love for the transient, but love for the Eternal that will be our real succor, our true sustenance, for it alone will bring us lasting peace, both here and beyond.

Karma and Transmigration

Many Saints describe this world as a field of karmas to which the soul has to return again and again, to reap the fruits of its past actions.

> As one sows, so shall he reap;
> Such is the field of karma.[16]
>
> —*Guru Arjan*

> If you plant a cactus,
> How will you reap mangoes?
>
> —*Kabir*

> The world is based on the law of karma:
> Whatever actions one performs,
> He has to taste the fruits thereof.
>
> —*Tulsi Das*

Similarly, in the Bible it says, "Whatsoever a man soweth, that shall he also reap."[17]

Deeds, whether good or bad, cannot release the soul from its captivity. They only bring it back to this world, into the realm of birth and death. We are brought back into those forms where we can best fulfill the results of our actions, our karmas, all the while the soul continues to suffer the anguish of separation from the Lord. While we are completing those karmas, we are also continually making new karma, and as a result, we continue to come and go, always remaining in the prisonhouse of this world.

As Christ tells us in the Bible, whatever sins we commit, they become our master and we become their slave:

> Verily, verily, I say unto you, Whosoever committeth sin is the servant of sin. And the servant abideth not in the house for ever: but the Son abideth ever.[18]

A slave has no option before the master, he has to do whatever his master commands. Christ is explaining that we have no choice now, because the sins we have committed have become our master and we have become their slave. We have to go where our master commands us to go: we shift from house to house, from body to body, in the endless cycle of transmigration.

This whole world of transmigration has been called the prison of eighty-four lakh species, the jail of *chaurasi.** Indian mystics have used the word prison or jail, and Christ also uses the same word:

> Agree with thine adversary quickly, whiles thou art in the way with him; lest at any time the adversary deliver thee to the judge, and the judge deliver thee to the officer, and thou be cast into prison.
>
> Verily I say unto thee, Thou shalt by no means come out thence, till thou hast paid the uttermost farthing.[19]

Christ means that we cannot escape from this prison of birth and death until we have cleared all our karmas, all the seeds that we have sown, because even a little thing can pull us back to this world. That is why he suggests that we should ask forgiveness of those we have wronged, while we are still living in this world, while we are "in the way" with them. Otherwise, we will have to face the judgement of our actions, which means that we will be thrown into the prison once more—for whether we come as a debtor or as a creditor, we cannot gain release until our entire account is cleared.

* Literally, eighty-four. The eighty-four lakh (84 hundred thousand) species into which the soul may incarnate; the wheel of transmigration of the soul.

Escape from *chaurasi*, the wheel of eighty-four, is possible only when the soul merges back into the Lord. We can only be one with the Father when we have been able to clear every action and sin we have committed in our past lives. With each birth we come carrying the weight of previous karmas. Until our entire karmic account is cleared, until all our sins are washed, though the Lord is within everyone, the soul can never shine and become whole, it can never become one with Him. To experience and realize that we are of the essence of the Lord, we must "repent," as Christ said. "Repent: for the kingdom of heaven is at hand."[20]

However, to repent truly we must know what we have done; but our past deeds have been completely forgotten, and mere words of being sorry for our past actions are not sufficient to invoke His grace or His forgiveness. We can only repent by worshiping the Father; and worship of the Spirit, the Sound and Light within, is worship of the Father. No other worship pleases the Father.[21] We must attach ourselves to the Spirit, to the Shabd and Nam within, in order to worship the Father, in order to repent for our forgotten sins. This Spirit, although constantly resounding within every one of us, can only be contacted by going within, through the practice of meditation as instructed by the Master.

Journey of the Soul

Our spiritual journey starts from the soles of our feet and goes up to the top of our head. In this body, the spiritual Journey has two stages: the first is up to the eye center, and the second is from the eye center to the top of the head.

In our body, the seat of the soul and the mind knotted together is at the eye center, in the wakeful state. From here, our consciousness is spread into the whole world. Even when we close our eyes we are not here, we are never still. Rather we find ourselves thinking about our worldly ambitions and worldly affairs, about our relations or our daily activities. And about whomsoever we are thinking, their forms automatically appear before us. Therefore, by thinking, by contemplating on the forms of the world, our consciousness has spread outward into this world of illusion. Guru Ram Das says:

> Wildly, the mind keeps running in this world
> of illusion;
> It takes not abode in its home, the eye center.[22]

Unless we withdraw our attention to the eye center, we cannot concentrate within and take even the first step of our spiritual journey Homeward.

As Christ mystically expressed it: "Seek, and ye shall find;[23] knock, and it shall be opened unto you."[24] We seek the Path leading to our Home, and once on that Path, we ultimately find the Lord. We finally merge into that One for whom we have been so ardently searching. The first step, then, is to withdraw our consciousness to the eye center. The Lord is within. It is we who have kept our attention focussed outside, in this world. We must knock from outside so that the door leading to our Goal within may be opened. We have to withdraw our consciousness from the world and bring it back to the eye center. Only then can the door be opened.

The eye center, where we come in contact with the Holy Spirit or Voice of God, has also been called by Indian Saints the "tenth door." Guru Amar Das says:

> Stop the mind from running out
> through the nine portals
> And open thou the tenth door,
> Which will lead thee to thy true Home.
> There the Divine Melody ringeth day and night,
> And it is through the instruction of the Master
> That thou canst hear it.[25]

That Spirit, that Shabd and Nam, is within every one of us, forever resounding in resplendent glory. Unless, through meditation, we withdraw to the eye focus, we can never be in touch with that Divine Melody. But having once contacted it, we find that Sound Current so fascinating, so charming and tempting, so captivating, that immediately we become attached to it, and automatically we become detached from the senses.

Christ said,"If therefore thine eye be single, thy whole body shall be full of light."[26] When we are able to open that single eye, to withdraw our consciousness to the eye center and open the door to the kingdom within this temple, we shall see that Light and hear that Divine Sound, about which Namdev says:

> Where the effulgent light is seen,
> there rings the boundless Shabd...
> The Unstruck Melody has the lucency
> of the sun.[27]

And with the help of that Light and Sound, we ascertain the direction of our Home and travel the Path leading there. By seeing that Light and hearing that Sound we are able to truly repent for all our past sins, thus releasing the soul from the snares of the mind. Then only can the soul once again become whole and shine in its own pristine brilliance; then only are we able to go back to the level of the Father, to become absorbed in the Ocean of absolute bliss and everlasting peace.

When we are able to withdraw our consciousness to the eye center, our mind, just like a needle drawn to a magnet, catches that Sound, that Melody within. When we are attached to that Melody, automatically we are detached from the senses. Now the tendency of the mind is downward, towards the senses. The senses are always pulling our mind down to their level. But when we are able to withdraw our mind to the eye center and attach it to the Holy Ghost, the Spirit within us, that attachment automatically creates detachment.

By austerities, by disciplining the mind, it is impossible to withdraw permanently from the senses, for detachment cannot create attachment in anybody; only attachment can create detachment within us. When our mind is attached to that Divine Music within and it sees that Light within, automatically that attachment creates detachment from the senses and frees the mind. Soami Ji says:

> On hearing the Sound within,
> the mind becomes calm and still.
> Through a million other means,
> the stubborn mind refuses to yield.
> Only on contacting the Shabd within,
> does the mind become docile.[28]

The technique for withdrawing the consciousness to the eye center and joining it to the Word, the Shabd within, is available only from an Adept, a perfect Master. For such is the Lord's design, that though the treasure is within each one of us, it can be obtained only with the help of the Saints and Adepts who have themselves traversed the inner Path. The Maker has placed the key to the treasure in the hands of His beloved devotees, the true Masters, who alone can impart the secret to us.

> The Master alone has the key;
> None else can open the door.[29]
>
> —*Guru Amar Das*

> Without a Master, no one can obtain the Name;
> Such is the law laid down by the lord.[30]
>
> —*Guru Amar Das*

> Let no one be under any illusion:
> Without a Master, none can cross the ocean
> of existence.[31]
>
> —*Guru Arjan*

The Master

Whatever we learn in the world, we have learned from a teacher. Even a child learns how to sit, eat, walk and talk through the guidance of his mother. He then goes to school and learns how to read and write from his schoolteachers; and later, to become a qualified engineer, doctor or technician, he has to undertake a long course of training under the supervision of a specialist in that particular field. Spirituality is a most difficult and intricate subject, where a teacher, a Master, is indispensable. We do not achieve anything in this world without a teacher or a guide. How can we achieve God-realization without a spiritual teacher?

The Master has himself traversed the inner regions and realized the Lord, and he alone can tell us how to follow the Path, and how to succeed in overcoming the many barriers and temptations of the inner journey. Maulana Rum says:

> Seek a Master, for without a Master
> This Journey is fraught with dangers
> and calamities.
> Whosoever treads this Path without a Master
> Is led astray by evil spirits
> And falls into the well of Illusion.
> If you take not the protection of the Master,
> O foolish one,
> Then the call of Satan will lead you astray.

A Master actually means, a living Master. We need a Master because we are not at the level of the Lord. Only somebody at our level can give us the way to go back to the Father; can fill us with His love and devotion; can put us on the Path; can guide us back to the Father. It is necessary to go to a Master because we cannot be at the level of the Father, and the Father in His real form cannot come to our level.

The living Master, however, while being one with the Father, is also at our level. As Christ says:

> He that hath seen me hath seen the Father... Believe me that I am in the Father, and the Father in me.[32]

Guru Arjan expresses the same idea when he says:

> Within me the Father has revealed Himself;
> Father and Son have met and become one.

Says Nanak, when the Father is pleased,
The Father and the Son are dyed in one hue.[33]

And when a disciple asked Jesus how to find the way back to the Lord, Jesus replied:

> I am the way, the truth, and the life: no man cometh unto the Father, but by me.[34]

In other words, it is only through a living Master that we can know the Path and reach the Lord.

The Masters of the past cannot carry out the task of taking us back to the Lord. A dead doctor cannot prescribe for our ailments today, howsoever great he may have been during his lifetime. A dead school-teacher cannot teach us today. We need a living doctor, a living teacher. We are living human beings and only a living human being can speak to us, guide us, teach us and show us the Way.

Jesus also said, "As long as I am in the world, I am the light of the world."[35] He did not say that he was the light of the world for the future and forever. He was the light of the world only for those who came in contact with him when he was living, and others who come after his time have to find another living Savior.

Herein lies the need for a living perfect Master: just as we cannot complete a journey by simply reading a timetable, nor build a house merely by studying books on architecture, similarly we cannot taste that Divine Bliss merely by reading about it. We must learn the technique of going within from a true Master, carry out his instructions with love and devotion, and, in his company, travel the homeward Path.

We are always influenced by the company we keep. The company of good people has a beneficial influence on us, as we try to be like them, but if we keep the company of bad people, we are influenced by their bad thoughts, and we go astray along with them. We need a Master to build that atmosphere of devotion around us, to inspire us to follow the Path and go within.

Word Made Flesh

Our real Master is the Word, the Logos, Shabd, Nam, the Audible Life Stream, or whatever name one may choose to give it. The Master is that Power manifested in human form. We need someone in the human form who has merged himself in the Shabd or Word, who is "Word made flesh," and who can in turn connect us with that Power within; and that someone is the living Master. Soami Ji says:

> Radhasoami, the Supreme Being,
> descended to earth as a man;
> He came as a Master to initiate souls
> into the mystery of Nam.[36]

The relationship of the Master with the Lord is that of a wave with the ocean. Guru Arjan says:

> The Lord and His Servant are one and the same,
> Make no distinction because of human form.
> The Masters are just like waves
> that rise in the ocean
> And merge back into it again.[37]

Waves come from the ocean and merge back into the ocean. Wave and ocean are one. Christ says, "I and my Father are one."[38] He does not say that his image is different from the Father. He is explaining that Saints are waves of the same ocean, that Saints and the Lord are one. Similarly, talking of his Master, Bulleh Shah says:

> The Lord has taken the form of man,
> He has come to awaken the world.

The Master, through initiation, connects the soul of the disciple to the Sound within, and puts him on the Path to the Lord. Initiation is not a ritual nor a ceremony; it is the birth of the soul into the Shabd within. Christ says:

> Verily, verily, I say unto thee, Except a man be born again, he cannot see the Kingdom of God.
>
> Verily, verily, I say unto thee, Except a man be born of Water and of the Spirit, he cannot enter into the kingdom of God.[39]

Here Jesus tells his disciples how to find the Lord within themselves. You must be born again—but not physically. What he means to say is that it is necessary to be baptized or initiated by a living Master who can put us in touch with the Holy Ghost, the Shabd, the Sound Current within. That is being born of the living Water or the Nectar within, and of the Spirit.

This Nectar is contacted at the eye center. Unless we get in touch with that Shabd or Nam within ourselves, we always remain the victims of the mind and senses. Christ advises us to get initiated through the Son of the Father, and thus get in touch with the

Spirit within. That is what he means by being "born again."

> That which is born of the flesh is flesh; and that which is born of the Spirit is Spirit. Marvel not that I said unto thee, Ye must be born again.[40]

The day of our initiation is the day of our spiritual birth. Then, through spiritual practice, we grow and grow to become one with the Lord. As a child grows into a man, so, after initiation, the disciple grows spiritually to become the Father. That is why initiation is referred to as a new birth, being "born again." And unless we take a new birth—that is, get initiation from a living Master—we cannot go back to our Father.

According to Guru Nanak, the cycle of "coming and going," the cycle of transmigration, comes to an end for the disciple who is "born again":

> Birth through the Master
> ended my coming and going.[41]

The Master does not leave or forget the disciple after initiation. He is always with him, guiding and leading him. In his Radiant Form, he helps the disciple at every step, accompanying him throughout the spiritual journey. The Master not only guides and helps during the disciple's lifetime, but stays with him even at the time of his death, and afterwards.

Dying While Living

At the time of initiation; the Master teaches the

disciple the technique of withdrawing his consciousness from the entire body, up to the eye center, where he comes in contact with the Sound Current. The Mystics refer to the process of vacating the body and withdrawing the consciousness to the eye center as "dying while living."

When death comes, our soul withdraws upwards from the soles of the feet and comes to the eye center. Then only does it leave the body. First the feet become cold, then the legs become cold, then the body becomes cold, but the soul is still in the body and sometimes we are still conscious of it. When the soul is able to withdraw up to the eye center, then only is the body without the soul and we die.

By the same process, we have to withdraw our consciousness to the eye center. While living, we have to die; while living, we have to vacate the body and bring the soul current to the point between and behind the eyes. That is "dying while living." Unless we are able to withdraw our consciousness to the eye center and attach it to the Spirit within, we do not die while living. And unless we die while living, we do not get everlasting life. Maulana Rum says:

> Die thou, O friend, before thy death
> If thou desirest to live.

Guru Amar Das expresses the same truth in these words:

> Who dieth while living
> And from death cometh to life again,
> Such a one attaineth salvation.[42]

The essential difference between ordinary death

and dying while living is that the soul's link with the body is not broken. The organs of the body continue to function, and the soul returns to the body at the end of the meditation time. An adept who has perfected the art of dying while living can leave the body and return to it at will. Hence, St. Paul says, "I die daily."[43]

After vacating the body and coming to the eye center, the soul's real journey homeward begins. When the entire life consciousness leaves the lower body and we go through the third eye, we are out of the physical body and we enter the astral world. Without thus dying while living, we cannot go within, get attached to the Holy Spirit and return to the Lord.

Christ refers to the state of dying while living when he says that the dead shall rise from their graves:

> Verily, verily, I say unto you, The hour is coming, and now is, when the dead shall hear the voice of the Son of God: and they that hear shall live ....
> for the hour is coming, in the which all that are in the graves, shall hear his voice, And shall come forth.[44]

The human body has been called a grave by Persian Mystics also. Shams-i-Tabrez says:

> What a blessing it would be
> If you were one night to bring your soul
>   out of the body,
> And, leaving this tomb behind,
> Ascend to the skies within.
> If your soul were to vacate your body,

You would be saved from the sword of Death:
You would enter a Garden
that knows no autumn.

When the attention is functioning below the eyes, we are dead as far as the Lord is concerned; but when it is withdrawn and concentrated at the eye center, we become alive to the Lord, and are dead as far as the world is concerned. Dadu describes that state in these lines:

Die thou, O Dadu, ere
The messengers of death arrive;
What uncommon is there in dying
As others do.

Christ describes this spiritual awakening as the dead coming to life. He says that the dead will rise, the deaf will hear, the blind will see, and the lame will walk,[45] when they see that Light, when they hear that Wind, that Sound within. We are all blind, deaf and lame, as well as spiritually dead; but when that inner eye is opened, we shall really see, hear, become alive, and walk straight on the Path leading back to the Lord. "The dead shall hear the voice of the Son of God: and they that hear shall live."[46]

Before we come to that Realization, we have eyes but see not; we have ears, but hear not.[47] We do not see the Lord. What is a blind man? One who cannot see something that is in his presence. We all know that the Lord is within every one of us, He is in every particle of the creation; but we do not see Him—neither inside nor outside. That is why Mystics call us blind. When that inner eye and that inner ear are open, we see the Light and we hear the Sound, that silent music, which makes the dead rise.

Guru Angad Says:

See without eyes, hear without ears,
Walk without feet, work without hands,
Speak without tongue—
Thus, while living, die,
And realize the Word, O Nanak;
Then alone the Beloved you'll meet.[48]

Maulana Rum expresses himself in almost the same terms when he says:

I fly without wings,
I journey without feet,
Without mouth or teeth, I eat sugar;*
With eyes closed, I behold the inner worlds.

When, by means of concentration with love and devotion, under the directions of a living Master, we finally reach our destination in the highest region and merge with the Lord Himself, then we die to live forever. Prior to that, we are subject to the law of reincarnation and even transmigration into the lower species, depending on the actions and desires we have involved ourselves in, not only in the present life, but in countless previous births.

Thus, when we reach the eye center, we start living; and when we reach our destination, we live forever. Guru Amar Das says:

---

* Divine Nectar.

The entire world is afraid of death.
Through the Master's grace,
Whoever dies while living
Understands the Divine Order.*
O Nanak, who dies such a death
Attains life everlasting.[49]

All Saints have stressed the importance of withdrawing the consciousness to the eye center and going within. They all teach that meditation is but a rehearsal to die, in order to live forever. Their teachings bring out this point very clearly, as indicated by the quotations that follow.

Kabir says he has overcome death by dying while still alive:

The whole world keeps dying after death,
For no one dies the real death.
Kabir has died a death
That will make him never die again.

Maulana Rum expresses the same thought:

O soul, wake up!
Rise above before death overtakes you,
And behold the kingdom
of everlasting peace and bliss.

Saints maintain that the final goal is reached by dying while still alive. The human birth of one who has attained this state is fruitful. Guru Amar Das says:

---

* *Hukam:* Literally, order or command: the word has been used by the saints to mean Shabd or the Creative Power.

O Nanak, one who has died to live,
His coming here is fruitful.[50]

And Paltu says:

All die; without exception
dies the whole world,
But few there be who know how to die.
One who dies while living, O Paltu,
Crosses the ocean of the world with ease.

Bulleh Shah states that "if thou diest before thy death, such a death will bear fruit." And Kabir says it is a rare one who obtains the fruit, by dying while living:

Tall is that tree,
Its fruit is in the skies within;
Rare is the bird who tastes it.
He alone will eat that fruit, O Kabir,
Who dies while living.

In the Koran, it says, "Die thou before thy death." Maulana Rum says, "So long as man does not come out of his body, he will remain ignorant of the inner vision." And Paltu adds:

O Paltu, die thou before thy death.
All have to die,
But they conquer death
Who die before their death.

Hafiz also speaks of the inner journey, which begins when one leaves the body:

You who do not come out of the caravanserai
of your body,
How will you pass through the spiritual lane
within?

Soami Ji says, "There is no other way save Shabd to free youself of this clay pot of the body....Your Abode is where the physical body exists not—why are you then tied down to this body?"[51] Or, in the words of Guru Nanak:

The Home you wish to reach after death,
Attain it through dying while still living.[52]

Maulana Rum says that the soul has passed through the gates of death numerous times, but could not get released because it did not know how to die while living:

As long as you do not die while living,
How will you obtain the true benefit?
Therefore die, and come out of your body.
O man, you have died many times,
But still you remain behind the veil,
For the method of true dying
You did not learn.

Guru Ram Das says that his Master showed him the way to cross the terrible ocean of the world:

I asked the benevolent Satguru:
"How am I to swim the difficult ocean,
O lord?"
Live in the Will of the Satguru
and die while living.

Die while living, swim across the ocean
of existence
And merge thyself into the Guru's Name.
Such a fortunate one, by devotion
to the True Name,
Attains union with the Supreme Being.[53]

It is only after the Master connects the soul to the Word that the disciple can die while living. Withdrawing the consciousness and merging into the Divine Melody within is possible only through the Master's grace. Guru Amar Das says:

Through Guru's grace alone, one dies
while living,
And having thus died, becomes alive
through the practice of Shabd:
Such a one attains the gates of salvation
and rids himself of ego.[54]

Die through the Shabd
To live forever,
And never again face death;
With the nectar of Nam
Mind is sweetened forever—
By Shabd alone can one attain it.[55]

In homage and gratitude, Namdev addresses this poem to his Master, Visoba Khechar:

Through the Word imparted by the Guru
I have realized my true self,
And while still living,
I have learned to die;
I have now no fear of death.

Visoba Khechar says: "Death we transcend,
O Nama,
When we experience it while living."[56]

The Saints say that one who thus dies while living knows all the mysteries of the worlds within, and enjoys the grace and blessing of the Lord:

If you die while living, you will know all,
And experience the Lord's grace within.
Such a one, O Nanak, attains true esteem,
And recognizes the Lord within all beings.[57]

—Guru Nanak

Saints come to the world by the grace and mercy of the Lord. They do not come to make it a better place, nor to improve its lot, but to free us from our bonds of attachment, and turn our attention towards the Father. They come to make us blind to this world and give us the sight to see the Lord.

Were it not for His grace, we would never even think of our separation from Him, nor would we desire to return Home. But for His grace, we would neither meet the Master nor follow the Path. His grace comes first. He creates the desire in us to meet Him. He pulls from within. We think we search for Him, when in fact He creates that desire in us to search for Him. With His grace, we develop faith in the Master. With His grace, we put forth the effort to practice, to attend to meditation with love and devotion. Without grace, we could not move one step at any stage. The guiding hand of grace is always with us. With His grace we realize within our self the true identity of the Master, the Word made flesh. And with His grace we reach back to the level of the Lord and merge with Him. We truly fulfill the purpose of our human life. No longer separated from our Source, we return to our eternal Home of peace and bliss, to be one with our Father, forever.

> O Nanak, when the Lord is merciful to someone,
> He brings him in contact with a Satguru;
> Such a one, through the Guru's grace,
> Dies while living,
> And never faces death again.[58]

2

The Divine Design

The Divine Design

1 Q. Master, you tell us that the purpose of meditation is to seek the Lord within, to follow the Path within back to the Father. But I can't seem to fully comprehend the idea that meditation takes us within, that the Lord, the Creator, is within me.

A. When at night you sleep and you have a dream, where are you? Is the dream within yourself or is the dream outside your body?

Whatever the impressions of your previous experiences are; but is whatever you see in a dream within the body or somewhere outside the body? Do you go out of the body to see that, or do you see all that within your body?

No doubt it is the reproduction of outside associations, but what you see, how you behave, and how you act in a dream—is all that drama within yourself or somewhere outside? Do you leave the body and go outside to see all that?

It's purely within. So if a dream can be within the body, why can't the Radiant Form of the Master or spiritual experience be within the body? And yet when you dissect a body, you won't find any drama of the dream within the body. It's not physical at all.

We say the Lord is within in the sense that unless

we reach a certain level of consciousness within ourselves, we will not see the Lord. We have to advance to that level of consciousness within ourselves and not somewhere outside. And when you advance within yourself to that particular state of consciousness, then you see God.

It is also said that when you see Him within, you see Him everywhere. He's not confined only to the body—He's everywhere—but you have to reach that particular level of consciousness to see Him within, and then you see Him everywhere outside in the world. Similarly, you have to reach a certain level of consciousness within yourself to have all these spiritual experiences. The experiences are within yourself and not somewhere outside, and by being outside, you cannot reach that level of consciousness within yourself.

The whole creation is within ourselves. You have read in the Bible in St. John that nothing existed before the Creation; only the Lord existed.[1] All that we see is nothing but His own projection. The creation has come out of the Father. Everything has come out of the Father and everything is within the Father, and the Father is within us. So through meditation, we withdraw to the eye center, we contact the Master within, and we see for ourselves that everything is within us.

Through meditation we withdraw to the eye center and contact the Master within.

2 Q. This I intellectually understand when I read in all the books that you're there and that you're waiting for me to come to the eye center. I would just like to hear you talk about it, though.

A. The difficult thing to understand is thinking that probably the body of the Master will come into our body. It's not the body which is the Master; it is the Shabd, that Creative Power, which is the Master. Our real Master is the Shabd, the Word, which is within every one of us. So the inner Master projects himself from that Shabd, from that Light and Sound, and we see the Radiant Form of the Master.

You have read in the Bible where Christ says: I have taken abode in you. Now I am in you and ultimately you will be in me, and then both of us will be in the Father.[2] When the Master initiates, he takes abode in us in the sense that our soul is connected with the Sound within, and the Sound is our Master. That Creative Power which has created the whole creation is the real Master, and we get connected to that. The Master projects his own form from that Shabd within us, and appears to us in his Radiant Form.

Now we are not acquainted with that Power, that Shabd; we are acquainted only with the physical form of the Master. By meditation we get acquainted with that Power through the Radiant Form of our Master, whom we naturally can recognize. As Christ says: my sheep know me and I know my sheep, so they recognize my whistle.[3] The Master knows us and we know the Master, hence we recognize our Master within. He has to be recognized, so he takes his form from that Shabd and manifests himself from that Power.

Christ says that ultimately you come in me and I come in you, which means we lose our identity and merge into that Being, we merge into that Shabd, into that Creative Power. Call it Master, call it God—in the end, it comes to the same thing. We have to merge into that Being and lose our own individuality, our own identity.

Our problem in trying to understand this point is when we think of only the physical form of the Master. Then naturally he can't come within us. We have no other concept of the Master. The real concept is that of Shabd, the Radiant Form. Now for example, when you sleep, you see so many persons within you in a dream. Where are they? We are in the body when we sleep—we don't leave our bed or go out of our room—yet when we are dreaming, we meet so many people within us. After all, where are they when we meet them, when we talk to them, when we laugh, we enjoy, we weep, we cry? Where are they? Where are we? It must be at some level of consciousness within. So if they all can be within us, why can't the Master be within us?

3 Q. Master, would you speak to us about equanimity, tranquility, peace of mind?

A. Peace of mind? The purpose of meditation is nothing but to obtain that peace of mind. Actually, all this tension and depression that we feel is due to the scattering of our mind. When our attention is scattered we become very restless, unhappy, and we lose that peace. The more we concentrate at the eye center and the more our attention is upward, the more peaceful we become, and only then we enjoy that bliss and happiness within. The more the mind is scattered from the eye center through these nine apertures into the outside world—whatever the reason may be—the more we become depressed, unhappy and miserable.

The only way to obtain peace is to withdraw our consciousness to the eye center and keep our attention upward rather than downward. We get peace only beyond the eye center, upward; as long as we are below the eye center, we are miserable. The Lord may give all gifts to us—everything—but we can never obtain peace.

Peace we can obtain only when all coverings are removed from the soul, when the soul shines and becomes whole, and it becomes worthy of merging into the Lord. Only then do we find peace. As long as the soul is separated from its Source, we can never have peace. And the soul can become worthy of merging into the Lord only when it leaves the association of the mind, when all the coverings of karma and of sensual pleasures are removed. Only then the soul shines; only then do we obtain that peace, and radiate that peace.

In order to get tranquility and peace, the only method is meditation, which takes our mind back to its source, thereby releasing us from the mind and removing all coverings from the soul. We can never find permanent peace in worldly objects and sensual pleasures. They are short lived, these so-called pleasures, and the reaction to them sometimes makes us more miserable, more unhappy. So the only way to obtain everlasting peace is to go back to the Father and become one with Him.

In fact, everything is at rest only when it goes back to its own source. As long as we are separated from our Source, we can never be at peace. For example, the physical body is made up of five elements: earth, water, fire, air and ether. When the five elements of the body merge into their origin, then our body is at peace, and we are rid of all disease. So long as the five elements in the body are separated from their original source, the body is not at peace. Similarly, when the mind is separated from its own source, Trikuti, the mind is not at peace; and as long as the soul is separated from its own Source, from the Lord, the soul is not at peace. Hence, we get bodily peace, mental peace, and peace of soul, bliss of soul, only when each merges into its own source.

4 Q. Master, what type of prayer does the Lord like to hear?

A. Meditation. Meditation will help you to live in the Will of the Lord, and that is the best prayer—to live in the Will of the Father, to adjust to the events of life, and to accept with grace and a smile everything which He gives to us. That attitude can come only by meditation, and the prayer which the Lord accepts is meditation. Just your complete unconditional surrender to the Father, submission to the Father—eliminating your individuality, merging into the Being—that is prayer, that is meditation. There's no other prayer in the world which pleases the Father. Only one prayer pleases Him—that we want to become one with Him—and only meditation makes us one with Him. So this is the best prayer.

There is no set prayer which you can repeat four times a day or five times a day. No language is required, no words are required in prayer. Prayer is a language of love from the heart to the Father, and nobody exists then between you and the Father. You're not conscious of the world when you pray to Him. He exists and you exist. That is real prayer, and that is only possible at the time of meditation when we try to forget all that we are and where we are.

Prayer is not when we ask the Father to fulfill our desires and satisfy all our worldly ambitions. That is no prayer at all, it is just asking Him to condemn us to this creation again. If we pray to the Father to fulfill our worldly desires, we actually expose ourselves to come back to this creation again and again; and we can come back to this creation even without praying to the Father. So, ritualistic prayers, or requests concerning our worldly desires, do not lead us anywhere.

The only prayer is that we should become one with Him. Right from the beginning of the creation we have been condemned, we have lived separated from Him. We have felt the separation all through, and now He should make us one with Him, merge us back into His Being. That should be our only prayer.

That is why Christ says, if you don't hear me, if you don't follow my teachings, don't think that I'm going to condemn you to the Father, because you're already condemned.[4] "Condemned" means we are part of this creation. He says: what more can I complain to the Father about you, because you're already condemned. Now we want to get out of this condemnation and rise to His level.

We do not know what is in our best interest. We pray to the Father to satisfy certain desires, and if by any chance He fulfills them, then we become so frustrated with those very things that again we have to pray to get rid of them. Again we have to bend down on our knees to get rid of what we had prayed for before.

When we clearly don't know what to pray for, then

why not leave everything to Him? Why show our lack of faith in Him? We should have faith that whatever He gives us is in our best interest. The loving child always gives himself entirely, when he is in his mother's lap. He doesn't have to ask for anything at all. The mother is most careful about that child. She's always concerned with what time she has to feed him, what time she has to bathe him. She will take care of the child in every way. The child doesn't have to ask the mother for anything—he knows that she loves him. If we unconditionally surrender ourselves to the Father, we will know that He also loves us and that He will give us what is in our best interest, and we should accept whatever He gives us with grace.

Our only prayer is that we should become one with Him, that we can't bear this separation any more. Christ has given a very beautiful example. He says: you are asking the Father for bread and so many other things. Doesn't He feed the birds, the insects and all living creatures? Doesn't He feed the grass, which is just cut and burned in a minute? Won't He then feed you and look after you—you being the top of the creation?[5] Why should we show such a lack of faith in Him by praying to Him every day for worldly things?

If your servant works very diligently, lovingly and patiently in your house, you're always anxious to reward him, to give him more and more. But if he's constantly demanding something, you want to get rid of him. That is our attitude, and the same is the attitude of the Father. If we will just be loving to Him and do our duty, then He is even more eager to give to us. When we don't want to do our duty and are always demanding and demanding, He wants to get rid of us and send us back to this creation again. That is why all Mystics say that we must live in the Will of the Father.

Somebody told Christ: your mother is standing at your back, perhaps desirous to speak to you. In one way or another, Mystics or Saints always find some excuse to give the teachings. Christ said: who is my father, who is my mother, who is my brother? I have no father, no mother, no brother. He said, those who live in the Will of my Father are all my brothers; they are my mother, they are my sisters, they are my real relations.[6] Those who live in the Will of the Father, with them my relationship is eternal, because for them there will be only one shepherd and one flock. They will never separate from one another. So the real prayer is to live in the Will of the Father, and that comes only by meditation.

5 **Q.** Maharaj Ji, is it beneficial to pray to the Master for success in meditation before we start, just as a mood-setting type of thing? Or is that just a lack of faith?

A. No, you can do it. There's no harm in praying to the Father for His grace. If a child won't ask his father, whom will he ask? But instead of praying to the Father to give us grace in meditation, why not start with the meditation? Meditation itself is praying to the Lord. The actual prayer is meditation; praying with words is a means towards meditation.

When you go to a house, instead of first praying to the Lord, "I am going to knock at your door," why not just start knocking at the door? Ultimately, you want to knock on the door, whether you start by knocking, or you first tell the Lord, "I'm going to knock on your door." You can even knock first. The main thing is knocking, and that is meditation.

6 **Q.** At the time of meditation, what thoughts should we have?

A. I think we should have no thoughts at all. The purpose of meditation is to get rid of all the worldly thoughts which are bothering us day and night. We have to withdraw ourselves from all these daily thoughts. But the first question is, what is meditation? Unless we know what meditation is, we cannot know on what we have to concentrate.

Meditation means withdrawing our consciousness to the eye center and holding our attention there; then attaching ourselves to the Shabd or Nam, the Sound Current, which is within every one of us, and with the help of that, detaching ourselves permanently, forever, from the lower senses. That is meditation.

7 **Q.** You have said that the mind is a slave of the senses. Is that referring to the lack of concentration or is that referring to our desire for pleasure?

A. You mean in what way is the mind a slave of the senses? The senses pull the mind to their own level. Any sensual pleasure pulls our mind to its own level, which means the mind is a slave of the senses.

The seat of the soul and mind is here at the eye center, and from here the tendency of the mind is downwards towards the senses. The mind runs to the senses for pleasures, for happiness, and all these sense pleasures pull the mind to their own level, making it a slave of the senses.

Q. Including things like sight, feeling?

A. Sight, feeling, touch, taste; in fact, all the senses and sensual pleasures.

Q. Doesn't it all start in the mind first? Don't all the sensual pleasures start in the mind first?

A. That is right, because the mind starts responding to the senses, so it runs to the senses. The mind is tempted by the senses. It starts with the mind; but then, the senses are also a part of the mind.

Q. Through meditation, we're cutting all of that off?

A. Meditation means trying to hold our attention here at the eye center and not let it come down to the senses. That is concentration, to keep the mind steady at the eye center and not let it come down. The purpose of keeping the mind here is to attach it to the Divine Melody within so that with the help of that Sound, the mind can go back to its own origin.

Since the mind is fond of pleasures, it refuses to go to the senses when it gets a better pleasure than the sensual pleasures. And by attaching itself to that better pleasure, that Sound and Light within, the mind comes to its own origin, which is Trikuti, the second stage. Then the soul automatically gets released from the mind. That is why Socrates hinted: Know thyself. For God-realization can come only after self-realization; the soul can realize itself only when it gets released from the mind.

Now the mind is dominating the soul, and the mind itself is dominated by the senses. But with the help of meditation we have to reverse the whole process, so that the soul dominates the mind, and the mind dominates the senses. That is the purpose of meditation.

8 Q. Maharaj Ji, nirat*, I understand, is a quality of the spirit, of the soul; but is there a nirat, as well, of the mind? I want to link this to the basis of the realization of the self first, and then realization of the Creator. Is there a parallel in these?

A. The mind and soul are knotted together, so nirat and surat are both for the soul and mind together. Because the mind and soul are together, the faculty to see (nirat) and the faculty to hear (surat) affect both the soul and mind. The mind also sees the Light and hears the Sound. The mind is the first to catch the Light and the first to catch the Sound. Only then the soul can see its own Light and can catch its own Sound.

Meditation, to begin with, is for the mind; and the soul naturally gets its advantage as the mind becomes purer and purer, for then the soul gets released more and more from the mind. The inclination of the soul is always towards its own Origin, but the mind is a weight which is keeping the soul tied down to the creation. So meditation, this Light and Sound, is to purify the mind, because the soul is always anxious to go back to its own Origin.

9 Q. If someone is initiated and he fails to meditate, can he do something else to compensate for it?

A. What do you mean by something else?

* Nirat: the seeing faculty of the soul.

Q. Some sort of seva* or some sort of other thing to compensate for meditation.

A. All these other types of seva will lead you to meditate. They are means, but the means can't substitute for the end.

Q. So there's no substitute for meditation.

A. No. I'm sorry to say, no. The Creator has determined how we are to go back to Him, and we cannot take any short cut or any other route. He has ordained that we must seek a Perfect Master, and be initiated by him while both the Master and the disciple are living. Then through meditation we must please the Master, we must eliminate our ego, and merge with the Father, become one with the Creator. So meditation is the only way.

This is all His plan, it is the Divine Design. I'll explain further. As Christ has said in the Bible: to sin against the Holy Ghost can never be forgiven.[7] If you turn your back to meditation, you can never be forgiven—forgiven for what stands between you and the Father. That cannot be eliminated. Unless we are forgiven for those karmas which we have done in past lives, the soul can never go back to the Father. And Christ says that if you sin against the Holy Ghost, if you don't attend to your meditation, then you will never be able to clear that layer of karma and your soul can never go back to the Father.

Christ says: to sin against me can be forgiven. It means that if you have no faith in me you can be forgiven, because when you attend to meditation you

* Service.

will automatically develop that faith in me. But if you don't attend to your meditation at all, then how can you be forgiven? If you have medicine but don't use it, how can your illness go? Friendship with the doctor won't eliminate your illness; you have to use the medicine, howsoever bitter it is.

So, "to sin against the Holy Ghost can never be forgiven" means that you can't bypass meditation. You may do other types of seva—they are strong means to meditation—but ultimately you have to meditate.

10 Q. Sardar Bahadur Ji has said that if you miss just one day of meditation, you'll step back for one month.[8] Exactly what did he mean?

A. He means the same thing that Christ said: to sin against the Holy Ghost cannot be forgiven.[9] Christ made it very clear in the Bible—if we turn our back to meditation, then how can we be forgiven for the karmas which we have been collecting from life to life, from age to age? How can we be forgiven?

These are all ways and means to induce us to attend to our meditation. Take it literally, take it devotionally, take it in any way—the main thing is that we have to attend to our meditation.

Saints generally explain the teachings according to the background of particular people. Some people are very orthodox; they won't accept things easily. Probably Saints may have to frighten them before they will accept the teachings.

Some people are very simple and accept the teachings just by simple statements, which make as good an impression upon them as any other statement. Some people will accept the teachings only if you very lovingly tell them to do these things.

Some people are very intellectual; unless you explain the teachings to them intellectually, they will never understand anything at all.

The approach of the Mystics has been different in different times according to the people to whom they were explaining the teachings. But the main theme of every Saint is that we should attend to our meditation.

They know best how they have to succeed in convincing us, but actually, they want to impress upon us the importance of meditation. They do this through parables, through stories, through intellectual discourses, through simple talks, through discussions. These are all means. The main thing is to impress upon us the importance of meditation, and we should look only to that, and not try to analyze these little things.

11 Q. You have said that simran* should not be done mechanically but with love, faith and devotion. But also you said that Christ said that if you sin against me I can forgive you, but not if you sin against the Holy Ghost. If we do not have faith in the Master but attend to meditation—

A. My explanation has been a little misunderstood. Christ said: if you sin against me, it can be forgiven, but if you sin against the Holy Ghost, you can never be forgiven. He didn't say that you *should* sin against me. He meant, even if you have no faith in me, you can be forgiven, in the sense that you will develop that

* Simran: repetition.

faith if you keep on attending to your meditation. But it is one thing if you have no faith in me and another thing if you don't even attend to the meditation; then you can never be forgiven.

Q. But meditation must be mechanical to begin with, because love and devotion develop very gradually.

A. If you go on attending to the meditation, if you don't sin against the Holy Ghost, then love and devotion will develop, and will be strengthened.

As Christ said elsewhere, now you ask so many questions, but when you will see me, which means that when you will come to that level of consciousness where you will find me in my Radiant Form, then you will have no questions to ask.[10] It means that now you have all sorts of doubts about me, but when you see me within, then you will have no doubts at all. So, even when we love the Master, even when we have devotion and faith in the Master outside, still something within us doesn't allow us to have complete faith, still some doubts are always creeping in.

All doubts can be dissolved, or resolved, only when you see the Radiant Form of the Master. Then there is real conviction. Before that also, you may have love for the Master or faith in the Master, because you have satisfied your intellect. Satisfaction of the intellect has given you a certain faith, but you can have the real faith only when you see the Master within. Then even if the whole world turns against you, you don't bother about any of it. The faith which we develop by satisfaction of our intellect or reasoning can be shaky at times, but that inner faith can never be shaky.

12 Q. When a satsangi does meditation it is seva of the Master. How is it seva of the Master?

A. Because you please the Master. Master wants you to become pure and clean so that you can merge back into the Father. What is seva? Seva is to get the pleasure of the Master; anything which pleases the Master is seva of the Master. It pleases him that you are burning your rubbish, you are burning your load of karma every day, you are becoming lighter and lighter, and that you will eventually be in a position to fly back to the Father. Meditation pleases the Master because ultimately he's responsible to take the soul up, and it pleases him if we are decreasing our load every day. Naturally it pleases him.

When a tree is yielding fruit, the gardener is the happiest person, but what does he get? The gardener does his best to put a dry, withered tree in order by means of chemicals and other treatments. When that tree bears fruit it belongs to the landlord, no doubt, and not to the gardener; but the gardener is the happiest person, because even that tree has started yielding fruit. That tree has pleased the gardener, and naturally the owner of the garden is also pleased.

Similarly the Master is pleased when the soul works hard to go back to the Father, though ultimately the soul belongs to the Father. Of course, the Father will be happy to get the soul back; but the Master is also happy that the soul, which had gone astray, which was a slave of the senses, which never knew anything about the Father, which was blind to the Father, has started realizing the Father within. It has become lighter and lighter, and has started shining, and is now in a position to merge back into the Father. The Master gets the highest pleasure out of that also, and so meditation is the seva of the Master too.

13 Q. Master, can we live a life of service to the Master—of body, mind and wealth—before our mind has risen to a higher level?

A. Sister, the time we give to meditation is nothing but service to the Master. You cannot serve the Master in a better way than by following his instructions and living his way of life—attending to your meditation. That is the best service to the Master.

You have seen the gardener working harder on the trees that don't yield any fruit, than on those trees which yield fruit. Those which yield fruit are actually helping the gardener by not demanding much of his time. They are serving the gardener. And those which dont't yield any fruit at all, are making him work harder and harder, more and more.

So we can serve the Master by following the teachings, and by living the teachings, thus bearing the fruit for which this human birth has been given to us.

14 Q. Sir, how is meditation the seva of the Lord? Isn't it our own seva?

A. Whatever we do for ourselves we do also for the Lord. Ultimately we are going to become the Lord. God is a higher consciousness, so service to our own self, or service to the soul, is service to God. The soul is a part of that Divine Ocean. Any service to the soul is service to the Lord. Anything which takes us back to the Father is service of the Father.

Unless we serve our soul, we cannot get released

from the clutches of the mind, and meditation is service of the soul. To take pity on ourselves, to take pity on the soul and to do something to release it from the mind is a service to the soul. That is meditation. And when you serve the soul, you automatically serve its Source also; so meditation is service of the Lord.

15 **Q.** Master, a man who has desire is not free. I am leaving Dera, and by next week I will be back home. I know that from now on I am going to have a still bigger desire to see you in my meditation. Is this to be free?

A. Would you like to be free of this desire? The purpose of meditation is to be with the Master always. That is the purpose of the Master, and this desire grows and grows with meditation. As Christ said, blessed are they that mourn, for they shall be comforted.[11] When do we mourn? When we feel separation from somebody, then we become restless to be with the one we love. Then we mourn. Only when we are filled with that type of love and devotion and desire to be with the Master will we get rest from birth and death. And this desire grows and grows. In spite of the pain it carries, there is something in it which you won't like to get rid of.

16 **Q.** One thing that I didn't understand from the books was that one of the attributes of true love and devotion is that the soul is getting restless. When we're in this restless state all the time, how do we sit still for meditation?

A. It is restlessness *for* meditation, restlessness for being one with the Father, and meditation is a means to put an end to that restlessness. How can you avoid that means? When the pull is there for the beloved, your feet automatically walk towards the beloved. Walking is a means to reach the beloved, to reach that end. So, just as you automatically walk towards the beloved, similarly, you meditate in order to become one with the Father. When the pull is there, the restlessness is there.

3

Creating the Atmosphere

Creating the Atmosphere

This world is not our true home, it is merely a field where we come to work out our karmic obligations. Everything that we see here is transitory and impermanent. Nothing of this world has ever followed anyone beyond death, even though one's entire life may have been wasted in its pursuit. Only meditation and the Master are eternal, and they alone are deserving of our attention.

We are told by the Saints to make the best use of our time: the human form is a blessed opportunity to enable us to realize the Lord within, and escape this prison house of birth and death. While working out the karmic credits and debits, our attention should always be focused on our love and devotion for our Master. We must constantly feel the separation from our Beloved, and continuously yearn for our Creator, the Lord of our soul.

The Master and the Path should always be kept in view, and meditation must become our primary concern in this life. Our every action should reflect the teachings and build that holy atmosphere in which we attend to meditation, and become receptive to His bounty and grace. To this end, we must adjust our entire life, for success requires a complete transformation of the disciple. We should keep a balance, and meet our worldly duties and responsibilities; but our spiritual duty to the Master is foremost. We learn to live on the edge of this world as spectators, and do not allow ourselves to be drowned in its sensual pleasures. We learn to be in this world, but not of it, by vigilantly keeping our attention directed towards our goal.

The seed of Nam is planted within every initiate, and it must sprout. We are advised to protect this crop and preserve the sanctity of this treasure. A crop in an open field will certainly grow without protection, but it remains vulnerable and is easily plundered. We must, therefore, surround our crop, which we grow through meditation, with the fence of satsang, the company of the Masters and Saints and their devotees. Satsang provides an impregnable shield against robbers and thieves who may wish to have us squander that spiritual wealth. Powers, which develop in us through the practice of the Sound Current, must never be arrogantly displayed, nor cause any show of vanity. If we preserve and protect this treasure, its flow from Him becomes more and more bountiful.

So we must daily continue to build that atmosphere in which we attend to meditation with ever-growing love and devotion. We must become strong on the Path and mold our lives according to the teachings. Thus, pleasing the Master, we become fit for the Court of the Lord, and fulfill the very purpose of our human existence.

ESSENTIAL PREREQUISITES

17 Q. Master, how do we effectively build an atmosphere for meditation?

A. How to build the atmosphere for meditation? We try to build an atmosphere for meditation by reading books, by attending the group meetings, by meeting satsangis and discussing the teachings and the philosophy and being a source of strength and help to one another. It is all building an atmosphere for meditation.

We are always influenced by the company we keep. If we start mixing with criminals, with bad people, we will start thinking along those lines. If we mix with good people, with noble people, with devotees, we will start thinking in their way, because we're always influenced by the company we keep.

So this is how we build an atmosphere for meditation—by the group meetings, by satsang, by discussion, by meeting satsangis, dissolving our doubts, helping one another. That's all building an atmosphere of meditation, filling one another with love and devotion.

18 Q. Then to create the right atmosphere for meditation, would it be more helpful to meditate in the country or small towns rather than in the big cities?

A. One has to build one's own atmosphere around him in which he has to meditate, because everywhere you can't get satsang, you can't get group meetings—you can't get the right type of group meetings, I would say, or the right type of atmosphere that is conducive to meditation. You don't always get the right type of satsangis or the right type of devotees where you can build your meditation.

Actually, one has to build one's own atmosphere for meditation. You have to create that atmosphere yourself by reading the books or by seeking the right type of people with whom to mix, who talk about the Lord and meditation and all those things. You yourself have to create that atmosphere.

19 Q. Master, I know a satsangi in the entertainment business, and he tells me that the kind of people involved seem to be of quite low morals and very much immersed in the world and the senses. Can this satsangi build that atmosphere for meditation, and still stay in that business?

A. Brother, if he doesn't compromise with the principles of Sant Mat. If the foundation is there, only then you will be able to build. Without a foundation you will not be able to build at all. You can't build on sand; as Christ said, you have to build on rock.[1] The principles of Sant Mat are the foundation on which you have to stand in order to build; but if you think there is a danger of your slipping when in such a business, naturally it won't be conducive to your meditation. If your mind is always scattered, if your mind is always in such a place where there's a chance of slipping here and there, then it is never conducive to meditation. The right type of atmosphere is very essential for meditation. If you find that right type of atmosphere in such a business, then it's all right. You can know better.

20 Q. Master, we take a vow to lead a clean and chaste moral life in mind and body. Why is this vow so important?

A. Sister, all the vows are very important. If we don't have good moral character outside, we can never make progress within at all. There are so many temptations within. If you're weak outside, you'll be more miserable and weak within; you'll never be able to make much progress.

Then, if our attention is always dropping to lower centers, it is difficult to withdraw our consciousness up to the eye center. Unless we lead a good, clean life, and unless we are able to concentrate here at the eye center, we can never make progress at all.

And we are also sowing seeds. Christ made this very clear in the Bible when the people were about to stone some lady caught in adultery. Of course he saved her, but he advised her also: go, and sin no more.[2]

Then Christ also explains how to account for what you have done. He says, "If thine eye be single, thy whole body shall be full of light."[3] Withdraw your consciousness to the eye center and see that Light within yourself. That Light and Sound will help you to purify your mind, by pulling it from the senses and taking it back to its own source.

21 Q. Would you give us directions for seekers when they ask us what they should do about the vow of meditation? Some newcomers to the Path are actually sitting in meditation before they're initiated.

A. I personally think they should not try to do any meditation at all. They should try to understand the philosophy thoroughly and make a full investigation, and once they're convinced about the Path, then they should try to follow the Path. Trying to do meditation just by reading books doesn't make much sense.

22 Q. Master, I think this is in *With the Three Masters*, on page 111. Great Master* says that twenty-four minutes with a Master is equal to a hundred years of meditation.[4]

A. That means something very different. The company of Mystics for one *ghari*, twenty-four minutes, is better than meditating for a hundred years *without* having a Master. The Great Master means to say that if you go on meditating by yourself without any guide, even for a hundred years, it's useless. It's much better to be in the company of the Mystics for twenty-four minutes than to meditate without a Master. I often quote in satsang that if the path is towards the east and you run to the west, you will only keep going farther away. So that is what is referred to, but we always try to find the meaning which suits us.

23 Q. Master, when I meditated before, I could manage to go in right away, but after the initiation today, I tried to use the new method, and I cannot go in.

A. And how were you meditating?

---

* *Great Master* is a title of respect and endearment for Maharaj Sawan Singh. It originated from the title of Dr. Julian Johnson's book, *With a Great Master in India.*

Q. I focused between the eye brows.

A. And where did you use to go?

Q. I felt I was going inside.

A. You just practice as has been told to you today, and slowly and slowly you have to withdraw, and then you will be able to go up. It's not so quick that if you were initiated today then by tomorrow you will be able to control the mind and hold the attention at the eye center and go up.

Q. Should I get rid of the old way of meditation?

A. Yes, absolutely just forget about it and make this a habit now.

24 Q. Maharaj Ji, a friend of mine once told me that if you really want it bad enough, to be in Trikuti or any other spiritual plane, you could just be there. By devotion, by bhakti, love, wanting. Is it true?

A. Simply by wishing you can't go there. Only the Shabd, only the Light and Sound within can pull you to that level of consciousness—nothing else. Your wish won't help. Your practice will help, your faith will help.

25 Q. Master, when we were initiated, we were told that it has been said as strict instructions given at the time of initiation that after six months we would have enough conviction and faith in the Path to know that we definitely are on the right path.

A. That is right. If we are really honest about the initiation and about the teachings, and steadfast on our principles, and we attend to our meditation with love and devotion, we definitely get conviction about the Path within six months—even much earlier.

26 Q. Master, if a satsangi has been predestined to have many lives after initiation, is there a way to shorten it by meditation or by detachment?

A. Sister, the first thing is, how do you know that disciple is destined to have many lives after initiation? How do you know that? We cannot be aware of all that. We shouldn't try to analyze these things. Once we are on the Path, we should be sincere within ourselves and attend to our meditation. That's the only thing, and then we should not worry about anything at all. Don't worry about any birth or any death or anything. Just attend to your duty, attend to your meditation.

27 Q. Master, I've heard it said that we must use the intellect to rise above the intellect. I was wondering if you would comment on that?

A. Intellect is a great barrier in our way, but we have to pierce the barrier of intellect with the help of intellect. An intellectual man will not accept a simple truth just by a simple statement. He wants to be convinced. But once conviction comes, nobody can shake him. So reasoning convinces us and then we become firm in our faith and we attend to meditation.

Intellect cannot lead us anywhere, but the satisfaction of the intellect will give you faith and practice. If you try to brush aside your intellect and try to attend to meditation, you will never succeed. Intellect will always jump in the way. But if you satisfy your intellect with reasoning, then faith will come and practice will come, which will then take you to your destination.

And once this conviction is there, once the satisfaction of the intellect is there, then you have no fear as to the correctness of your direction, as to the truth of the Path and the teachings.

Therefore, before coming to the Path we must satisfy our intellect. We must be satisfied that this is meant for us, that this will lead us back to our destination. Otherwise, all sorts of questions and doubts and so many things come in our way. We must satisfy our mind. And once this mind is satisfied, automatically the faith will come, automatically the practice will come.

If you want to follow the Path without satisfying your mind, then questions and doubts arise, and whenever you sit in meditation all those things will come before you. They won't let you sit in meditation at all. "Why should I sit in my room, why should I close my eyes, I have so many friends, I don't know what I am doing, whether it is right or wrong." All those questions will come in your mind and you will not be able to make any progress at all. So intellect will not lead you anywhere at all. In fact, the unsatisfied intellect is a barrier in your way.

If you tell a simple person in a simple way, he will follow it. To an intellectual person, if you tell him in a simple way, he will never follow it. He's so intellectual he cannot accept simple things in a simple way. It must be put to him in a very complicated way. First he creates a problem with his intellect, then he wants to solve that problem with his intellect, then he takes pride in solving it or feels frustrated in not solving it. That is the fate of an intellectual person.

But if an intellectual person is convinced, it is just like building on a rock. Nobody can shake him. For a simple person, however, even though it may be easy for him to understand, because he is so simple, yet he's shaky also, and consequently he is easily led astray by any other person.

So that is the difference. There's nothing wrong with the intellect. You can't brush aside your intellect and follow the Path. You have to satisfy your intellect. That is why we have so many meetings, so many satsangs, so many books, so many questions, so many inquiries. They are just to satisfy the intellect. They are not leading us anywhere. If you say by reading the books you get something—you get, in fact, nothing. If by attending the meetings you feel you'll get something—again you get nothing. It is only the satisfaction of the intellect that you get.

But once convinced, then you have that faith, then you can practice. And through that practice, through meditation, through living the teachings and molding your life after them, you get what you want—not by merely satisfying the intellect, but by faith and practice with love and devotion.

28 Q. Maharaj Ji, it is often said that we should do more meditation with punctuality, regularity, and love and devotion. But love and devotion seem to be out of our hands.

A. Sister, by love and devotion I mean that you must have faith in the Path which you are following, that this is the Path which goes back to our destination, and faith in the one who has put you on the Path, that he's put you on the right path and he's always with you to guide you to the right destination.

Unless you have that faith, you will never practice meditation.

If I know that a road leads to New York from Washington. I'll go on driving at full speed. If I have no faith that the road will go to New York and I feel that it may go in some other direction, it becomes very hard for me to drive. I have to ask people for directions at every step. Sometimes I look at the map, sometimes I look at the roadsigns, sometimes I ask pedestrians; then I go astray.

Faith doesn't take you to the destination. Practice will take you to the destination, but faith will make you practice. Without faith, you can't practice. You will not be able to drive at full speed without faith. Full speed will take you to the destination, but faith is helping you to drive at full speed. Similarly, love and devotion is to have faith in the Path and the Master. Then we practice also, and then we get the results from that practice.

29 Q. I want myself to surrender absolutely and unconditionally to the Master, but I do not know how to develop this absolute love and devotion for the Master, because I find that sometimes I am not as much devoted to the Master as I ought to be, although I want to be exclusively devoted to the Master. What should I do for that?

A. Well, brother, the main question is: how to strengthen our love. The only way to strengthen love is by meditation. There's no other way, because the love which we get by experience cannot be compared to any other type of love. Intellectual love is all right; emotional love, which is influenced by other people, is all right. Any type of love is all right, but nothing can surpass the love of your own experience; and for that experience, meditation is necessary. You can build love and devotion only through meditation, not otherwise. Meditation builds everlasting love, and that is building on a rock, and not on sand.

Q. But before that kind of love comes, don't we first have to be absolutely convinced or have faith that this Path will lead us to that love?

A. Yes, first is the conviction in the philosophy, which creates a desire in you to follow the philosophy. Everything, of course, is with His grace; but first is the conviction that what you are going to follow is right. That conviction will lead you towards practice, and then naturally you will practice only when there is some elementary love and faith in you. But real love, strengthening of devotion, comes only by meditation. Everlasting love, the depth of love, can be had only by meditation.

30 Q. There are some people, Master, who have not seen the Master and who have not tried to delve deep into the philosophy of Sant Mat, and still, somehow or other, they have spontaneously an enormous amount of love for the Master.

A. What do you know about the depth of their love? How do you know? How do you compare their type of love with the depth of love?

Q. Apparently it seems that—

A. It is good if they apparently feel so, but that love may be only on the surface. It may be shaky. You can't say.

Once someone is convinced that an animal is a horse, then even if the whole world says it's a buffalo, he doesn't care at all. The whole world is against him, but he knows it's a horse. As long as he's shaky, if ten people say it's a horse he'll say it's a horse; if twenty people say it's a buffalo he'll say it's buffalo; so he's always wavering. He needs support from twenty others that what he feels is right. But the love developed through experience doesn't need the support of anybody else in this creation. Even if the whole world is against him, he's not shaky; he knows that it's a horse. That type of love and faith you can develop only by experience, not otherwise.

31 **Q.** Then if love for the physical form of the Master is necessary for progress on the Path, what about the people that are initiated but have not seen or may not ever see the physical form? How do they develop this love for the physical form of the Master?

A. Even if they have not seen the Master, with the help of meditation they will develop that love for the Master. If they keep on attending to their meditation, even with an intellectual faith or an intellectual belief, they will be able to build that faith. But if they don't attend to meditation at all, then how can they develop that love?

Love for the Master leads us towards meditation, and meditation strengthens our love for the Master, it deepens our love. So, meditation is the main thing. If the Lord gives you that deeper type of love, you are fortunate. Otherwise, if you know the Path, you should attend to meditation, and automatically that faith will come. Automatically that devotion and love will come, with the help of meditation.

32 Q. If one has met you it is very easy to love you, but the ones who have not been here, is there a reason why they're not here?

A. There's no question of a reason why they're not here. They will get the same advantage if they will carry on with the meditation. They may not be here, but their Master is with them.

33 Q. Master, we are told that this Path is one of love, of bhakti, of devotion. In regard to this love and devotion then, which seem to be an essential aspect of the Path, in *Spiritual Letters* it says, "Even after a hundred years of bhajan, one does not get so purified as by an intense longing for darshan," and he continues to say, "Bhajan does not purify so soon as does true love for the Master and a true longing for his darshan. Rather, Satguru himself is Sat Purush."

It seems to me that maybe longing for darshan is more important than bhajan.

A. Brother, longing for darshan will come only out of meditation. Otherwise, this emotional upheaval doesn't lead you far. Sometimes you feel, sometimes you don't feel. Sometimes while being in the presence of the Master, you don't even want to talk to him or look at him; sometimes while being far away from him, you are very anxious to go back to him. But meditation will create real longing in you for darshan. Only meditation will create the desire for that real darshan within.

34 Q. But if the Satguru himself, is Sat Purush, then our looking at him, physical darshan, is also very very helpful.

A. It is helpful, no doubt. Who says it is not helpful? The object of meditation is to create love, and the meaning of love is to eliminate your ego and to become another being. That is the purpose of love. And the purpose of meditation is also the same: to create that love which will eliminate your ego or your individuality and will ultimately make you merge into the other Being. That is love, and that love you can get only by meditation.

Emotions are all right, to some extent, in order to be in touch with the Sound within or to attend to your meditation, but emotion is not the end-all of love. It may be a means leading to love, but the ultimate darshan is within.

Christ has also given the importance of this darshan when he said: it is expedient for you that I leave now.[5] It is expedient for you that I leave my physical body, because this physical body has a certain purpose to play: to create love and desire for the Master in the disciple. That is the purpose of the Master's physical form, and when you don't have the presence of that physical body of the Master, what will you do? You will turn within to the Radiant Form of the Master.

This longing for the physical form, this longing which you cannot fulfill, leads you within towards the Radiant Form of the Master, which will ultimately take you back to the Father. So this physical separation serves its own purpose. As Christ said: you know where I'm going, and you also know the Path leading to me.[6] So, when we don't find the Master outside and we want to be with him, we have no alternative but to attend to meditation and see him within—and that is real darshan.

And then there is also a difference between darshan, and darshan. If you really have darshan of the Master, which is thinking of him as God, then I don't think you need any meditation at all. But I don't think anybody can think of him that way. One moment we think of him as a human being, another moment we think of him as less than a human being, another moment we think of him as God. So it is just academic or intellectual to say that Master is God, for the mind doesn't believe it. It doesn't. If we really believe and really are convinced and really feel that he is God, then we don't need any meditation at all—but it's impossible. These are only things to say, but they're not practical. Nobody can do that.

Q. Perhaps it might be more possible if the Master would not conceal himself so much.

A. No, it's not a question of concealing. It depends upon that real love which you can build only by meditation. As you know, Christ says in the Bible: now you ask me so many questions and you have so many doubts, but when you see me within, then you will have no questions and you will have no doubts.[7] Naturally when we find someone like us in the flesh, how can we think of him as God? It's impossible. Unless we reach to a certain level of consciousness, we cannot.

Academically we all say God is everywhere, but we don't believe what we say. We do so many bad things in this world, which we would not dare do before a child. If we believed that God really is omnipresent, we would never do all these heinous things.

Intellectually, we say He is everywhere, but we don't really feel convinced. We say God is watching us, He's always with us, but then why are we like this if we believe He's watching us and He's always with us? Why are we imperfect then? Aren't we frightened of Him, awed by Him, that He's watching us? We do bad things only when we think that nobody's watching us, and that we don't have to account to anyone.

An academic belief in these things is all right, but only meditation will give you real conviction about these truths. These are simple truths, but you have to experience these simple truths. Only by meditation can one do it.

Guru Nanak also says the same thing. He says: if you see the Master, all your sins will be washed and you will be able to go back to the Father. But, he says, seeing the Master as what? Only when you think of him as God will your sins be washed. If you see him as a man or a guide or a lover or an intelligent man, then what? If you really believe God is here on earth, then all your sins will be washed. That is real love, and that real love can grow only by meditation. There is no other way of engendering that love. We would like to feel that the Master is God, no doubt, but wanting to feel that is something different from what we actually feel.

Without meditation we are not led anywhere. That is why Christ said that to sin against the Holy Ghost cannot be forgiven.[8] Sinning against me can be forgiven, he says—which means that if you have doubt in me, if you doubt that I am the Son of the Father, if you doubt that I am also at the level of the Father while being at your level, then you will be forgiven—but to sin against the Holy Ghost cannot be forgiven. If you don't attend to your meditation, then how can you be forgiven?

Forgiven for what? Forgiven for whatever you have done in past lives. Forgiveness is for those karmas which we have been collecting in every birth and which we have brought with us today. Forgiveness is removing the coverings on the soul. Unless we are forgiven for all those karmas, the soul can never go back to the Father. Christ says, this can be forgiven only by the Holy Ghost, which is why sinning against the Holy Ghost can never be forgiven. If you turn your back to meditation, then how can you expect to ever be forgiven or to ever go back to the Father? If you go on attending to meditation, even if you have some little doubts in the Master, those doubts will automatically be resolved and conviction will come within. For then you are truly building on a rock, you are absolutely unshakable on the Path.

WAY OF LIFE

35 **Q.** Master, regarding our worldly obligations, how much attention do we give to our jobs? How much do we exert ourselves for our work, our careers?

A. This is not the end-all and be-all of life, the purpose of our life. We work because we have to live in this world, but the purpose of living in this world is something different. We have to see proportionately how much time we have to give to these worldly things to maintain ourselves, but at the same time we also have to look to the main duty for which we have come here.

Q. But we have an obligation to the job itself. We're being paid, and therefore we owe a certain amount to that job.

A. Yes, there is no harm in working. I'm not against work. We should work, but we should also give regular time daily to meditation. If you won't work, how will you live in the world? It is how you utilize your whole time that makes the difference. If one is free and spends his whole time in gossiping and sitting in clubs and all sorts of merry-making, how is he going to earn his living? But if you're devoting your allotted time to meditation, to service for humanity, to love and devotion for the Lord, then you are making the best use of your time.

36 Q. Master, I've often heard that if something interferes with our meditation, we should eliminate it, and I was wondering that sometimes we seem to get caught in worldly duties which appear to be really interfering with our meditation. Let's say a job for instance—the job requires so much of our time that it is difficult to do simran during the day and to put in our full time. Should we try to continue to do the worldly duties?

A. Well, brother, you have to adjust your timing, your engagements, your liabilities, your responsibilities. You have to adjust with all those things and then find time for your meditation too. Meditation is primary, but you have to do worldly things also, you have to do both duties. You have certain responsibilities as a wife, as a husband, as a daughter, as a mother, as a citizen, and yet also you have a duty towards the Lord. So you have to adjust everything.

Q. Well, to put it specifically, say that the time for simran is twelve o'clock, and at that particular time a friend needs help. Which takes the priority?

A. It depends upon the situation. After all, the friend doesn't need help during the whole day. But generally, we remember these obligations only at the time of meditation. We never remember these obligations when we are absolutely free. When we are going to a movie or gossiping or sitting in clubs, we don't think about these obligations; these obligations bother us only when we sit in meditation. These are all justifications of the mind to run away from meditation—nothing else. But otherwise, if one wants to, one can adjust everything. One can discharge the worldly obligations, and one can attend to one's own spiritual duty as well.

37 Q. In the books, often it is said that we should adjust our life to attend to our meditation regularly and punctually. Could you speak about the benefits of regularity and punctuality?

A. Well, brother, there is hardly anything to say. You know the advantage of regularity and punctuality. Now when lunch time comes, whether we are hungry or not we quietly go to the dining table, because we have formed the habit of eating at that particular time.

Similarly, we have to form a habit of meditation. If you say, "When I feel the urge I will meditate," you would perhaps never meditate. If you think, "When I feel the right atmosphere, then I will meditate. I will sit in the morning, I will sit at noon, I will sit in the evening," you will always go on giving excuses to yourself; you will never attend to meditation.

Just as you have made a habit of going to the office at a particular time, of going for a walk at a particular time, of going to the dining table at a particular time, similarly you should make a habit of going at a particular time for meditation. Then your mind slowly and slowly is disciplined to attend to meditation. That is why so much emphasis is laid on regularity and punctuality.

If you say,"All right, today I don't feel like meditating; I'll sit tomorrow," then tomorrow again you'll have some other excuse, and the day after tomorrow again you'll have another excuse. Then there will be gaps and gaps and gaps of time, and you'll think, "Oh, I have absolutely forgotten for months and months to sit in meditation." But if you force your mind to meditate and say,"Even if I can't give the proper time to meditation, let me give at least half the time, even if I'm busy," then you'll get regularity.

And punctuality is also important because we have associations with timing. If you have selected a particular time for meditation—for example, 3-30 or 4-30—you know that you have to get up punctually in the morning, and you will also be punctual in going to sleep at night. You will adjust your time in such a way that you get six or seven hours of sleep so that you can get up in the morning. Otherwise you know that you will miss your morning meditation. To this extent punctuality is essential. It should become a habit with us.

Unless we discipline our mind this much, our mind will always find excuses not to sit in meditation. We are regular in our other daily activities—"I have a time to go to the office; I have a time to go to lunch; I have a time to have a cup of coffee; I have a time to walk in the evening; I have a time to sleep"—then why not also have a time for meditation? It should become a part of our life, a part of our daily routine.

If you discipline your mind every day by attending to meditation punctually, then you won't miss meditation, and if you do miss it, then you'll feel miserable that day. You'll feel that something is lacking, and you will try to find some other time for meditation to make up for the lost morning time. Thus, regularity and punctuality are both essential, if we can manage it.

Even having a particular place to sit makes a lot of difference in our meditation. Now, a bed is associated with sleep. If you want to read in bed, the moment you are in bed you will fall asleep, because you have an association of the bed with sleep. If you sit at a writing table, you automatically feel like writing a letter to somebody, because you associate that table with writing letters. If you sit on a comfortable chair, you'll feel like relaxing; you associate relaxation with that chair. So also, if you find a particular place for meditation, then you will have an association with that place for meditation, and that place will remind you to attend to meditation.

These things are just to induce us to attend to meditation—nothing else. Otherwise, if you can keep to meditation without regularity, it is all right. If you can keep to meditation without having a particular place for meditation, it is all right. These are just inducements to the mind not to run away from meditation.

38 Q. Master, sometimes our mind just runs away from this duty of regularity and punctuality, and there is a sense of guilt in not having put our meditation first in our lives.

A. Naturally. We all try to be regular and punctual in our other daily activities. When you tell somebody you will meet him at a particular time, and you are late, you feel guilty. You say, "I'm sorry I'm late," because you feel you have not been able to honor the appointment which you had made. We should also honor the commitment which we have made with the Father, that we have a certain time to attend to meditation. We have to sit, whether our mind is still or not. Whether we have to fight with the mind or not is a different problem, but we have made a certain commitment with the Father, and we should try to honor it by giving our time to the Father at that particular time.

If we are sorry for being late even five minutes in our worldly commitments and we feel guilty within ourselves, then similarly we should carry that feeling of guilt if we don't attend to meditation. Then the next time you will not feel guilty because you won't miss meditation. If you are late today and feel guilty, then the next time you won't be late. If you don't feel repentant, then you will always have a habit of being late. The mind always wants excuses to run away from meditation, and we have to fight it by not giving any excuse to the mind.

39 Q. In the Indian scriptures the hours between 3 a.m. and 6 a.m., or generally the hours of the early morning, are called the "nectar hour." Is there an inner mystic advantage to that hour?

A. No, no. I follow your point. There's no particular time for meditation. Whatever time you can attend to meditation is to your credit, but the morning time has certain advantages over other times. When you get up in the morning, the first thing is you are absolutely fresh. Your tiredness is gone. Your mind is not scattered, and you are not distracted by outside disturbances. There's no telephone ring, there's no knock at the door and there's no hustle and bustle of traffic outside. So it's a quiet time. And then, when you are going to start a day, why not start it in the name of the Father? That atmosphere of bliss which you build by meditation should go with you the whole day to help you face the ups and downs of life without losing your balance.

But if you can't find any time for meditation in the morning, you can easily sit at noon. There's no harm. But then you have to attend to your office work. There may be a knock at the door, and somebody may come unannounced and may even spoil your meditation time. In the evening if you sit in meditation, naturally you have worked the whole day and you are tired. Your mind is scattered and you can't concentrate so easily. That is why the morning time has advantages over other times. But if you don't get the morning time, any time is good for meditation.

In India, at least in the olden days, people used to go to sleep at sunset and would get up before sunrise. So, three o'clock is a very good time for meditation because the day starts at six. Then, before the day starts, one can attend to meditation. And if one has his evening meal, then sleeps fairly early, one easily gets seven to eight hours of sleep.

Q. I wondered, because in some of the Saints' teachings it says that you get a much greater advantage as to concentration, and there's less effort required to get in a spiritual mood.

A. That is what I have told you. Of course less effort is required. Your mind is not scattered. When you get up fresh in the morning, your body is absolutely fresh and your mind is not scattered. It's concentrated. You have forgotten all the ups and downs and all that happened to you during the previous day.

Sleep is a great redeemer. When you've had a good sleep and you get up, you are absolutely fresh, howsoever agitated or perturbed you may have been during the previous day. You forget all that. But if you sit in the evening and your mind has been agitated the whole day, fighting and quarreling with people, doing this and that, then everything will appear before you. So it becomes difficult to concentrate. Hence, that advantage you get in the morning.

40 Q. Is there a stronger working of the Shabd when you are meditating between three and six a.m.?

A. Shabd is always the same. There's no question of the Shabd being particularly strong at that morning hour or the Shabd not working in the evening. At every second, at every moment, it is there. We have to be at the eye center to hear it. There's nothing in a particular hour. But the morning hours are generally calm and quiet, and we are fresh, and nature is so peaceful in the morning, that naturally you feel like sitting for meditation.

41 Q. Maharaj Ji, my question concerns my practice of simran and bhajan. There seems to be a great discrepancy between my practice and the ideal, and these following quotes express to me about the same idea. The first one is from Guru Nanak. It says, "The house that you get after death, reach there by withdrawing your spirit from the body in your lifetime. Nanak, die, withdraw your spirit while you are alive." The second quote comes from a tape recording. "One should sit with the body relaxed but very still, and if after some time, after the first small discomfort, we make a move, one slight move of the spine, the blood circulation returns and we have to start all over again in the process of withdrawing our current upwards." The third one comes from a satsangi who said that as practitioners of Sant Mat meditation, we should strive to sit still for as much as two or three hours without moving. The fourth one is from Tulsi Sahib:* "Physical death is like being stung by a thousand scorpions at once." I understand that day by day we as satsangis should endure a little pain, die early day by day, and another source says there's no gain without pain. My meditation doesn't come close to this. In my busy daily life at home, getting up early, getting home occasionally, frequently by wedging my simran and bhajan at odd hours, at different times and different days, I wonder if I could be deceiving myself in hoping for progress this way.

A. At the time of initiation, we are instructed that we have to give two hours and thirty minutes for meditation at a stretch, and out of that I generally advise to give one and a half hours for simran and one hour for hearing of the Sound. I also advise that if you can't sit for this long at a stretch because you're not used to sitting for so long, you can divide your meditation, to begin with, into two sittings or three sittings. And along with that I also say, try to stretch your time in the morning so that you ultimately give two hours and thirty minutes at a stretch.

In the beginning it is very difficult even to sit still for so long. The mind rebels and wants to go out of the room; it doesn't even want to sit in the room, what to say of doing meditation. I would say, you should not fight so much with the mind that there is a reaction and you leave the meditation altogether. Just give some time, and then at some other time you can give more of your time; but go on stretching your morning time, go on increasing your morning time.

* Tulsi Sahib 1764–1845—a well-known saint who lived in Hathras.

Then you will get into the habit of sitting and giving the proper time of two hours and thirty minutes.

Besides that, you can make use of simran at whatever odd time you get, but we should get into the practice of giving two and a half hours in the morning, not by fighting with ourselves but by slowly and slowly training our mind to sit.

And as far as changing the posture is concerned, we should first find a posture which suits us, then we should try to sit in that posture as long as we can. When it becomes very uncomfortable, very uneasy and you just can't sit still, then it is better to change than to fight with yourself. Because if you start fighting to retain that posture, then naturally your attention is fighting with the body to retain the posture, and your mind is scattered. Then it is much better to walk two or three minutes and to sit again in the same posture, but we should try to sit as much as we can in that particular posture without disturbing ourselves.

And there is no discrepancy at all in what you have read. Guru Nanak said the same thing: that you withdraw your soul current to the eye center, and this way you will go back to your House. And whatever Tulsi Sahib has said—that you have to die while living—means also the same thing: withdrawing your consciousness to the eye center. That is dying while living.

Q. What about the scorpions?

A. He has given an example to show that you should practice dying while living, because it is easier than the death you have to face at the time of death. At the time of death, the pain that you face is just like the pain of scorpions' stings so keep that in mind. In order to avoid *that* pain, now bear this pain of meditation. He has just given this as an example to show generally how much pain we have to go through at the time of death. He says in order to avoid that, a little discomfort now is much better. So we shouldn't mind this discomfort or pain in the body while sitting at the time of meditation, because otherwise we may have to face that pain of the scorpions. It is just a way of explaining to us.

Q. So I shouldn't jump up when the first little discomfort comes, but at the same time I shouldn't torture myself.

A. That's what I say. You try to sit in that particular posture as long as you can and try to extend your sitting in that posture as much as you can. But when a stage comes where it becomes very very uncomfortable for you and in order to keep that posture your attention is scattered, then it is better to change that posture rather than to let your mind scatter out.

42 Q. Ultimately our meditation really should be done at a good, solid stretch?

A. At least solid time should be given. We should try to give two and a half hours at a stretch, but since we are not in the habit of sitting so long, one hour is enough, rather than letting the mind find the excuse, "I can't sit so long." From that point of view, don't give any excuse to the mind not to do meditation. If you can't sit more than an hour at a stretch, then give some more time at some other time and try to extend your morning time until you get into the habit of giving the full time.

43 Q. Master, how important is a healthy body when you're trying to make spiritual progress? Could you expect to go in if you didn't have such a healthy body?

A. That's not the point. Even if you have a very frail body or a weak body, going in depends upon your concentration. The concentration helps you to go in—not how much health you have. But in the beginning a healthy body naturally helps in meditation. A sick person can't sit in meditation easily. He might find it difficult to attend to this daily practice.

Q. Well, what I was thinking about was a degree of health finer than just the obvious kind like if you have a cold or if you're sick to your stomach and can't sit in meditation. I've done other kinds of reading that may be have put some funny ideas in my mind, and sometimes they talk about finer degrees of health. Like, if you have weak kidneys or something, it would be difficult to become so balanced and concentrated that your energy could go up.

A. No. It has nothing to do with that. You don't have to be very strong to sit in meditation, but a healthy body naturally is better. Otherwise you can hardly sit for half an hour before your body starts aching and you feel uneasy, you can't sit, you want to lie down, you feel sleepy.

That is why these yoga asanas were all invented—to maintain health. Rishis and munis used to retire to caves in the mountains for meditation. They didn't come out of their caves, and their needs, which they could meet there, were very few. While being in their caves, they could do all these exercises and keep healthy and attend to their meditation.

44 Q. Master, you said that it is okay for us not to sit in the bhajan position for meditation because we're soft Americans, but isn't this position better for keeping alert and withdrawing the currents?

A. Brother, posture is not important in meditation. It is recommended only from the health point of view, because there are certain postures where you become very lazy and you feel sleepy. But you people are not used to sitting in our Indian way; even most Indians are not now used to sitting in the Indian way. So you can sit in any way which suits you.

Sit in any comfortable position, but not in such a way that you are lured to sleep, that you easily fall asleep. If we can squat (sit cross-legged), then we don't need a chair, and we can sit anywhere. We also sit in the bhajan posture very easily because we don't need the help of anything at all. You can't carry a chair everywhere you go. That is why these are convenient postures.

Even in our daily work, we are advised to keep the spine straight. At our desk and table where we work, the chairs are always straight. If they were very comfortable and you sat on a sofa to work, you would just go to sleep because you would become too lazy. Even dining chairs are straight. Similarly, in meditation we try to keep our backbone straight, and that is from the health point of view. There is no special spiritual advantage in that.

Spiritual advantage will be in the concentration. If your concentration is all right, you will get all the spiritual advantages, whether you are sitting in the Indian posture or in any other posture. Ultimately you forget in what posture you are sitting and whether or not you are even in the body. You have to forget your body. You have not even to be conscious of what position you are sitting in; and unless you come to that stage, you cannot become one with the Divine Melody within.

45 Q. Is it better, if it's possible, to sit without leaning against something?

A. The main thing is, our spine should be straight, from the health point of view, from the alertness point of view. If your backbone is straight, you're more alert and you are not easily lured to sleep. But if your back stoops when you sit, then there's always a danger of getting sleepy, and if we lean against something, sometimes the backbone is not straight. Even if you work sitting in a chair and your backbone is straight, you can work much better. The main thing is, one should try to keep the spine straight.

46 Q. The problem of sleep seems to be the biggest one.

A. Yes, that is right. The problem of sleep is a big hurdle in our meditation, and that practically everybody has to face. Hardly anybody can escape it, because when we sleep, our whole attention is at the throat center, and when we try to concentrate in meditation, our whole attention is at the eye center, and there is very little difference between the eye center and the throat center. The moment we try to concentrate at the eye center, the consciousness slips down to the throat center and we fall asleep.

It is a big problem no doubt. That is rather the only big problem for a disciple, but so many factors help us. One thing—we should never try to sit in meditation at the cost of sleep. We don't want to cut down our other activities for sleep, but we try to cut down our sleep and sit in meditation, and naturally the body needs a certain amount of rest. It varies with the individual's type of work, but everybody needs not less than six hours in any way—sleeping hours, not lying hours.

And then we are not punctual about our time of sleep and getting up. Sometimes we sleep at eleven at night, sometimes at eight at night. The body, however, becomes used to getting up at a certain hour if we are punctual. When we don't remain punctual, then we always find it difficult to get up.

Then, also our food goes a long way in affecting our alertness. If we eat very fatty things, fried things, heavy things, they weigh heavily at the time of meditation. Sometimes, according to what I was told by one doctor, a lack of protein also causes drowsiness and lures us to sleep. So we have to adjust our diet.

In addition, when we get up in the morning, we can move about a little. If we try to sit in meditation in our own bed, and are too lazy to get up and leave the bed and sit down, that also induces us to sleep, as we have an association with the bed for sleep. Associations work a long way. We have an association with the bed just to sleep, so we again are lured to sleep. If you leave the bed and move about, go to the bathroom and wash your face a little and be somewhat active, and then you sit, you will be able to overcome sleep. But one has to fight with persistence and perseverance.

Regularity is the main thing, but in this modern way of life it's very difficult for us to maintain regularity and punctuality, so naturally we go to sleep. But I don't think we sleep when we watch TV or go to a picture house. So our staying awake also depends upon the interest, and the extent of our interest to sit. There are so many reasons that we fall asleep, and we have to find out the cause, and deal with it accordingly.

47 Q. Master, I was told that if one is doing very heavy manual labor, that perhaps you'll get tired because you're doing this type of work, and that it's actually a little harder for you to withdraw from your body because you're more attached to it, having to work very hard with it.

A. I don't think physical exercise, physical work, has anything to do with your withdrawal within. In fact, it has nothing to do with it. It is your attachment to the senses which makes it difficult to withdraw to the eye center. Hard exercise doesn't make it difficult to withdraw from the body, because the body does the exercise, not the mind. It's wrong. Do you mean to say that weaker people who don't do any manual work withdraw more easily?

The only problem is that people who work very hard get too tired, and they should not try to sit in meditation at the cost of sleep. Physical work makes no difference at all in withdrawing.

48 Q. How many grams of protein does our body need daily?

A. It may vary from individual to individual, but still, doctors can advise you better. Most of the protein we can get from our daily food, taking milk and curd and cheese and so many other things. But still, if there's any deficiency, you can consult some doctor or dietitian. They can tell you better.

49 Q. I've heard that meditation on a full stomach is harmful because in meditation the blood goes to the head and therefore does not allow the food to properly digest. Is this true?

A. We don't say meditation is harmful, but if you meditate with a full stomach, you may feel sleepy. Otherwise, you can do meditation at any time—with a full stomach, with an empty stomach; it is all right. But naturally with a heavy stomach you'll be yawning, you will go to sleep, you'll be lazy, so you may not be able to concentrate.

50 Q. Would a cup of hot coffee or hot tea before we meditate be advisable to get rid of drowsiness?

A. If that helps you to keep awake, it is all right.

51 Q. Maharaj Ji, I think it was Jagat Singh Ji Maharaj who said, "Eat less, sleep less, speak less," and I've had a question: I understand the *eat less* and I understand the *speak less*, but I don't understand the *sleep less,* because when I sleep less, it seems to interfere with my meditation. Could you explain that?

A. You should control your sleep. We shouldn't try to sit in meditation at the cost of sleep. We should cut down other engagements of our life, but the body must have six to seven hours sleep.

Q. Do some people need more than that?

A. They should give more time then.

Q. So what does "sleep less" mean?

A. "Sleep less" means that you shouldn't unnecessarily go on sleeping. Some people sleep ten hours or twelve hours, so for them, six or seven hours is less. If you will eat less, you will automatically sleep less. If you will speak less, the mind will not be so scattered. Speaking tires you and scatters the mind, and eating too much makes you sluggish.

52 **Q.** If one wakes up, let's say, at one or two o'clock and is very refreshed, and you know that if you're going to get up and sit for meditation, you have to go back to bed again before six or seven o'clock, is it better to try to sleep and then get up again later, or still to get up and take advantage of the time, knowing you're going to have to go back to sleep again?

A. Do take advantage of that time and attend to meditation. No opportunity for meditation should ever be lost under any circumstances. After that there is no harm in going to sleep.

53 **Q.** If we sit for meditation, but in the two and a half hours we fall asleep for part of the meditation, and if we don't try to make up that part during the rest of the day, is that breaking the vow to do two and a half?

A. Brother, the vow means that it is our good intention to give that much time to meditation. That is the vow. But when we take a vow on ourselves and wo don't attend to meditation, we carry a sense of guilt, that we have not done our duty. That sense of guilt will help you to sit in meditation again, and then you will be able to give more time to meditation. But don't be too rigid about these things. If you have not been able to give the full time in the morning, give more at noon or in the evening, whenever you feel like.

54 Q. If a person falls asleep after meditation, it seems that increased concentration makes the falling down into sleep harder, and people often have vivid dreams or visions, or they sleep so that when they wake up they're much more *tamasic* than they would be ordinarily, and sometimes the lower chakras seem to get aroused. Is that possible?

A. Sister, with concentration you get better sleep, deep sleep. Generally one becomes sleepless when the mind is scattered, and then you take tranquilizers or sleeping pills just to relax and sleep. But concentration relaxes you, and you get better sleep with concentration. If you try to eliminate the worldly thinking, naturally you will relax and go to sleep. If you go on thinking about worldly matters, you will be tense or excited and you won't get sleep at all.

Dreams are a part of sleep, and hardly anybody can avoid them. But you get better dreams if you sleep after meditating or reading some good literature, Sant Mat literature and all that.

Also, when you are sleeping, your body doesn't hold much of your mind as it does when you're awake. In the sleep state, the mind leaves the body, and sometimes you have dreams of flying or going very high, and sometimes you have visions. Even in sleep you sometimes get visions, because it is easier for the mind to leave the body in the sleep state.

But one thing I can tell you: if you don't get

sleep, start doing simran and you will fall asleep. Instead of taking pills, simran is a better "pill."

55 Q. Master, you said that we're supposed to meditate with a relaxed mind, but supposing at the time of meditation all that we have is a tense mind?

A. Then relax it. That is why it is generally recommended that before sitting in meditation we should read *Sar Bachan* or some other devotional Shabd or books, just to fill ourselves with that devotion, with that love, and to forget the misery of the world and our part in that misery, and just to relax the mind before we attend to meditation.

That is why Sardar Bahadur often used to advise us that when we get up from satsang, we should go and sit in meditation, because in satsang your thoughts are all towards the Father and your mind becomes relaxed, spiritually and mentally, so you should take advantage of it for meditation.

56 Q. May songs of devotion be used to put one in the right frame of mind for meditation?

A. There's no harm. You can use those songs of devotion; you can read *Sar Bachan;* you can read any letters from *Spiritual Gems;* you can read anything which creates or generates that devotion in you for meditation. Then sit in meditation.

57 Q. Master, when satsang is given back in our home, is there a devotional time before satsang and after satsang too? A time of quiet and meditation or simran before the meeting and after the meeting?

A. Well, you can sit at any time. There's no question of before or after. Whenever you find it convenient, you can sit in meditation.

Q. Master, I mean for the whole group of people.

A. You mean as a group meditation? Group meditation leads us nowhere, practically. Group meditation is only to create a little atmosphere of holiness to hold the meeting, just to prevent gossiping, bickering and criticizing anybody and unnecessarily hurting anybody. That is the advantage you will have from it. You don't get much spiritual advantage by group meditation because you are always conscious of one another, as to who's to your right and who's to your left and who's snoring and who's breathing deeply. Your mind is not there in meditation at all. Meditation should only be done when alone. That is why it is always advised to retire to some solitary corner for meditation, so that you are not conscious of anybody.

58 Q. What about a husband and wife meditating together in the same room? Is that a good idea?

A. It's all right, sister, if you're not conscious of each other. That is the main thing. If they can forget each other's presence, then it is all right.

59 Q. We talked about meditation not being possible with other people or in a crowd and that we need a small room for silence, but it would seem that with meditation, surely it should be possible to get to the stage where you could meditate instantaneously and therefore do it permanently, anywhere, at any time.

A. We should try to find a lonely place, a quiet corner where we are not disturbed, where we're not conscious of anybody's presence. When you reach to that stage when you're in tune with the Father, then every place is good for you, but that's a very high stage. You can't begin with that. You can end with that.

60 Q. Maharaj Ji, does it make much difference in meditation if you completely cover your head with a blanket? Does it make any difference?

A. How can it make any difference? Whether you keep your head bare or covered, what difference does it make in meditation? Meditation has something to do with the concentration of the mind. You won't get a better concentration when you cover your head or when you uncover it. There's no ritual in Sant Mat.

Q. I read that in a book, Maharaj Ji. I read that it would help to isolate you.

A. No, no, that covering is something different. People cover their head so that they can become unconscious of their neighbor. But if you can become unconscious of your surroundings without covering your head, then there is no need.

Why do we close ourselves in a room? So that we may become unconscious of our surroundings. We just go to a room for meditation because then we don't see anybody, our attention is not drawn to anybody. Otherwise we can sit in the open, in public. Because the public distracts our attention, so we cover our head and face sometimes just to become unconscious of our surroundings. Otherwise there's nothing in it. It's not that you have to do it or that there is any advantage in doing it. That's just to give you a feeling of seclusion, that you're alone. That's the only advantage.

61 **Q.** Maharaj Ji, why is it so very difficult to try and meditate at the Dera?

A. There's no question of any difficulty here. There are no worldly activities to distract you, and all activities that keep you away from meditation are of your own creation. Don't create them and you will get enough time for meditation.

62 **Q.** Master, the other day when I was by the banks of the river outside of the Dera, it seemed to me a good idea to have meditation nets so that one could be closer to nature while meditating. Now, is there not, in fact, some project like this that you have in mind?

A. Brother, actually, we have made this whole Colony, the whole Dera, a project for meditation, but it is for us to keep that atmosphere of meditation here. That is for us to determine how we use it. In fact, this whole Guest House and the whole Dera is made from the meditation point of view. There's no other activity in the whole Colony, but it is up to us how we keep this Colony, how we make use of this Colony.

I'm glad you have asked me this question, because I wanted to tell this to the residents of the Guest House, since I'll be leaving tomorrow, that those who are staying here should try to make best use of their stay in the Guest House. You should try to keep the sanctity and the spiritual atmosphere of this place in the Guest House also, and not create problems unnecessarily.

63 **Q.** Maharaj Ji, quite a few have asked me, is it necessary to attend satsang while you're away, and I said, yes, because it occupies that hour.

A. The question is, what else have they to do here? Otherwise, they will just sit here and gossip. If they can utilize their spare time for meditation, then it is all right, but they can't sit in meditation the whole day.

I'll be having meetings held in my absence every day at whatever time suits you. It may not only be at evening time—even in the day time—because you're free, so you can set up any time which suits you every day. You can ask questions and discuss Sant Mat literature.

And try to do additional meditation in whatever time is left rather than moving about aimlessly in the Colony. It's better to make the best use of your time. In my absence you can read the books, you can read the literature. We have so many books, the library is filled with the comparative study of religions, and we have a lot of books in our own Guest House here for the visitors, so try to make the best use of your time.

64 **Q.** Master, if somebody withdraws the attention from the senses and keeps the mind constantly clean, would this be a great help in focusing the mind at the eye center? By clean I mean that the mind does not go out.

A. Naturally, where will the mind stay then? Here at the eye center. Unless the mind runs out, it is here at the eye center.

65 **Q.** Master, I often have the urge to use creative talents that are in me. I was wondering, is it better that I curb these tendencies and just try to rechannel this energy to the eye center and sit in meditation?

A. No, you can use this creative energy and also meditate. After all, the whole day you can't sit in meditation. If you won't put your talent into art, you will put it to something else. There's no harm. Also attend to your meditation. We have to plan about twenty-one hours in a day, and meditation will only come to about two to three hours. The rest of the day what will you do? We have to do something practical.

66 **Q.** You have said that our whole life must be meditation. Is it a different type of meditation than actually sitting down and withdrawing?

A. That atmosphere which you're building by leading a noble home life induces you to meditate. Otherwise you won't feel like attending to meditation if you're always gossiping and quarreling with one another. But if the atmosphere is good, naturally you're induced towards meditation, and that meditation naturally helps us in every way.

67 **Q.** Maharaj Ji, I have no question, but I should like to thank you for Nam, which I received three years ago today.

A. The real thanks we can give for initiation is to practice it and to live it and to mold our pattern of life accordingly. That is the real, actual thanks we can give to the Master. Mere words are meaningless. They don't carry us anywhere.

68 Q. Master, can you advise us how to mold our life and to carry the teachings with us throughout the day as a sense of seva, a sense of service to the Lord, in our daily life?

A. Sister, the question is, what is seva? Every satsangi should do some seva. Seva is of four types: with the body, with the mind, with wealth, and with the soul. They are all seva. The first three sevas are the means to the real seva, which is seva of the soul, or connecting your soul with the Sound within. That is the real seva. Seva means that service which is done to please the Master, and what pleases the Master most is when we attend to our meditation. Withdrawing our consciousness to the eye center and connecting it with the Sound is the real seva, which is impressed upon us by every Mystic or Saint.

We do seva with the body so that we may be able to eliminate ego from within ourselves. We feel more humble when we are working shoulder to shoulder with the masses. When we sit with them, at their side, naturally we are filled with humility, we feel we are at their level. So, we work with our body for the congregation or for our fellow human beings. We try to be helpful and useful to them just to create humility within us.

And then we do seva of the mind, which means withdrawing our consciousness to the eye center with the help of simran and dhyan, and leading a Sant Mat way of life—being steadfast on the principles of Sant Mat on which we have to build our foundation for meditation. That is seva of the mind.

We do seva of wealth because accumulating wealth usually leads us towards vices, and attachment to wealth creates an inflated ego in us, or a sense of superiority in us, or a sense of possession in us. If we use wealth for the well-being of the masses, for the congregation, it is to our advantage. If some people are filled with love and devotion for the Father directly or indirectly by means of our wealth, that is to our advantage.

Any seva that anybody can do is most welcome, but the real seva is to attend to meditation, to connect your soul with the Sound. These three sevas of wealth and mind and body are the means to that end. If you forget the end, the means will only clean the vessel but will not fill it. Real seva is to clean the vessel and also fill it. Some people give emphasis only to the means without worrying about the end, which is wrong. We clean a cup or a utensil not to see it clean, but because we want to use it—we want to put milk into it, we want to put coffee or tea into it. We want to use that clean vessel. That is the purpose of cleaning the vessel. If every day you go on cleaning a vessel but again it gets dusty, and again you clean it, then why clean it? What is the use if you don't use it, you don't fill it?

So these three sevas which I have explained to you are only the means to an end, and the real seva is Surat Shabd Yoga, connecting your soul to the Sound. That is the seva that is the most pleasing to the Lord and to the Master. The first three sevas should lead us to the fourth seva, which is the real seva.

69 Q. We're told and we read the importance of doing simran not only during meditation but all the time, and this is not easy because we forget. How important is it to try and do simran all the time?

A. If simran had not been so important, Saints wouldn't have impressed upon us the necessity for it. It is important. If you let your mind run out and think about worldly things the whole day and you want to pull it back to the eye center in just an hour or so, how can you succeed? After all, it takes time then to withdraw. If you don't let the mind run the whole day, then it becomes easier to pull it up to the eye center. That is the main reason.

And then it also frees us from many worries and unnecessary miseries. Either we are miserable thinking about the past or we are worried about the future. We don't want to spend this present moment happily. There is something wrong with us. We never want to be happy at the present moment. Either we are worried about what we have done or about what is going to happen to us. We don't want to make best use of the present moment.

If we make this moment happy, our past automatically becomes happy, and we have no time to worry about the future. So we must take life as it comes and spend it happily. Every moment should be spent happily. And simran helps.

70 Q. If we're faced with temptations and we say simran, how does that help?

A. Well, sister, what is simran? Simran is a means to concentration at the eye center, and we are tempted by the senses only when our mind is scattered. When the mind comes from the eye center downward to the senses, only then are we tempted by these senses. When it is not scattered, when it is collected at the eye center, automatically you will save yourself from all those temptations. In that way simran helps. It keeps you concentrated at the eye center; it keeps your thoughts at the eye center.

71 **Q.** If we think that the Lord is present in this world and in all things; if we feel that this world, in a way, is a manifestation of God's bounty and love, then can't we also indulge in the contemplation of that beauty? If we do simran all the time, how can we do any creative work? How can we compose music or poetry or enjoy the beauty of nature?

A. No, no, brother. I said whenever your mind is free. If you're doing any creative work, naturally you need your mind to work there. If you have a duty as a clerk in a bank and you're working with the accounts, how can you say, "I refuse to do it; I must do my simran"? Do simran whenever you're free. Saints don't say that you have to leave your worldly work and all that. Do simran when you're mentally free.

For example, you're going for a walk; your mind is free. Instead of gossiping with a friend, you can easily do simran. You're traveling by air; you're going by train; you're going by car; you're sitting on a lawn and just enjoying the sunshine—why can't you make use of that spare time? So that is what the Mystics mean—when we are mentally free we should try to make best use of that time by doing simran.

72 **Q.** Can't we say, Master, that an atmosphere of beauty is conducive to meditation?

A. It depends upon the attitude of the person. Some people are so lost with so much beauty around that they just can't concentrate. But on the other hand, this beauty helps some people to concentrate. It depends upon the individual, his approach and the concept of beauty is also one's own.

73 **Q.** Would you say that an attitude of inner contemplation, reflecting on God, thinking of Him, of His kindness and love, also has value in some way?

A. That's right. That will automatically induce you to do simran. That will help you to do simran, naturally.

74 **Q.** Often I feel like I could do simran more, but I'm afraid that somehow things are going to get out of hand unless I'm really concentrating on what I'm doing.

A. No, only at the time of meditation you should attend to simran with concentration. When you are doing mental work, then you can't do simran, but if you are doing work with your hands or just walking, then of course your mind is free and you can attend to simran. When your mind is occupied, how can you do simran, unless you have reached the stage where it goes on automatically in your subconscious mind.

75 **Q.** There are some jobs where you either have to actively use your mind all the time or you have people coming at you all the time with questions and things, and you feel like you're being nibbled to pieces sometimes. I absolutely cannot do simran under either of these circumstances.

A. Sister, one has to adjust one's daily activities, daily life, daily engagements. One has to adjust. We have to do our worldly duties also. If I say,"I won't like to come to the evening meetings," how can I escape, howsoever comfortable I may be in my bed? I have to come here, I think it's my duty. We have to fulfill certain responsibilities, certain obligations, but still we have so much spare time when we unnecessarily make ourselves miserable by thinking. At least that time should be spared for simran. We're not constantly busy with work.

76 **Q.** Doesn't the simran revolve twenty-four hours a day in one's head once one gets advancement? Even when one goes through one's pralabdh karmas, doesn't the simran revolve?

A. It can if one is in the habit of doing simran. Then even unconsciously one is doing simran. You get into the habit of doing simran so much that even unconsciously you are attending to it.

Q. Does the Master do it for us in those circumstances?

A. You mean the Master should do the simran and you should just feel free?

Q. Only when we can't do it.

A. Do we ever do it? We are only an instrument to do it. The Doer who's forcing us to do it is always there.

77 **Q.** Master, last night someone asked a question about having conversations with the Master in their own mind, and you said it was just the mind. Is this a good or bad practice? Should we try to stop it when it happens or just ignore it or what, when we carry on these conversations with the Master?

A. Doing simran is better than the conversation. If you don't want to do simran, then you can converse. But simran should have preference over conversation.

78 Q. Maharaj Ji, Baba Ji says,"Once again you're enjoined to note that there should be no time when you're not having bhajan and simran," and at other places he says specifically,"While walking, sitting, sleeping, continue your simran." And you have mentioned that you should continue to have meditation in your dreams. My question is, how do you do simran when you're sound asleep?

A. No, no, I said one should not forget the Path even in a dream. It's a way of explaining. *Even in a dream* means that generally in a dream you forget everything of the world. I said we should not forget meditation even in a dream, which means it should never be forgotten.

Q. Well what did Baba Ji mean,"While walking, eating, sleeping, you should attend to your simran"?

A. In your daily life at all times, you should not forget the teachings.

79 Q. While on simran I have another question concerning it. It's supposed to be constant, and if simran does have to do with the attention, then in the business world when you're forced to concentrate your whole attention on a particularly difficult, intricate problem, how can you do simran at that time?

A. No, you are taking it too literally. What Baba Ji means to say is that whenever we are free, we should always be doing simran. Whenever we can. The words are, even in a dream you should not forget the Lord, which means that under no circumstances should you forget the Lord. In your daily activities you should not forget the Lord, you should not forget the teachings, you should not forget your bhajan and simran. In your daily activities with the world, under any circumstances, under any direction that you're working, you should not forget the teachings.

80 **Q.** I was reading in *Spiritual Letters* that Baba Jaimal Singh said to Great Master, "I'm responsible for your simran and bhajan when you're doing your official duties." Could you tell us what that means?

A. Those letters are from one Master to another Master in the making, so you and I can't generalize those letters. What he means to say is, you think that whatever work you are doing is your Guru's work, and that your Guru is in everything. In whatever you are doing in life, in all your activities, your Master is there. He's associated with everything you do during the whole day, and whatever you do then is bhajan and simran for you. Don't forget your Master in any activity of life.

Q. That means it was meant for Maharaj Ji?

A. It means don't forget your Master and the Path and the Sant Mat way of life at any moment, in any activity of life. Then all that you do is bhajan and simran. That's what Baba Ji has written to the Great Master.

81 Q. I find that bhajan makes the daily living very difficult for me, because when the bhajan is truly concentrated, I find that my mind, my spirit, or my soul, whatever it is, is reluctant to once again re-enter the swirl of daily living.

A. We have to do both things. We have to live in the world, but we have to meditate also. We have to keep a balance between the two, because there is a certain load of karmas which can be cleared only by facing life and not just by attending to meditation. When we become absorbed too much in meditation, sometimes the Master also withdraws the grace so that we may work in the world, we may not leave our worldly work. Rather, we may even be pushed to the world to face the world.

It's a very strange thing—I can tell you a little from my personal experience also. First, we have no love for the Path, we have no love for the Master. The Master forces us to love him, he creates love for the Lord in us. He holds satsangs, he makes us work, he makes us do seva. All these things he does just to fill us with love and devotion for the Father. And when that love arises in us, when we become a victim of that love, then he conceals himself. Then it's a game of hide-and-seek. He does not want us to be so much absorbed in that love that we leave our worldly duties and worldly work.

As a child I got my education while living here in the Dera. Probably I was just five or six when I was brought here by the Master, and naturally as a child everybody is fond of play and of his friends. We used to play and run about on the river banks here and there, and a man would always be sent to bring us in from where we were, and we would be made to hear the satsang. We were made to sit in the front, and if we were noisy, we would have to sit in the back, but we could not leave the satsang. We had to sit in the satsang, and when, slowly and slowly, slowly and slowly, things started making their way in us and we realized what we were getting, we were pushed out of the Dera and told by the Master, "Go and practice law here and do jobs there and don't come to Beas for six months, and then don't come every month."

This is a game of very strange hide-and-seek. As children we were all right; we used to play with friends. We never thought about the Path and the Master and love and God and all that. First the Master created all that in us. When he succeeded in that, then he pushed us into the world to face the world. So this happens; there's nothing new to it. The Master would like us to keep the balance.

82 Q. Master, when one realizes that he is helpless, what should be his next move?

A. The next move is to sit in meditation. When one finds that he's absolutely helpless, then he should really become helpless and submit himself to meditation and leave his intellect. That's the only move one should make.

PROTECTING THE TREASURE

83 Q. Would you please explain how satsang is building a fence around the crop of meditation?

A. What it means is that by meditating we are building a treasure in heaven. We get all sorts of powers within ourselves—with the help of meditation we can perform miracles, we can do so many jugglery tricks—but if you go on losing it like that, then you remain a pauper. If you earn ten rupees in a day and in the evening you just spend it all, you are back to where you started at the beginning of the day.

Satsang will help you to preserve that treasure of meditation. Satsang will help you to remain humble and not to become the rival of the Lord, "He didn't give you a son and I have given you a son. He deprived you of this boon in life and I am giving you this boon in life." You are just trying to become a rival of the Father by performing miracles. But satsang will help you to remain in His Will, which is real humility and meekness. It will help you treasure all of the grace of the Father that is within you.

The more you treasure and digest within yourself your wealth of meditation, the more He showers His grace upon you. When a son grows and becomes an adult and starts his business, a responsible father will give him a small sum of money to invest in the business. If the son is rightly handling the accounts and not wasting the money, and is giving proper time to the shop and to the business, the father is happy to give him more and more. Ultimately, the father gives all that he has to his son, when he thinks that the son can handle it. If, however, on the very first instance the son starts squandering the money and not giving any attention to his business, then the father also withholds his hand.

We do achieve results in meditation when we start honestly on the Path, and if we are able to digest and treasure that bliss and peace within, we get more and more grace within; but if we waste it, if we squander it, then He also withholds His hand of grace from us.

84 **Q.** Then, Master, do we squander this treasure if we speak about our meditation?

A. You are doing meditation for your own good and not for impressing other people. To talk about it means you want other people to appreciate that you are a great devotee of the Father. You want them to praise you, and you want to inflate your ego.

Q. Then is there any harm in telling a lie to keep one's meditation a secret? I've read in *Divine Light* that one should never tell a lie.

A. You see, by concealing certain facts, we try to inflate our ego or we want to hurt somebody, knowing very well that it is wrong. But when that motive is not there, I don't think you are telling a lie at all. Just by avoiding a question, doesn't mean you tell a lie. When you don't want to share certain things with some people, I don't think you are telling a lie.

For example, if you don't want to share your spiritual experiences with your wife or anyone else and you just smile or keep quiet, I don't think that is telling a lie. There's no motive to hurt anybody or to inflate your own ego or to show your own superiority by concealing certain facts. That motive is not there in your mind. But if by concealing certain things we gain for ourselves, and we try to hurt somebody else for our own gain, then of course it's not right.

85 Q. Maharaj Ji, would you please explain to us the importance of never divulging any inner experience? Because there are so many stories going on that so-and-so said he went up and saw Light, or other such experiences.

A. Sister, it is not in one's own interest to share one's inner experience with anyone, because even if not consciously, then unconsciously there is always ego. When you discuss or share with another person your own spiritual experiences, you think, "You didn't even see the Light? You couldn't even cross that?" So you definitely become the victim of ego, and the moment you become a victim of the ego, your progress stops and you lose what you had. That is the main reason for not sharing your spiritual experiences with anybody.

This is an individual relationship of the soul with the Father. It's nobody else's business. Nobody else comes between the soul and the Father. No one has any right to share that experience. That is just the relationship of the soul with its own Origin, its own Path. Why should we like to share? A wife doesn't share all the secrets of her husband with anybody else. How can you expect the soul to share all the spiritual experiences and secrets within with anybody else? It should be digested, and the more you digest it, the more grace you will find within, the more receptive you become to His grace.

And then if we start sharing our experience, there is always a danger of becoming a victim to performing miracles, because the ego inflates—"I can do this and I can do that"—and things do happen, because you have attained a certain level of consciousness within. You're not even conscious of your spiritual powers, but you say things and then they come true—not that you want to perform "miracles," but you have the power to perform them. Unconsciously you do those things, and you always do them at your own cost. So, it's always better to remain obscure and just digest within yourself all that you have. One can say, "I'm happy with my meditation," and that's all.

Moreover, when other persons know that you are quite spiritually advanced and you see the Light or that you are very happy spiritually within, they start humoring you and praising you, and then there's always a danger of your ego becoming inflated. They start showing you undue regard and respect, they take you as a great soul, a spiritual leader, and you also become over conscious of all that honor. Then the result is that you lose what you had.

That danger is always there, and people are selfish. They will be around you for their own selfish purposes. Not that they are happy about your spiritual progress, they simply want to take advantage of your spiritual progress. Some want a child; some want worldly fame; some want sickness to leave the house. That is why they are hovering around you—for their own selfish purposes. They think that they can use you because you have some spiritual experiences, spiritual powers within. Then you are likely to be tempted by all this, and ego creeps in when you start getting importance from people, and you lose everything.

The Great Master used to tell us that the sadhus leave everything in the world, but they cannot leave self-importance. They always want self-importance, and people, due to their own selfish purposes, are anxious to give it to them. The moment any importance is given to anybody, there is a danger of his falling. So it's always better to remain obscure.

86 Q. Is running after the Master out of love for him the same as outwardly expressing our inner experiences and feelings of devotion and love?

A. Running after the physical form of the Master is something very different from having love for the Master. Running after the Master doesn't mean that you have love. You may be empty within and still you may be running after the Master. Yet, you may be filled with love for him and you may not move even an inch. You would like to remain in discipline, but that doesn't mean you have no love. Running after the Master doesn't show any special love.

Love is always within. When you try to dramatize your love, you lose the depth of the love. You have to digest that love within. If you have that love within, the moment you try to dramatize it, you lose its depth.

87 Q. Maharaj Ji, there is a metaphor used to explain that emotions in Sant Mat are like a river that has to be controlled, that emotions have a force in Sant Mat.

A. I don't know what you mean, but emotions are all right if they lead you to devotion, but they should be channeled. If you let loose your emotions, they become a nuisance. If the river flows within its banks, only then it is useful. But when the river floods, it overflows its banks and creates devastation everywhere.

In the same way, emotion is very useful when it is channeled, when it is disciplined. But if your emotions get out of control, then they are just like the flood of a river which does more harm than good. So we should have disciplined emotions, disciplined love for the Master.

88 Q. If one begins to feel love for the Master, should one try to hide this, keep it inside and try to not let it show?

A. Would you like to publicize your love or go to the roof and shout about it? Love has to be within, sister. It will reflect in your actions. Your face will betray you, but you don't have to shout.

Q. Should you try to hide your face from showing it?

A. If you can, but there is no need for that exercise at all. Love will definitely reflect from your every action. Your whole daily living will reflect how much you really love the Master. But love is not to be advertised or to be shouted to the masses. Real love is never dramatized. It flourishes and grows only in silence. It is just between you and Him. Why should anybody come between us? We don't love the Master to show it off to others. That approach should not be there.

4

Meditation

Meditation

The Lord is permanent and eternal. He is birthless and deathless. Those who remember Him and continually think of Him will also become immortal. They will end the cycle of births and deaths. We should, therefore, focus our attention between and behind the eyes by constantly repeating the Lord's Name, and should keep it there by turning our outward mental tendencies inward.

This practice is so simple and easy that a child of five or a man of hundred years old can do it without difficulty. We have a natural habit of doing simran, or repetition. We have merely to change it from simran of the world and its objects to simran of the Lord—from the transient to the Eternal. As a result, our thought currents are reversed and become concentrated at the third eye. But at first they will not stay there, because they are in the habit of dropping down and wandering out into the world through the nine apertures. It is difficult to keep the mind still in darkness and in emptiness, unless we give it some form upon which to contemplate.

But on what form should it contemplate? We become strongly attached to whatever form the mind comtemplates on. Bound by love for that form, the mind will go wherever that form goes. Therefore, the object or form that is most worthy of our worship and contemplation is one whose body is on earth, but whose soul is in heaven and is constantly in communion with the Lord. Such a God-man we find in the Master. Only he is worthy of our worship.

Through contemplation, the mind develops the habit of staying at the eye focus, or third eye. By contemplating on the form of the Master who initiates us, by loving him, we become attached to him. We imbibe his spiritual power and ultimately merge in the Lord. The drop, once separate, joins the ocean and becomes the ocean.

The real purpose, then, of dhyan, or contemplation on the form of the Master, is to assimilate the universal, timeless, and eternal teaching; namely, to join the soul with the immanent powers of the Shabd and Nam, the Light and Sound within. When we become concentrated and one-pointed at the eye focus, we discover for ourselves, through bhajan, or listening to the Sound within, that there is a Divine Melody, an Inner Music, which emanates from the house of the Lord.

This immanent Power recognizes no caste, creed or color, nor any geographical boundaries. It is the heritage of all mankind, whether they are rich or poor, young or old, man or woman. Everyone has an equal right to it. Whether one is Hindu, Muslim, Christian or Sikh, he alone is on the right Path who focuses his attention at the third eye and contacts this Holy Spirit, the Shabd and Nam within.

The Saints and Masters call this practice "dying while living." By withdrawing our consciousness to the third eye and listening to the Music of the Sound Current, the Audible Life Stream, our mind and soul together rise out of the tomb of this body and become free from it. By the grace of the Master, we cut asunder our attachments with the world and forget its troubles and miseries. Daily, through the practice of meditation, we die. We die to live, to enjoy the eternal bliss and peace of our True Home, and live forever.

CONCENTRATION

89 Q. Master, would you briefly explain how to meditate?

A. How to meditate? You have to close the eyes, so that your attention doesn't go out. And when you close the eyes, automatically you are where you should be. You close the eyes, and you are just at the eye center. Then, keeping your attention there, you should try to do simran. The idea is that your attention shouldn't scatter outside, it should be here at the eye center.

90 Q. Maharaj Ji, if the higher regions are above the eye focus, then why couldn't we concentrate above the eye focus instead of starting here?

A. Well, brother, when you are sitting midway up a hill, you just can't start your journey from the top, nor would you like to go back down to the bottom in order to climb up to the top. We are all sitting here at the eye center, which is the natural seat of the soul and mind knotted together in the conscious state.

Whenever you are thinking about anything, or you have forgotten something and you wish to recall it, automatically your hand goes to your forehead. You will never put your hand to any other part of your head or your leg. This is a natural habit. When you want to remember something, or think deeply, you automatically concentrate here, because the seat of the soul and mind is here at the eye center.

Hence, we want to start from where we are. Neither do we want to come down to the lower chakras, the lower centers, and start up, nor can we start from higher up. So we have to start from the eye center.

91 Q. Previously I once heard that our third eye is open while we're in the womb, and later on after we become initiated, we then become aware of its state of openness. Is this true, or is it that the third eye is not opened until after we're initiated?

A. The opening of the third eye means that we start seeing the visions or we have spiritual progress within. When you see the Light, the colors, the moon and all those things inside, there is something which sees all that inside, and that we call the third eye.

The third eye is known as such because we're in the habit of seeing through the eyes, but these physical eyes are not required inside. Some other perception is required, so we call it a third eye, but there's no eye at all which you have to find inside. Christ calls it the door of the hosue,[1] but then there's no door there either. These are just ways of explaining things. When you enter a house you need a door to go in. Without a door you cannot get in, and without the veil being removed, you cannot see anything inside. That is why it has been called the third eye or the door of the house.

92 Q. Maharaj Ji, you've written that the door at which we have to knock is the center between and behind the eyes. My question is, if the attention is kept in the darkness which is seen when the eyes are closed, will that attention at some stage of concentration automatically go behind the eyes?

A. You are automatically there. When you close your eyes, you are nowhere else but there behind the eyes in the darkness. Just close your eyes and forget where you're concentrating. You don't have to find that spot at all. Whenever you're thinking, you're automatically there at the eye center, so you close your eyes and you see the darkness, and being there in the darkness, do the simran. That is the point which is referred to. You're automatically there.

Q. So, during meditation one shouldn't make a constant effort to feel that he is located at the eye center, but should just look into the darkness and let that feeling of "being there" come automatically?

A. That's right. When you close your eyes, you are normally automatically here at the eye center, because the seat of the soul and mind knotted together is at the eye center. When you close your eyes, you are here in the center of the darkness in the forehead, and being there, you do the simran. You also feel that your Master is there and that you are there in the darkness and you are doing simran in the presence of the Master, if you can't visualize his form. So be there and also feel your Master is there, and that will hold your attention there in the darkness.

93 Q. I have read that at the time of meditation we should imagine that we are sitting at the eye focus. Should we do that rather than just try to be at the eye focus?

A. They're the same thing, brother. Just be at the eye focus, which means to try to concentrate at the eye focus or to think that you're at the eye focus. They are the same thing. It is a way of explaining.

Q. I thought it was different in that we're actually picturing ourselves in our mind's eye as being at the eye focus.

A. No, you be at the eye focus, which means to be in that darkness. When you close the eyes, you are there where you should be. Being there, you should do simran. Whenever you close your eyes, you are where you should be. Be there and do simran.

94 Q. What do you mean when you say to look into the darkness?

A. You close your eyes; you see nothing but darkness. Be there and do simran. Being in the darkness, do simran. That is what I mean by looking at the darkness.

95 Q. When you're looking at the darkness while you're doing your simran, as long as you can see that darkness, can you be sure that you're at the eye center, that you have not dropped to the lower centers?

A. As long as your attention is there in the darkness, you are there, but when you start thinking about all the problems of the world, you are not there, whether you see the darkness or something else. When your attention is there, you are there. If your attention is not there, you are not there.

96 Q. Is it difficult to hold the attention there when we're sick? It seems that the mind becomes more imaginative when we're a bit ill.

A. Probably because you don't have anything else to do. When your mind is absolutely free, then it starts imagining all sorts of things, but when it is busy, then naturally it doesn't imagine so many things. That is why they say that a vacant mind is a devil's workshop. The mind is never still, even if you close yourself in a dark room and lock it from the outside. Your mind is never there. It is always running about in the world imagining all sorts of things.

97 Q. Master, when I try to concentrate in the darkness, my mind flits about. I'm wondering then if the attention can be in two places at once?

A. Not only two places—the mind can run to a thousand places. While you're talking, even if you're giving a lecture, your mind is thinking about something else. The mind has the faculty to think about many things at a time. You're doing simran and your mind is wandering in the whole world, thinking of all the worldly problems—that also is the mind. So the mind can be not only in two places, but in many places at a time.

98 Q. I read that we should hold the mind still in meditation, but that we shouldn't concentrate on a physical point for the eye focus. You have said that it's a mental position. Then how do we know what to concentrate on if it's in the mind?

A. When you close your eyes, you are there where you should be. Being there, do simran, concentrate.

When you close your eyes, you are nowhere outside. You are just here at the eye center, unless your mind is scattered somewhere outside. When you close your eyes, don't try to find any particular point. Don't try to invert your eyes physically and focus at any particular point or try to search physically by inverting your eyes. The eyes should not be strained physically at all. When you close your eyes, you are automatically there where you should be, so being there, you should try to concentrate.

99 Q. Is it wrong for the eyes to turn upward?

A. You don't have to invert the eyes physically in order to find any particular object within, because these physical eyes have nothing to do with what you are going to see inside. These eyes are meant only for the outside, so you don't have to invert your eyes physically, nor do you have to focus them at any particular point, because you will then strain your eyes. Just close your eyes and forget about them, and being at the eye center, do simran, with the attention there. Only when you are able to hold your attention at the eye center, will you be able to catch the Sound. Rather, the Sound will pull you upward, and you will be in the Light.

100 Q. When doing dhyan, if the physical eyes want to go together and it's not a strain, is that all right, or should we make an attempt to not let them go to the third eye?

A. You should not be conscious of your eyes at all, no question of not letting them go or trying to bring them together. Close your eyes and forget about them.

There should be no strain on the eyes from any point of view. Just forget about them. When you sleep, you don't strain your eyes to sleep. You just close them and then you sleep. So just close your eyes and do simran.

Q. And another thing is that when I try, my concentration drops down and I feel that my attention has dropped, and that's why they say to make an effortless effort. And I didn't know whether to insist, even if there is a little strain.

A. Yes, a little strain will be at the forehead. That is why we are advised that after meditation, we can rub our forehead and our eyelids lightly to relieve any little strain there might be. But the strain is insignificant.

101 Q. When we make an effort to hold our attention inside, does that mean that we are allowing the mind to scatter away from the eye center?

A. No, you have not followed my point. I didn't say that when we make an effort we are not at the eye center. I said, if you make an effort trying to find a particular point, then your mind will wander out.

Effort we have to put forth to concentrate, to do simran. Doing simran is an effort you are putting forth, for when we do simran, we have to forget the whole world. We are concerned only with the darkness in our forehead. We close our eyes and we see nothing but darkness, and when you close your eyes, you are there where you should be. Keeping your mind in that darkness, do simran.

Don't try to find any particular point in that

darkness such as two or three inches up in the darkness, two or three inches down. Then you are lost in that, you are always conscious of finding a point, and you don't concentrate. Just forget your eyes, even forget your body. Close your eyes—you are automatically there where you should be, and then do simran.

What I was trying to say was that we generally think that the center is in the forehead physically and that we must try to find that physical center within, but then we are lost in that. The center automatically will come with our concentration.

102 **Q.** Maharaj Ji, some of the yogas teach that the pineal gland and the pituitary gland are seats of soul consciousness. Is there any truth to this?

A. Well, brother, actually, we have to concentrate at the eye center, and they try to explain those things physically, that this gland is here and that gland is there. We shouldn't get mixed up at all with that. When you close your eyes, you are automatically there where you should be, and you have to be there, you have to still yourself there.

Q. Then a loss of one of those glands wouldn't affect—

A. No, certainly not. Even if that gland is damaged or taken away, that doesn't mean you can't concentrate at the eye center.

Q. It's necessary, isn't it?

A. That gland may be physically necessary for living, but I know people who are deaf, who can't hear these outside noises at all, and yet they are hearing the Sound.

103 Q. Master, in the journey from the eye center to the top of the head, which you often talk about, during the course of that journey, does anything chemically or physically happen in that section of the head as a reflection of what happens spiritually?

A. Yes, there are physical symptoms of withdrawal, and these are explained at the time of initiation.

104 Q. But Master, up till that point the current is withdrawn to the eye center, right?

A. That's right.

Q. And then does it leave the body there, or—

A. No. Everything is within the body. Your consciousness comes to that level.

Q. But does it rise higher then? Does the consciousness rise to the top of the head also?

A. You can say it is rising higher, but where is the beginning and where is the end? Consciousness doesn't physically start from the eyes and physically end at the top of the head. We mean that from a lower level of consciousness you go to the higher level of consciousness. From wherever the level of consciousness starts, from there now you are going upwards in your level of consciousness. That's what is meant.

105 Q. I think the books also say that the head is the laboratory of the whole creation.

A. Yes, because without having your concentration at the eye center, you won't understand anything about the creation, so everything comes from the head. Your whole mind is scattered, being pulled down from the eye center through the nine apertures. If you forget anything and you want to recall it, automatically you will put your hand to your forehead. You won't touch your legs or any other part of the body. This place has something to do with our thinking center, and we have to withdraw our consciousness to that very thinking center. From there your level of consciousness will move upwards.

106 **Q.** Maharaj Ji, are there centers at the top of the head which are affected by one's meditation other than just the third eye?

A. Sometimes we do feel some sensations in the head at the time of meditation. This is because unconsciously, unintentionally, we are straining our eyes. We feel warmth or a tingling sensation there, but there's nothing to worry about.

107 **Q.** Maharaj Ji, some of us were discussing earlier the sensation when one begins to meditate of sometimes feeling nauseous. Could you explain something about this?

A. I don't know what exactly you mean by a nauseous feeling, but when you are withdrawing the soul current upwards from the throat center, you have a certain choking sensation in the throat, to begin with, and you feel as if your throat has become dry or parched by too much speaking. If you have a little sip of water, or you swallow, or if you gently rub the throat with the hand once or twice, the feeling goes.

And then also when we try to concentrate here at the eye center, there's a little, insignificant pressure on our eyes, because unconsciously the eyes start inverting inside, but one can easily remove it by rubbing the eyes once or twice lightly. And there is also insignificant pressure in the forehead, which one can relieve too.

A feeling of nausea can come if you have eaten something that doesn't suit you, or if you are sitting in a closed room and the air is not fresh, or if you are synchronizing your simran with breathing. Then a nauseous feeling will definitely come. But we should never think about breathing at the time of simran. Now you are listening and I am talking; neither you are conscious of your breathing, nor I am conscious of my breathing. It is a normal function of the body, and we should never give any attention to it at all.

108 Q. Maharaj Ji, during meditation suppose several times you experience one of these sensations of say, the parchness of the throat, and then for a long period after that you never experience this again. Does it mean that you haven't achieved that real concentration again?

A. No, sometimes we feel it, sometimes we don't feel it. If now you have been able to overcome it, you may get it again sometime. But whenever you are confronted with such a situation, you can always help yourself just by rubbing the throat a little or by swallowing a few times, or by sipping a little water.

109 Q. Some people, at the time of meditation, become hot or cold. What is the reason for changes in temperature of the body during meditation?

A. I don't think you feel any heat or cold. Sometimes we feel a little cold when we withdraw to the eye center. Then there is a little difference in temperature, but it's not so much that you start shivering. Otherwise, the normal temperature remains the same.

110 Q. Master, sometimes during meditation there's a sort of sensation, like someone taking their hand and rubbing it up the center of your spine. Is this something to worry about?

A. We start feeling many types of activities and sensations in the body. Sometimes you feel that type of sensation at the backbone, but just ignore it.

111 Q. Sometimes the body jerks when we're in meditation. Could you explain that?

A. Sister, we do jerk sometimes. Sometimes with emotions or devotion we try to hold our attention, and we do succeed in concentration, but we are spread out so much into the body that we find it difficult for the soul to pull up, so sometimes we start jerking and some people even fall unconscious.

But there's nothing to worry about in the least. No damage comes to the body. You will again get up. If you feel such jerks, you can lean against something hard or sit in a comfortable chair with some support, and then you can attend to simran. Sometimes these jerks do come, but they ultimately will leave you.

112 Q. Maharaj Ji, I have heard that after ten minutes of sitting, you should make a habit of then adjusting your posture, and then you'll sit longer.

A. You are not even to be conscious of that changing of the posture or of that adjustment. Sometimes when you're thinking about some serious problem, you are not conscious of whether a fly has come to your nose or even that you have removed it with your hand. You're not conscious of who has come to your room or who has gone from your room. You're not conscious of anybody, because you're so much absorbed in that thinking. So similarly, we should get so much concentration with the simran that we're not even conscious of a little change in the posture—that from this leg you have moved the other leg. You don't even know if the body moved. You're not even conscious of it.

When I become conscious of the posture—that now I am keeping my one leg here and I am feeling very uncomfortable and I say I'm not going to change it whatever may happen—I may be able to retain that posture for one hour, but I'm fighting to retain it. My concentration is not there, I'm not in the simran at all. From that point of view it's better to change the posture rather than to lose your concentration.

113 Q. This question pertains to numbness of the limbs, Maharaj Ji. There is a physical cause, as I understand it, such as pressure on the limbs or lack of circulation of the blood, and this is a numbness; and secondly there is withdrawal of the soul currents through concentration, and this produces a numbness in the limbs. My question is, is there a difference between the two types of numbness? Do both assist in concentration?

A. There is a little difference. The type of numbness we need is the withdrawal numbness, when the soul withdraws from the nine apertures and comes upwards.

Numbness, means that you are not aware of that part of the body. Sometimes when you are absorbed in your own thoughts, thinking about some problem, and somebody comes to the room or goes away, you don't even notice who has come and who has gone. If anything crawls on your leg, you don't even feel it, because you are so much absorbed in your own thinking. That is numbness of the body—you become completely unconscious of the body. You're not concerned in what position you're sitting. Your absolute withdrawal is there; your concentration is complete at the eye center. That is withdrawing your consciousness from the body.

It may not be physical numbness at all. You are not aware of your body, you are not even aware of the way you are sitting, you're not aware of yourself. You're so much concentrated and so much one with that Shabd or Nam within that you're not even aware of any part of the body. If you are aware that this part has become numb and you have withdrawn from this, then that is not right concentration. Numbness means you're absolutely not aware of the body.

Physical numbness naturally is all right, but that is not the end-all and be-all. The real numbness is withdrawal of the soul currents. Then you're not even aware of the body.

114 Q. Is there a length of time in meditation, sitting absolutely still, before this will start to happen?

A. You can't say that there is a certain length of time. It may take you two minutes to withdraw the soul current to the eye center, or it may take you a very long time, so you can't fix it by the length of the period. This is true even in the worldly sense: sometimes our mind is so scattered that a very minor problem takes us hours and hours to solve. Sometimes we are so concentrated that it hardly takes us a second to make a decision on that point. It's not a question of the time limit; it's your concentration. Sometimes you're upset, your mind is absolutely scattered, and you just can't solve that problem.

115 **Q.** Many times when I feel that I'm just starting to get somewhat concentrated and the breathing is slowing down, I find I have to just suddenly take a deep breath. It's almost involuntary, like a gasp or a sigh. When that happens, am I sending the consciousness back down into the lower parts?

A. No, you don't send any consciousness down, but this deep breath definitely happens sometimes. While we are trying to concentrate, sometimes unconsciously we take a very deep breath.

Q. Yes, it seems unconscious. Should we try to control it?

A. I don't think you can help it. You should try not to be conscious about that deep breathing. It's just a normal function of breathing, and if there's sometimes a deep breath, just forget about it. Don't be conscious of it at all. This won't spoil your concentration. But if you're conscious about the deep breathing, then of course your concentration goes.

Q. Well sometimes it surprises me. I take a deep breath and I'm surprised that I do it.

A. That's right. Just be unconscious about it. Just forget about it. Sometimes when you are talking to somebody and you are attentive, you may take a deep breath, but you are hardly aware of it. In meditation, if you pay attention to it and think, "Why have I taken a deep breath? What is wrong with me?" then of course you lose the simran and concentration. It's the normal function of the body, and sometimes it does happen. Even when you are doing nothing, you are just sitting, sometimes you take a deep breath without meaning anything.

116 Q. When we are at the eye focus, is it possible that the body becomes completely lifeless and that the heart may stop beating?

A. No. The heart doesn't stop beating, but you feel the withdrawal in the body, that something is missing from your lower limbs. And sometimes some people have a feeling of nausea, something like fainting, but actually it is not fainting or nausea—nothing of the sort. If you go on practicing meditation every day, eventually you won't have that feeling. You will be able to overcome such feelings. But the heart will be functioning, and you are connected with the body in the same way during meditation.

117 Q. But does this phenomenon of the heart stopping beating happen with certain yogis?

A. They have a different technique. They try to slow their breathing. A very feeble breathing remains, and maybe for a second you feel that he is not breathing at all or the heart has stopped working. That is in pranayam and hatha yoga and all that. With those techniques people may be able to slow the heart beat; but we should not try to synchronize the breathing with simran or be the least bit conscious of the breathing or the heart beating or anything about the body. We have to forget about the body altogether.

118 Q. Master, in meditation, can you tell the mind to ignore the body?

A. What do you mean by telling the mind to ignore the body? Meditation itself is explaining to the mind to rise above the body. Meditation, simran, is the means to withdraw your mind from the nine portals and to concentrate at the eye center. You are training the mind to leave the body and to come to the eye center. That is the purpose of meditation.

119 Q. Should we have a desire to go within during meditation?

A. If you're always thinking about that, you may not be able to concentrate. You should sit in meditation with an absolutely relaxed mind, with a calm mind. When we are sitting in meditation, naturally the desire to go within is there. That is why we're sitting in meditation. Otherwise, why should we sit in meditation if that desire is not there? That desire is forcing us to sit in meditation, but we shouldn't feel excited and start discussing with our own self, "What am I going to see now?" and "It hasn't come yet."

120 Q. What is the difference between expectancy and desire? Should we have no desire to see any visions inside?

A. No, we have a desire, but if we are always feeling excited—"Now I'm going to see light; now I'm going to see colors; now I'm going to see this thing"—we're not concentrating at all. What I mean to say is that we should have absolute concentration. Those things will automatically come, whether you desire them or you don't desire them. They will automatically come with concentration.

Q. But desire puts earnestness and zeal into our meditation.

A. There should be a desire and earnestness to meditate, but at the time of meditation when we sit, the mind should be absolutely relaxed, because one's mind can also start feeling frustrated: "I have been sitting for three hours and I haven't seen anything, so why should I sit?" If you sit with that idea, then there are chances of frustration. But if you just sit and try to concentrate instead of thinking about all those things, then even the slightest sign of progress will make you happy.

121 Q. Then, there's not only no expectancy, but would you say you've got to have an absence of any attitude?

A. No. There should be the attitude of love and devotion and faith when we sit for meditation.

Q. But how can there be an attitude without imagery and without various accompanying body tensions and the current running downwards?

A. The mind is always running up and down. That is different. I'm not trying to say that the mind doesn't expect all that, but what I mean to say is that generally we should try to sit with a relaxed mind. Excitement, however, is always there if you see anything, but if we have less excitement for what we see, it will be better.

122 Q. When I try to feel love or think of love and devotion, my attention drops. I want to do my meditation with feeling, and when I put a little effort in, I feel that my attention drops.

A. Actually, these things you can't analyze or discuss. It's very hard to analyze these small things. We have to sit in meditation for the love of meditation, for the love of the Father. When we do our daily routine work, we sometimes work with love for the whole day; sometimes we feel that the work is just a duty, and without our mind in it, we just go on working. When we are meditating, we should feel that the mind is there. The mind should be absorbed in meditation. If the mind is running away, then it is mechanical meditation. It should not be just mechanical meditation. But when the mind is absorbed in meditation, then naturally there is love and devotion in the mind for meditation.

123 Q. When you're meditating, you may get a feeling of elation; you may get a feeling of going up or whatever. If this takes place and excitement comes in just from the slightest change in the meditation, how do you control the excitement, because the excitement would tend, like you say, to scatter the mind. All of a sudden you're caught in the excitement instead of in the simran. How do you prevent this from happening?

A. With those experiences within you get just bliss

and peace. You may be excited in that bliss and peace, but you are not so excited as to have your attention outside.

Q. So that excitement in itself isn't actually going to pull you outside?

A. It may be everybody's experience that if at night you're very excited, you don't get any sleep. Sleep comes with concentration, and if we can't concentrate—if we are angry or worried—we don't get any sleep. If we are excited and happy—to some extent we are also excited about that happiness—we cannot sleep, because concentration is not there. With too much excitement, there is no concentration, which is why we should sit in meditation with a calm and relaxed mind.

124 Q. Maharaj Ji, you've said not to sit in meditation with any expectation, and that we cannot judge what is bad meditation or good meditation. But I believe you have said that when we eventually do go inside, it will happen when we least expect it. Could you explain that?

A. I don't know what there is to explain. What I mean is that you shouldn't sit in meditation with excitement, excitement to see or to achieve. Then your mind is always running in excitement and it's not steady or still, and unless the mind is still and steady at the eye center, it doesn't get any results. If you are always excited to achieve or to see or to visualize something—always anticipating that now you are going to see, now you are going to see—then your mind is running out. You should relax, and without any tension, try to concentrate here at the eye center. When it comes, it just comes. Sometimes you get visions when you least expect them, and sometimes when you want them, you are just blank; so that you leave to Him. We should attend to our meditation without any tension and excitement.

125 Q. In some of his letters, Baba Ji says that we must strive hard, work hard in our meditation, meaning with effort. The word strive is used, I think, two or three times, and yet we should also approach meditation in a relaxed manner and in a relaxed position.

A. "Strive" means every day you must sit. You must give time, you must work hard for meditation. Give as much time as you can. You must strive to sit every day. But sit with a relaxed mind.

126 Q. Once I had a breakdown due to undernourishment, and before that major breakdown I sometimes saw a little white light in front of me. I would like to know if that white light was due to meditation or if it was a warning of that mental breakdown.

A. Light is within every one of us, irrespective of whether one is initiated or not. It is at the eye center, within, and the moment we have the least bit of concentration, we will see it. Concentration may be by reading; concentration may be by emotions; concentration may be by any other means, by meditation. The moment we are able to concentrate at the eye center, we will see that Light, and sometimes we see the Light due to our past associations with the Path, our associations with spirituality in past births.

Q. Majaraj Ji, what is strange is that since this breakdown, I have not seen that Light.

A. Naturally. This is because you have not earned to be there to see that Light, you have not worked to be at the eye center to see that Light.

127 Q. Regarding concentration, during the daytime when one is in their worldly work, does the feeling that the Sound is coming and going depend on the concentration one has?

A. The Sound is always there; it makes no difference whether it is day or night. The Sound is always there, and when our mind is attentive, we hear it. When our mind is not attentive, we don't hear it. With the help of simran, we make our mind attentive to listen to that Sound.

128 Q. Can we also get that inner concentration by reading a book or other means?

A. No, that is not our concentration. Our concentration is here at the eye center. Otherwise there is no concentration, from a meditation point of view. Concentration means withdrawing your consciousness up to the eye level. That is concentration within.

Q. But if you sit still in any position for two hours, maybe reading a book, you'll withdraw.

A. You would not withdraw here to the eye center, you would withdraw to the book. You have taken your attention from everywhere else and concentrated on reading the book. That is also concentration, but not at the eye center. Without concentration you can never follow what you are reading. Sometimes you read three or four pages without concentrating and then you feel that you have skipped over four pages, and you don't know what you have read.

129 Q. Master, as a Catholic I used to say the rosary, and with a rosary you can concentrate at the eye center.

A. You can concentrate with a rosary, provided you keep your attention at the eye center. But if you keep your attention in the rosary, how can you concentrate at the eye center? Then you concentrate on the rosary. If you are always conscious of how many times you have taken the round of the rosary, how can you concentrate here? You are always counting.

130 Q. Maharaji Ji, I heard someone talking about sitting in meditation and looking at his watch. How can one sit in meditation and avoid looking to see how much time has passed?

A. Actually, what is meant is that when you are sitting in meditation, you should concentrate all your thoughts in meditation and not always be conscious of how much time you have been sitting, wondering when it is going to be one hour and when it is going to be two hours. You may not always be looking at your watch, but you are always wondering whether or not you have sat more than your allotted time. When your mind is thinking of how much time you have to sit and how much time has already passed, then you are not concentrating. You are always thinking about that. Therefore, you should eliminate all thoughts of the world and just put your mind in simran.

It is the quality in the meditation that is important—not the quantity. If you are sitting with love and devotion and full concentration even for one hour, that is much better than sitting for five hours with your mind always wandering or running about, thinking about all the worldly problems or pleasures. So we should try to get into the habit of concentrating fully, eliminating all thoughts.

131 Q. Maharaj Ji, would you say that it would be more beneficial to, say, do three hours in one sitting than, say, five hours spread out a little throughout the day, to attain concentration?

A. Well, brother, ten minutes of concentrated meditation with full attention and devotion may be of more value than five hours of meditation with scattered attention. It is the quality that is important, with what devotion and love you are able to concentrate and be one there in the Shabd—that's more important than sitting for even ten hours and thinking about all the worldly problems.

But when you are sitting and giving so much time, naturally you will get something out of it: quality will come from quantity. After all, how long will you sit without doing anything? Then you will try to concentrate, you will try to be at the eye center.

It's a constant struggle with the mind. Don't take it from the point of view that five hours of scattered meditation will be more beneficial than three hours at one stretch. One should try to give one's time to meditation and not think about these things.

Give as much time as you can, and as much as you can conveniently arrange. But it should be done with love—you feel like sitting and you want to be there. You feel the bliss of sitting. Just bolting the door from inside and forcing yourself not to go outside, with the mind running out every second, is not of much use. Even one hour, one and a half hours, with devotion and concentration and *being there* in meditation is more useful.

132 **Q.** But I was under the impression that our two and one-half hours meditation only clears off the karma that we build during the day. So to go beyond the realm of mind and Maya we must either meditate for many, many hours more than two and a half, or—

A. Who told you that?

Q. I've considered all the possibilities, Master.

A. No. Two and one-half hours of deep meditation.

Q. Deep?

A. Yes. "Deep" means with love and devotion, with concentration. Devotion clears much of our karmic load. It goes a long way in lightening our karmic burden.

DYING WHILE LIVING

133 Q. Master, would you explain what it means to die daily the living death?

A. Saint Paul said, "I die daily."[1] In meditation, we withdraw our consciousness to the eye center in the same way that we all die when death comes. First the feet become numb, then the legs, and slowly and slowly the whole body becomes numb. When the soul withdraws from the nine apertures and comes to the eye center, it leaves the body. To die daily means to practice the withdrawal of the consciousness to the eye center every day. That is why meditation is known as dying daily.

As you have read in *The Book of Mirdad*,* Mirdad said, die to live. You must withdraw to the eye center, and then you will live forever. Otherwise, you are just living to die. Every time you live, you have to die, so die to live. Learn to die so that you may begin to live, and live forever.

134 Q. Master, when we die daily in our meditation, do we really die as far as the body is concerned?

A. The silver cord is the last link with the body. When you draw your consciousness up to the eye

---

* *The Book of Mirdad*, by Mikhail Naimy, reveals the teachings of an ancient Mystic named Mirdad. Whether or not Mirdad is fictitious, his teachings are those that have been taught by other Mystics throughout time.

center in meditation, you don't cut the silver cord. Otherwise you would be dead. Those people who withdraw their consciousness to the eye center and are in touch with the Shabd don't die. They still breathe. The pulse is beating, and they are still in touch with the body. Only at the time of death are you completely detached from the body. Then you have no contact with the body at all.

135 **Q.** When one dies like this and withdraws to the higher state of consciousness, can one come up and down at will, or can one stay up there without control, perhaps for days or weeks?

A. No, you go up and down at will. As Christ said: I can take the body when I want to and I can leave the body when I want to.[2] He does not mean death. He actually means, I can be in the body whenever I want to; I can leave the body and be with the Father when I want to.

136 **Q.** Sometimes during the day, a focusing feeling overcomes me, and I have to meditate, even in the middle of a conversation or while being alone. What is the meaning of this? It's a magnetic, pulling feeling. Sometimes that feeling comes by itself, very frequently.

A. You mean something's pulling you upward?

Q. Yes.

A. Then give yourself to it. Just submit yourself to it.

137 **Q.** I'd like to know more about death, real death. When the soul leaves the body, how can one be sure that he'll go to the same regions, the same places, where he went during his meditation?

A. This meditation is nothing but a way to be sure about that. Actually, this meditation is a process of dying daily. Meditation is nothing but a preparation to leave the body. That is the real purpose of meditation. Before you play your part on a stage, you rehearse the part so many times, just to be perfect. Similarly, this meditation is a daily rehearsal to die, so that we become perfect at how to die and when to die. Meditation is nothing but a preparation to die.

138 Q. Master, we were told after we were initiated that nobody ever dies in meditation.*

A. We die daily in meditation.

Q. But not the real death.

A. Are you frightened of sitting in meditation for that? Who wouldn't like to die in meditation? Meditation is actually a practice of rehearsing during the whole of life to die. Meditation is nothing but a rehearsal during one's whole life for that end: death. We are practicing how to die every day, and that is meditation.

When you go up, don't be frightened that you'll never come back to the body—then nobody would sit in meditation. This whole Sant Mat way of life and attending to our meditation is nothing but a preparation for that particular time, and it's good if

---

* A discussion about the death of the Guest House gardener preceded this question. The Master said he was told that the gardener had died in bhajan with a smile on his face.

one dies like that. It's a daily death. Meditation is nothing but dying daily; and now he won't have to die daily any longer.

It is very strange. Every day we sit in meditation and prepare ourselves for death, but when that particular time comes, those who have not died while living start crying and protesting and weeping, and say they don't want to die. The purpose of meditating every day is to prepare for that time, to meet that eventuality, to go back Home. It is all a preparation, nothing else. When the Lord gives the opportunity now to leave the body and to materialize the effect of meditation, then we should make use of it.

139 Q. If we have been doing our meditation every day throughout the years, is death still terrible for us?

A. Death should not be terrible. Why should death be terrible when we are trying to experience that same death every day? Unless we start preparing ourselves for that time, death is terrible and painful. But when we sit in meditation every day, it means we are preparing ourselves. Even though we have no experience to our credit, we are preparing ourselves every day to leave the body, and when that achievement finally comes, then why should we be frightened? What is there to lament and weep about? At death, we are getting what we have been trying for our whole life. That is rather a happy moment.

SIMRAN—REPETITION

140 Q. Are the five holy names, the names of the Supreme Lord, or are they names of different lords of different regions?

A. We are told at the time of initiation that according to the attributes and qualities of those rulers, Mystics have given them these names. A Mystic may give you any name to repeat. It is immaterial. It will have the same effect for you. We're not worried about whether these are the right names or not. That is for the Mystic to select for you, and whatever name he gives you to repeat will have the power and the effect for you, whether it has any meaning or whether it has no meaning at all. That is for him to consider. We shouldn't try to dabble in the meaning of these things.

141 Q. Maharaj Ji, if somebody finds out the names by himself and tries to use them to meditate, will he get any benefit out of them?

A. A man with a little intelligence can find all the names from our books. There's no problem in finding them, but that is not going to help him at all. A bullet kills only when it comes through the gun barrel. It is the same bullet if you throw it, but it is not effective unless it comes through the gun. Similarly, it is only when the names are given to us by a Mystic that they have any power behind them—power to eliminate the ego, to purify our mind, to bring our entire attention to the eye center. Otherwise, the words in themselves have no power.

I'll tell you a little example: some king went to a Mystic for initiation, and the Mystic told him to say a word, to repeat a name of the Lord.

The Mystic told the king, "You can repeat the word Ram."

The king said, "I haven't come all this way just to hear this word, just to repeat Ram. I have read this so many times and everybody knows this word. What is the purpose of my coming all the way to you?"

The Mystic said, "Because it has come from me, you had better repeat it."

"But if I hear this word from somewhere else, won't it have the same effect?"

The Mystic told him, "I'll tell you some other time."

So one day the Mystic went to the king's court, and the king had all his generals and bodyguards and courtiers, standing around him. The Mystic said, "Arrest this king!" but nobody obeyed his order. He repeated, "I say, arrest this man! Put him in jail!" Nobody bothered about him.

Then the king said, "This man is overstepping his limits. Arrest this man!" and the Mystic was arrested.

Then the Mystic told the king, "You and I have said the same thing, but there was no effect in what I said. Yet the words are the same. We both used the same words, but you yourself can see the difference. So now you know the difference between words that come from me and words that come from you."

The words have to come from a Mystic. The

names by themselves don't carry any meaning, any power, at all.

142 Q. Master, we are told in the books that Kal practices the great deception and that he is doing everything he can to keep us from returning to our true Home. Now as I understand it, the first name we are told to repeat is just another name for Kal. How can I repeat that name with reverence?

A. You are not repeating the names of any agent of Kal. You are repeating only the names of the Master. The Master has given you those names to repeat, and you will not even see those rulers inside. For you, the Master is there, everywhere, so you are concerned only with the Master and not with any ruler of any region. Your Master is the ruler of whichever region you are passing through. Actually, you're repeating the name of the Master and of nobody else.

143 Q. Do all the Perfect Masters teach the same simran to their disciples?

A. They teach the course of simran. The words may be different according to the language or to whatever they think best. The words can be different, but they will tell you of the same process for concentration.

There may be many schools of thought for concentrating at the eye center, but from the eye center upward there is only one school of thought: Shabd, Sound Current, Spirit. For withdrawing the consciousness to the eye center, some people may have used different methods, but above the eye center there are no two ways, there's only one way: that Holy Ghost or Spirit.

This is how idol worship came about in India. People used to bring all their focus of attention on an image. When they were able to give their full attention to that idol, then they would forget about the statue and try to bring all that concentration to the eye center. Originally, they may have been able to do it, but now they have forgotten how to detach from that statue and bring the attention to the eye center, so they have started worshipping the statue.

All this was nothing but a process of dhyan. We visualize the form of the Master along with simran, but since the Masters were not present, people started contemplating on the form of statues or pictures. They got involved in it so much that they couldn't get rid of the image of that particular statue or picture. Then they couldn't bring their attention back to the eye center and they always remained outside. So there may be different schools of thinking for withdrawing to the eye center, but beyond that, there is no other way—only one: the Spirit.

144 Q. Master, what association should we have when we repeat the five names you've given us at initiation?

A. You should not try to associate them with anything. You should just keep your mind in those words and be at the eye center and still your mind. Don't try to think about the stages or about the forms of those rulers of the regions. We shouldn't get lost in those things.

For us, the only association is with the Master and the repetition of the words. Keeping the Master's form in view and repeating those names, we have to concentrate at the eye center, and we shouldn't let our mind think about anything else.

145 Q. Is it wrong to see the words when you're trying to do simran? If we can't contemplate on the Master, is it okay to see the words inside?

A. See those words in which language? After all, if you're going to see them, you must also think about some language in which the five words are written. Which language would you like to see?

You shouldn't worry about the words or the language in which they are written. Then your mind is slipping out. Don't worry about the words or the language or anything, for it won't help. You have to be mentally at the eye center, mentally concentrated in simran, not visualizing the words or the forms of the words or the meaning of the words. These things don't help.

146 Q. How can we do simran with the attention without using the tongue?

A. Mentally. During the whole day we are thinking about something or another and we never use our tongue. We always think mentally, so do simran mentally.

Q. It has to start from the tongue and throat.

A. The tongue is required only if you speak, but when you are thinking about some worldly problem, the tongue doesn't move, does it? In the same way, you have to do simran mentally.

147 Q. Sometimes you find that your simran is stuck at another center, like the throat center or the tongue. Should you try to force it up to the eye center? Do you try to find the eye center?

A. Sister, the throat center has nothing to do with the simran. You are to do simran mentally, not with the tongue. Try to keep your attention at the eye center while doing simran. It is the attention that has to do the simran.

148 Q. Master, sometimes when we're meditating, although the attention is up there at the forehead, the words sometimes seem to stay behind and the attention is broken. Is it best to bring the words in front?

A. No, no. You shouldn't be conscious about the words. Just be conscious that you are at the eye center and your attention, your thinking is occupied by simran. Just repeat the words and be in the darkness. Don't worry about whether the words are in the back or in the front, or what their pronunciation is and what the speed of your speaking is. You shouldn't be conscious of these things.

149 Q. I have a question about simran. I believe you said that paying attention to the pronunciation or to the speed would not help you to gain concentration, and then I was reading that Great Master said that the devotee should repeat the names as if one is calling out for the Beloved. And I'm just confused, because sometimes it seems to course through the mind very quickly so that all trace of clear pronunciation is gone.

A. We should do simran in a normal way, being neither conscious of our speed, nor of our pronunciation, whether it is right or wrong. Nor should we become conscious of the frequency of simran, that we have repeated the names so many times in such a short while. In a normal way, you simply go on repeating these words, keeping your attention at the eye center, feeling and thinking that you are sitting in the presence of the Master, and that you are calling him by these names. That is what the Great Master has written.

150 Q. What if all the words tend to merge into each other, until they're almost indistinguishable?

A. Your mind should merge into the words. Your mind should become part and parcel of that simran, and not that the words you repeat are different from your mind. Then only can concentration come. If you are repeating those words, and your mind is thinking about all the problems and activities of the world, concentration will not be there. It must merge along with the words. You should be *in* those words, not somewhere away from them.

151 Q. Maharaj Ji, I once understood from a satsangi that during meditation, the simran part, if an image of a person or group or something comes into your mind, you can make that image do simran. For example, if my child comes into my mind while I'm trying to concentrate—I can just transform the child and imagine the child doing simran, or if my mother comes into my mind, I can imagine my mother doing simran, so that I have every image in my mind just doing simran. Is this all right?

A. That is what we want to eliminate, sister. When we are doing simran, all the worldly forms come before us. We are always thinking about them, about our attachments, and the purpose of simran is to eliminate all those thoughts. The purpose of simran is not to bring in those thoughts but to eliminate those forms, eliminate those thoughts. It's just the reverse.

Q. So we should try to keep them away rather than have them disappear by themselves?

A. Even if we don't do simran, those faces are constantly with us, because our attachments always project those faces before us. We want to get rid of those forms, those attachments, with the help of simran and dhyan. But if we go on contemplating on their faces and doing simran, we are creating a stronger bond with them rather than eliminating them.

You find statues and idols in the temples and other places being worshipped because there was a school of thinking that believed in contemplating on those forms while doing simran. But with that practice, you get so much attached to that particular idol or statue that you find it difficult to detach yourself from it and then attach yourself to the Shabd and Nam within. You become part and parcel of those idols, so it becomes difficult to detach yourself from them. You are able to hold your attention by contemplating on them, but then that concentration doesn't take you up, because you get so attached to them that you can't detach your thoughts from the idols and attach yourself to the Sound Current.

We contemplate on the form of the Master, and the Master automatically takes the form of the Shabd. We don't have to detach our mind from the Master's form, because the Master is going to merge into the Shabd, into the Light and Sound within. Master is Shabd and is going to become Shabd, so our attachment to him rather helps us, whereas attachment to statues and other forms pulls us down and doesn't let us go ahead. But that school of thinking was to hold the attention by contemplation, then to detach from the statues, and then to try to attach to something else, which is very difficult to do. And even if you succeed in that method, it does not take you beyond the realm of mind.

152 Q. In the books it is written that several methods for concentration are recommended, but that simran is the easiest. Does this mean emptying the mind would be one of the methods?

A. Many people try to hold their mind by analyzing themselves, by not thinking about anything else. They try to adopt such methods, but it's very difficult. The mind cannot cease working. It's always thinking about something, so that is why the Saints say simran is the easiest method.

153 Q. Some often have difficulty to do simran right without being side-tracked by the mind, but when the mind is occupied with a beautiful thing, or what I think is a beautiful thing, like listening to concert music, it seems to be easy to do simran and rise to beautiful heights. Now, is this a good idea?

A. Brother, your mind is the same; when it is occupied with the music, how can you be attentive to simran? Because the mind enjoys that music, so you align yourself with the music, rather than with simran. No, simran is independent of music. The mind definitely enjoys music, and music gives us some sort of concentration, too, but it doesn't lead us anywhere. It's food for the mind but not for the soul.

Q. But I was side-tracking the mind so that the soul would go up.

A. No. It won't. The mind will just revolve with the music. It will remain with the music. The moment the music stops, you will be where you were before.

Q. No, it continued for quite a while.

A. There may be a little effect because you may be liking the music. Simran is very different. The purpose of simran is to still the mind, even to withdraw from such music and to be in touch with the inner Music. If the outside music is so fascinating, you can imagine how much better would be the melodious Music within, that silent Music within.

Our purpose is to hear that silent Music. These outer sounds are all poor copies of that inner Music. If we involve ourselves in this outer music, then we may not be able to reach that inner type of music. The purpose of simran is to hold the attention at the eye center and then to be one with the internal Music, which is the real music. You forget all these outer forms of music when you're in touch with that inner Music.

154 Q. If you're meditating in a place that is noisy, such as almost any city, is there anything wrong with doing the simran in the posture in which one listens to the Sound?

A. But what's the advantage of that?

Q. You can't hear the trains, for instance.

A. Yes, we should try to cut down outside noises wherever we sit. We need a lonely, quiet corner.

Q. So it's all right to do the whole meditation, if it's two and one-half hours, in the same bhajan position?

A. It's very difficult to sit in the bhajan position and do simran for so long. But actually, we should not be conscious of the posture or of outside sounds while doing simran, or even while hearing the Sound.

155 Q. Then can we take measures to use ear plugs and things like that when doing simran?

A. Well, if there's no alternative, then you may use these things. But after all, they are artificial things and we should not depend on them. There's nothing like natural surroundings.

156 Q. It has been suggested that one of the reasons for doing simran with ears open is to become accustomed to doing it within the world, and to be able to concentrate on simran but at the same time be sufficiently aware of those worldly noises that we have to concentrate to rise above them.

A. The object of doing simran without closing the ears is that we should eventually attune to the simran and concentrate at the eye center so much that even if drums are beating by our side, we won't be conscious of them. We have to practice so much that even if there is any loud noise around us, our concentration is not disturbed. But still, in the beginning we need a lonely, quiet place so we won't be distracted, because after all we have to work for that stage of concentration. We can't just begin with it.

157 Q. Master, when someone is meditating and he's doing his simran and all of a sudden he hears the Sound too and it's very strong, should he stop doing simran? He wants to avoid the Sound but he just can't, it's there.

A. Naturally when you're doing simran, the Sound will be there. If you are in touch with the Sound once, then whenever you do simran, the Sound will always be there. But if the Sound is not pulling you upward, then you should continue doing simran. If the Sound is very distinct and clear and it is pulling you upward, then you can switch from simran to hearing the Sound. Then you shouldn't resist that Sound. When the Sound is pulling you, you should give yourself to the Sound, submit yourself to the Sound, rather than resist it by keeping your mind in simran.

158 Q. Maharaj Ji, you say not to do simran at the time of Sound, but if one starts having visions of the Master or something of that nature during Sound, then we are told we should say our simran. But if the Sound is strong and the Master is there, then why say the simran? This point I've never understood.

A. You can listen to the Sound, but you should also repeat the simran, only as a test, just to be sure.

Just to be sure where you stand at that time, because the Sound can be misleading at times. If the sound is from the left side or if it is an imitation, it can be misleading, but with the simran you are never wrong. If you are seeing somebody and you use the sound as a test, you can be wrong. If the sound is coming from the left side and you are seeing some form within and you think that the sound is the test of that form, you can be misled.

159 Q. Can the Master be tested with the five names in a dream?

A. You can't. That form can be the mind, it can be anybody. In any way, it is not in your power to choose to do simran, in dreams. How can you trust the mind? If you have already formed the habit of doing simran at every moment, then naturally, you will automatically do simran even during a dream. That is a different thing. But until that stage is reached, it's not in your power to do simran in dreams. If it's there, it's just there. So good dreams are good dreams, but don't try to give any meaning to them.

160 Q. Maharaj Ji, the instructions are to do approximately two hours of simran and to spend the rest of the time listening to the Sound during meditation. If you can hear the Sound quite plainly, is it in order to listen to the Sound all the time and ignore simran?

A. There is no fixed timing as to how much time is to be given to simran and how much time to Shabd. Generally, what I advise is that three-fourths of the time should go to simran and one-fourth of the time should go to Shabd, hearing of the Sound. But when with the help of simran, the Sound becomes very distinct and clear and pulls you upward, you may switch from simran to the Shabd. You yourself will be able to decide when to lessen your time in simran and when to increase your time in Shabd.

But simran should be continued until a very late stage. You can't say that since you've started hearing the Sound, you should stop simran. Even then, simran should be continued. It may be only for half an hour or one hour, but it should be continued until a very late stage, until the second stage. Until you cross the second stage, simran should not be ignored. Simran should be kept, because you never know when the mind may slip out. Concentration is essential for hearing the Sound, so simran should be carried on.

161 Q. Master, when one is doing simran very poorly, what can one do? When one finds it very difficult to do simran, what can one do about it?

A. Brother, one should do simran! You can collect the wandering mind, which has become so wild, only by simran. Simran, though dry, is an essential part of meditation. It's only with the help of simran that we are able to concentrate at the eye center, and then we can be in touch with that Sound within which pulls us upward. Simran is an essential part of meditation, very essential.

Q. But Maharaj Ji, what if you can't hold onto the simran? What if you start the simran and it just goes away from you, it just disappears, and about an hour later you realize you should have been doing simran?

A. Then after an hour, again start. When you realize that you have forgotten the simran, that you are doing something else, again start. This is the habit of the mind: when you are doing simran, it will run away, it will start thinking about worldly things. Bring it back again and again. That is knocking. Slowly and slowly you're able to get into that simran and into that concentration.

162 Q. Maharaj Ji, if you sit there for two hours and about four times you've been able to repeat those words, you still can't call that two hours of meditation.

A. Well, if you give two hours to meditation every day and on the first day you're able to do simran for half an hour out of two hours, then the next day you may be able to increase that simran by five minutes or ten minutes. The mind gradually gets into the habit of doing simran, and there may be a time when the whole two hours will be in meditation.

163 Q. Even when sitting and meditating without concentrating—the mind may be wandering—does even that have its own value?

A. That has its own value. If we are always frightened that we will never be able to walk, then we will never be able to walk. Even if out of two hours you get only ten minutes of real concentration to your credit, it's worth having. The next day you may be able to get fifteen minutes of concentration; the third day you may be able to add another ten minutes. Slowly and slowly you will be able to increase your time. If during the first day you sit for two hours and you say, "I don't concentrate at all," and from then on you don't sit in meditation, that is no good. We must give our proper time to simran and meditation, every day.

164 Q. Then to not let the mind slip out, should we wrestle with our mind by doing the dhyan and simran forcefully and powerfully?

A. Simran and dhyan should be attended to with love and devotion. How fast you are doing simran or how loudly you are doing simran won't make any difference. With how much love and devotion you are attending to simran and dhyan—that is more important.

When you're doing simran, if your mind forgets simran and starts thinking about worldly affairs, worldly things, again bring it back, again pull your mind back to simran. Pull it back again and again. That is doing simran vigorously—not that you have to use any physical force. You have to fight with the mind to keep it in simran and dhyan.

But how fast a repetition you are doing or how loudly a repetition you are doing won't make any difference. With how much love and devotion you are doing simran—that is more important.

165 Q. Maharaj Ji, at first are meditation and simran generally mechanical until we get love? We're told to have love when we do our simran and do our meditation.

A. If we can't attend to meditation with love and devotion, it may be attended to even mechanically. Slowly and slowly that love and devotion will be built. To begin with we have to fight with the mind. We have to put the mind in meditation, and then automatically love develops with effort, and faith also comes. Some people are lucky, and start with faith and devotion; others have to build faith and devotion. That is due to the *sanskaras* of our past births, our past association with the Path.

166 Q. Master, could you please tell us about the course of simran that's given to every disciple at the time of his initiation? Does this mean you have to say your words so many times, a set number of times, until you see the inner Master?

A. It is not a question of the quantity of simran, but the concentration which simran is to give to you. It is not how many times you have to repeat these words before you can achieve your destination. That's wrong.

Simran is just to occupy our mind so that our consciousness withdraws to the eye center. That is why we're advised to do it with love and devotion. It should not be just mechanical. Simran with love and devotion will help you to withdraw to the eye center and will give you concentration. You cannot think, "Since I am repeating day and night mechanically, I'll withdraw, "for then you could turn on a tape recorder. That will not help you because you have to concentrate here at the eye center. It is the concentration which is important.

Whether you withdraw your consciousness with your devotion or emotion or with the help of simran, ultimately it comes to the same thing. Some people can withdraw just with the help of dhyan. They're so much in love with the Master that they withdraw their consciousness with the help of dhyan and come up to the eye center, but then they cannot stand that Light because they're not in the habit of withdrawing slowly and slowly.

Simran is a process where you slowly withdraw upwards. It is constant and practical and permanent. Many times in the satsang you have seen people, especially ladies, who hear the satsang and faint because they are very emotional. They become so emotional and full of devotion by hearing the satsang or having the darshan of the Master that they are able to concentrate and withdraw. But still, when they see a little flash of Light they faint, because they're not in the habit of seeing that Light.

167 Q. At the Dera people have withdrawn, falling over and lying down. Is this natural? If one goes within to this point here (the eye center), will the body keep falling over?

A. No. It happens only sometimes, especially with ladies. They reach to a certain stage with emotion, not with simran. If you were to throw a fine muslin cloth onto a thorny bush and then pull it up at once, very quickly, you would only give it a shock, and the whole cloth might be torn. But if you remove it from the thorns one by one, one by one, the whole cloth can be safely removed. When these ladies hear the satsang or talk about the Master, they become so filled with love and devotion for the Master that they at once concentrate through their emotions. They're not in the habit of slowly and slowly withdrawing upwards, so when they see Light suddenly or hear the Sound, they can't stand it. Sometimes they start shivering or crying, and sometimes they faint.

Just as if a thousand-candle lamp were suddenly put in front of your eyes, you'd at once faint. You'd be dazzled. You wouldn't be able to see anything. But if we start with one candle and slowly go on increasing the light, our eyes go on adjusting to the light. Then we can eventually see even a thousand-candle light without any strain on our eyes.

168 Q. In slow withdrawal, does the body become numb, actually stiff?

A. In slow withdrawal, the body becomes used to withdrawing from the nine apertures, so then there is no shivering or fainting. You go up and come down, ascend and descend at will. Otherwise, if the soul leaves the body suddenly and you're not prepared to face all that Light within, then you can't control it and you faint.

169 Q. When one has fainted, does that mean the soul has actually gone within?

A. The soul goes there, sees the Light, and then the person just becomes unconscious. Still the soul is in the body, of course. It has seen the Light, but as I said, if a dazzling light is placed before your eyes all at once, you can't stand it. Similarly, when the soul goes inside through emotion, it can't stay there. The person becomes unconscious, and then slowly regains consciousness again.

There's nothing dangerous about it. But sometimes people become so frightened of that Light that they don't even sit for meditation, because they're not used to seeing so much Light.

170 Q. I have been told that we do need emotion to get to the eye center, and I don't quite understand. If emotion like that—

A. Not just by mere emotion, but by emotion converted into simran. With emotion you attend to your simran and dhyan—with love and devotion. Sudden, built-up emotion may make you faint.

Now we have all adjusted to these candles,* but if

* Because of a cut in electricity, the evening meeting was held by candle light.

suddenly a bright light is brought before us, it will take a little time to adjust to that light. That is why the whole process of meditation is very slow. First we see flashes of Light, and then the Light stays a little longer, and little by little it becomes brighter, and then we are able to see more and more of it.

171 Q. Maharaj Ji, getting back to the idea of a special course of simran, I've heard that we each have a certain amount of simran to do in this life, say, a couple of million times to say simran.

A. Well, brother, I have never tried to calculate simran mathematically, but if you can count how many times your mind has run out, then you can also count how many times you should do simran within, because it should take at least ten times more simran than the mind has run out. If you can count how many times the mind has run out, then you can accordingly add ten times more simran.

Mathematical calculation won't do. We should devote our time to simran. Concentration is the main thing.

Q. Nothing mathematical, but I've heard somewhere that we have a certain amount to do, and the quicker we do it, the better for us.

A. There's no set amount. it's a whole life of struggle—that's the amount. A whole life of struggle. We have to withdraw our consciousness to the eye center, and then we have to hold our consciousness there, that it may not slip down again. That is why it is a lifelong struggle. Whenever the mind runs out, we have to withdraw the consciousness to the eye center again. And that naturally needs practice. Then we have to hold the attention at the eye center, we have to see that it doesn't drop again. So constant simran is required to hold the mind at the eye center, to be in touch with the Sound within.

172 **Q.** Great Master once said that you cannot rend the veil inside unless there is grace, longing and love. Does constant simran have the power to do that, or will simran develop the love to rend the veil to pierce within? Is it the power of simran alone, or will that just develop the love?

A. Simran or meditation without love doesn't yield much result. Simran and meditation with devotion yields results. That's why the Great Master says that if you just mechanically do simran and your love is not there, your faith is not there, your mind is not there in it, then you don't get much result. You have to attend to simran and to the whole meditation with love and devotion.

173 **Q.** What does Master Jagat Singh mean when he says that when we are repeating simran, we should do it as if we were putting precious things into a safe?

A. That's right. When you are doing simran, think that you are at the eye center and you are repeating the names as if you were putting some precious jewels in a safe. Your whole attention is here in the eye center and you are just doing simran, which is your precious treasure. That's what he means.

Q. Is that similar, then, to the story Great Master relates of how King Janak told a seeker that he always acted as if he had a bowl full of milk in his hands and he didn't want any of it to drop?*

---

* This story, "Sukh Dev and King Janak," is related in *Tales of the Mystic East*, by Maharaj Sawan Singh Ji.

A. Same thing. Sukh Dev's whole attention was in that bowl of milk. He was not conscious of the drums, the parades, and the merrymaking of the children that were going on. He said, "I have noticed nothing at all. I have seen only this bowl." His whole concentration was on that bowl. That means his concentration was one-pointed. When that type of concentration comes, when that type of love comes, only then we see the Radiant Form of the Master. Everything was there, but he wasn't conscious of anything but the bowl full of milk, lest he spill even a drop.

174 Q. Master, they say that when Sardar Bahadur said his simran he used to savor each word like it was nectar, and I think that, for myself anyway, when there's less love and devotion in the simran, it becomes very difficult to hold your attention. For most of us it is still a dry process. What is the way we can make the simran like nectar? They say that Sardar Bahadur Ji savored every word. He was so intoxicated with the love of simran that he could just go right to the eye center. You've said many times that if we don't have love and devotion for the simran, if it's just dry, it doesn't do us much good. We have to develop the love for it.

A. First you many start with a dry simran, and then ultimately you may end with a love simran. When a child is sent to school to learn the *ABC*, it's very dry for him. He is made to repeat it over and over. it's only later he loves to read, an enjoys pronouncing words. Simran is the same thing.

175 Q. Can the mind be conditioned so that simran doesn't have an effect on it? If a doctor is giving medicine to somebody to destroy bacteria, and after a while those bacteria become resistant to that medicine, could the same thing happen with simran—that the simran doesn't have an effect, that after a time the mind doesn't—

A. You mean simran won't have the same effect on the mind? No. Rather, the simran will have a greater effect on the mind. The more time you give to simran, the more effect you will find it has on the mind. It's not that the mind will become immune to simran.

176 Q. Maharaj Ji, I read a beautiful article on simran which mentioned that just simran—forgetting everything else for the moment—can bring great sweetness if it's done properly, and I'm wondering, some of your remarks have said so much about simran, and for most of us that's the main path right now. Can you give us any suggestions on how to increase love and devotion in simran so they're not just words?

A. Simran looks dry, but the concentration that you get with simran alone gives you peace and bliss and happiness. The more your mind is concentrated, the more happy you are; the more your mind is scattered, the more frustrated you are. As long as the mind is below the eye center towards the senses, you can never be happy—there's nothing but frustration and agony. But when you're able to withdraw your consciousness to the eye center and still your mind, you feel bliss and contentment and happiness. And simran is the only way that you can withdraw your consciousness to the eye center.

177 Q. Master, when a person is unconsciously saying simran—like if you've spent two or three hours saying simran and then you have your duties to perform, and you get up and you may have to go to the grocery market or down the street or something, and suddenly you realize that at the back of your head somewhere simran is going on automatically—is that of any real value to you, when it's just going on automatically?

A. Sister, the stage will come when it will go on automatically. Even if you are talking to people you will feel that you're doing simran; and we should get into that habit, because only then are we able to concentrate at the eye center. Only that will help us to become unconscious of the world, of what is going on around us. Then we will just move as actors move on a stage.

In this state we will feel that there is no reality. Sometimes you will be talking to a person and you will feel that you are not you. Somebody else is walking and talking with the other person. Simran helps to separate your individuality from yourself. Then the whole day you will see the world as a stage, as if somebody else is acting, talking, doing a husband's duty, a wife's duty, a child's duty, and you are somebody different from yourself. And that helps. That is the effect of simran, and that is ultimately what we want to achieve. We want to separate our real self from this world.

Sometimes you may feel that somebody else is sitting in meditation and you are watching somebody sitting in meditation, you are separate from the person who is meditating. That feeling does come.

DHYAN—CONTEMPLATION

178 Q. Would you speak about dhyan?

A. The purpose of simran is to withdraw your consciousness to the eye center, and the purpose of dhyan is to hold your attention at the eye center, because it is very difficult to hold your attention in a vacuum. The mind has the faculty both to think and to visualizing Whatever you are thinking about you are also contemplating on. If you are thinking about your friend, his form will appear before you.

These are the natural faculties of the mind, and we have to occupy both tendencies: thinking and visualizing. By thinking and visualizing we have all become attached to this creation, so Saints advise us that by the same process we have to withdraw our consciousness from worldly attachments and bring it back to the eye center by thinking about the Father—repeating His Name, doing simran—and by contemplating on the form of the Master.

Why the Master? Because we want to contemplate only on that form which will not pull us back to this creation again. If we contemplate on flowers or on friends or on some statue or on some worldly thing, we will be pulled back down to this creation again, because these forms are all perishable. We contemplate on the form of the Master because his real form is Shabd, he is the Word made flesh, and by contemplating on his form we are getting attached to the Shabd inside, to the Audible Life Stream of which the Master is the embodiment.

Physical darshan of the Master is very helpful for the purpose of dhyan. The ancient Saints attached great importance to having the darshan of Saints and Masters, who are the source and flow of love and light. Darshan makes an irresistible appeal to the inner being of the satsangi, even when he receives no verbal instructions.

The effect of darshan is dependent upon the receptivity of the seeker, whose reaction is determined by his own *sanskaras* and past connections. Often the seeker is satisfied with the darshan of the Master and has no desire for anything else from him. To derive bliss from the mere darshan of the Master is a great thing, because it indicates that the seeker has love—very essential for spiritual life. Having had the darshan of the Beloved, the devotee naturally desires nothing except to have as much darshan of the Master as possible, which results in drawing the devotee closer to the Master on the inner plane.

Thus, with the help of contemplation, our tendency becomes upward and we are able to hold our attention at the eye center. That is why contemplation is important in meditation, and it should be done along with simran. When we're doing simran, we should also try to contemplate on the form of the Master. Otherwise, if we occupy only the faculty of thinking, our mind will be contemplating on the forms of worldly persons, places and things.

Those who are fortunate enough to have seen the Master should try to contemplate on the form of the Master while doing simran. And those who have not seen him should not try to contemplate on his photo or on any imaginary figure, because then they will become attached to that photo, which is lifeless. We generally advise them to try to hold the attention in the darkness of the forehead, thinking that the Master is here in the darkness, while they go on repeating the five holy names. But those who have seen the Master can contemplate on the form of the Master. With that contemplation we are able to withdraw our consciousness to the eye center and are able to hold it there. And when we are at the eye center, automatically we will be in touch with the Sound and Light within, which will pull us upwards. That is the purpose of contemplation or dhyan.

179 **Q.** Master, in contemplation we develop love and devotion for the Master; we try to keep the physical form of the Master in our mind. We're attaching ourselves to something that is also perishable, aren't we?

A. By attaching ourselves to the form of the Master, we're attaching ourselves to the Power which is in the Master—that is the Shabd and Nam within. The danger of our physical attachment with anybody is that we are bound by that attachment, and we may have to come back to this creation due to that attachment. But since the Master does not have to come back to this creation, and his real form is Shabd and Nam, the Light and Sound, and he is to merge back into the Father, that attachment to him automatically takes our mind in that direction.

The purpose of the Master's physical form is to create love and desire for the Father within us, to put us on the Path, and to create that longing to be one with the Shabd and Nam within. That is why Christ said in the Bible: it is expedient for you that I leave you now, because then you will give more attention to the Holy Ghost within.[1] Now you are so much attached to my physical outside form that you're always running after me and you're not giving proper attention to the Spirit or Holy Ghost within. But when we can't find the Master outside, and we know how to find him within, naturally we will try to find him within. We know the way, we know the Path, so automatically we will go within to the Holy Spirit, the real form of the Master.

180 Q. Maharaj Ji, should simran continue during dhyan?

A. Dhyan and simran should go on together, simultaneously. You must synchronize dhyan along with simran.

181 Q. The Great Master once wrote or said to sit in dhyan for a new minutes before beginning the simran. Can you explain something further on that?

A. Dhyan means thinking about the Master, visualizing his form before you, feeling that you are now in his presence. And the purpose of all this is to create that atmosphere of bliss and peace in which we have to attend to our meditation. Our mind is intensely pulled in all directions, therefore, when we sit for meditation, we need some time to compose it, to push it on the Path, so to say, before we can start. So it will just create that atmosphere, and then to attend to meditation, you do simran and dhyan.

182 Q. Maharaj Ji, when doing dhyan, is there effort involved in trying to visualize the Master, or is it something that if it comes naturally, then hold onto it? Or must one try? Is there a certain amount of trying to visualize?

A. We have to try. In order to visualize the form, in order to hold the attention there, we have to try. Trying is always there. The mind even revolts against doing simran, but we have to make an effort to do it again and again. Similarly, we have to make an effort to contemplate on the form of the Master, again and again. Try to visualize; otherwise, you should feel that you are doing simran in the presence of the Master.

183 Q. The mind has a tendency to go to all the worldly forms, like beauties of nature, and it does everything it can to keep the attention away from the Master, because that's its duty. It doesn't go quite so naturally to the Master's form, even though the soul wants it to go to the Master's form. So, we have something against us right from the start. It's very easy to pick up forms of the world which you have no interest in or don't even care about. They come so easily and completely, but not the Master's physical form.

A. Well, no doubt it's difficult. I don't deny that. The form which you try to visualize generally never comes. The form which you try to eliminate is always there before you. But if you will gain a little concentration at the eye center, then it won't be difficult to visualize the Master's form. With concentration you are able to hold it. And for concentration, simran is the only method, the only way. Dhyan is not a "must," but it is a help to keep the mind in concentration. Simran leads the mind to concentrate, and dhyan holds it there, at the eye center.

184 Q. Master, why is it very difficult to visualize the form of the Master? It is the most difficult part of meditation. You may think of any other person or figure, but the Master is the most difficult.

A. It depends upon our attachments and love. We always easily visualize the forms of the people we love. We don't love the Master, so it becomes difficult to visualize him.

185 Q. Will that dhyan come as more and more we practice trying? Will that ability to visualize the Master come?

A. Yes, it comes with practice also, it comes with devotion also. Both are essential: devotion and practice.

186 Q. You have said that in doing simran, to visualize the form of the Master helps you to concentrate, but sometimes it seems to work just the reverse. The mind has two things to focus the attention on instead of one: one is the words, and one is the form of the Master, and this seems to divide the attention.

A. No, brother, actually they are not two things at all. It is in the nature of our mind that whenever we are thinking about anything, we are also consciously or unconsciously visualizing that thing. If you think about your friend, you will also think about the form of your friend. You can't help it. That's the nature of the mind. So, just to occupy these two faculties of the mind, it is advised that we repeat the five holy names and also try to visualize the form of the Master, just to hold the attention.

But if you personally feel distracted by dhyan, you can leave dhyan and keep on doing simran. But it is a little easier to hold the mind at the eye center with the help of dhyan. Otherwise, simran alone will help you to concentrate at the eye center.

It is difficult to hold the attention in a vacuum, unless you see some Light. When you start seeing the Light, then it is all right. Then you needn't do any dhyan, because you are occupied in seeing the Light and doing simran. There is something to hold your attention there. But when we are in a vacuum and void, it is preferable to contemplate on the form of the Master, because it is a little difficult to be there in the void and in the darkness. But if dhyan distracts you, you can just continue with simran. It's perfectly all right.

187 Q. It seems the attention jumps from simran to dhyan and from dhyan to simran, because to do it simultaneously is not so easy.

A. At the time of dhyan the distraction is in trying to associate the Master with outside activities. But if we just contemplate on the face of the Master, cutting down all outside associations, then it is not a distraction, it's a help.

The object of simran is to withdraw the consciousness to the eye center. The object of dhyan is to hold the attention there, and love holds the attention there. When we love somebody, our attention is automatically held by that person. We don't look anywhere else. We just still our mind, focus our mind on that particular face. We're not conscious of anything around the person whatsoever. That is dhyan, and only love can create that. Then dhyan is no distraction.

But when you associate the Master with outside

activities in the world, there's a distraction in simran and dhyan because it is not the Master you are contemplating. Then you are also concerned with associations which distract your attention, and that dhyan is not a complete dhyan.

188 Q. Maharaj Ji, I'm still confused. During meditation if it isn't possible to have dhyan, if the form of the Master isn't coming to us mentally, should we try to force the attention to focus something of the Master, or should we just continue looking in the darkness?

A. If you can visualize the form of the Master, it is a very happy state. Otherwise, just keep your attention in the darkness and go on doing simran. Automatically the form will appear. If you struggle too much to bring the form, your mind will run out. As I have told you this dhyan is actually the outcome of love, the effect of love. With worldly people, you can just close your eyes and at once start visualizing them, because you're so much attached to them.

Q. So in simran you only repeat the simran without trying to see the image of the Master?

A. No, no, you try to visualize the face of the Master but don't fight to locate him somewhere. To project his form takes constant effort. Otherwise, if you can't visualize the form, just feel that your Master is before you and you are sitting in the presence of the Master and doing simran.

189 Q. I've heard it said that when we do dhyan, we should try to contemplate on the face of the Master as it is in satsang. I was just wondering, when we try to contemplate on the form of the Master, should we just try to sit there and think that we are sitting in front of the Master and then let the form come before us, or should we actually try to visualize the Master in a certain situation?

A. You should try to visualize the face of the Master and you should not be concerned with his surroundings. If you can't visualize the face, then think that the Master is sitting before you as he sits in the satsang, that you're sitting in his presence, and go on doing your simran in his presence.

Q. So we visualize the form of the Master while he's smiling or what?

A. No, don't try to do that. Just as you see his face in the satsang—try to visualize that face and go on doing simran. Otherwise you will connect the Master with outside activities and your mind will run out.

190 Q. Maharaj Ji, in dhyan, should we struggle to bring the image of the Master into our mind, or can we picture ourselves in the situation where we receive darshan?

A. It's always better to contemplate on the face of the Master rather than to try to have some association of the Master with those surroundings or events. Your mind is likely to run to those events and associations and to forget the Master. At the most, you can visualize him sitting in satsang. And if you are not successful in contemplating on the form, the best way is to feel that you are in the presence of the Master and doing your simran that your Master is before you and you are sitting before the Master and doing simran in his presence.

191 Q. Master, sometimes when we close our eyes, we can visualize with our mind's eye the image of the person that we love. Then if we haven't seen that person for a long time, after a while the image starts to fade and blur and we just can't get a clear image of that person's features. When we close our eyes after we've been away from your physical presence for a long time, will the same thing happen?

A. The image of that person starts fading when love starts fading from your heart. If you think that by going away from the Dera your love will start fading, then of course you won't get the image. If you think the image will still be fresh and that the love will grow, then of course, it will always be there. It depends upon you.

192 Q. If your memory grows weak, can you refresh the Master's face from a photo to do dhyan?

A. How can we achieve contemplation? How can we achieve real dhyan of the Master? Without love you cannot contemplate on the form of the Master. The form of whomsoever you love automatically appears before you. You love your friend, you love your wife, you love your child. Whenever you think about the wife and child, at once their forms appear before you. But for that love, they won't come before you.

That is why they say, attend to your meditation with love and devotion. When you love the Master, his form automatically appears before you, and keeping that form there, you have to do simran. Minus that, you should try to think about the Master and do simran, which will automatically create love and dhyan in you. Memory means love. If love is there, the form is there. Otherwise, we can create love by meditation, and then the form will be there.

Q. So as long as you have love, the form will never go away from your memory?

A. It won't. It can't. You won't be able to get rid of it. You are obsessed by the love. When you love anyone in this world, you are obsessed by that love. You can't get rid of that idea, or stop thinking about that person. You're always thinking and talking about that person. The same applies with the Sant Mat teachings.

193 Q. Master, in this connection, I often feel that it is regrettable that because of modern conditions of life and perhaps because of the expansion of Sant Mat, it is so difficult to have any personal, lasting relation with the Master. The Master is a symbol who is so far away from us that we can only try to kindle that love in our hearts for him, but we cannot sit at his feet as the disciples of Christ used to sit at their Master's feet.

A. I understand. That is right. That is why we are advised to keep the attention in the darkness and do simran. That will automatically create that type of love. With the help of simran, that love will automatically be generated in you.

In the past, there were only a few people following the Saints. They had a personal touch with the Saints, and Saints gave their writings mostly from that personal touch point of view. That is why the Saints have given so much emphasis to love and devotion, which can be created through that atmosphere. But we can create the same love and devotion from within by attending to meditation.

194 Q. Maharaj Ji, I think I've heard you say before that a satsangi who has been initiated by a past Master cannot do dhyan of the present Master. Is it true?

A. A disciple must visualize only the form of that particular Master who initiated him, even if that Master leaves the body.

Q. There are so many who have been initiated by Great Master—

A. They must do dhyan of the Great Master. It is a "must." They can't shift to another Master. For them, he is their Master. Anybody else may appear within; anybody else may come along with their Master within, but a disciple has to look only to his own Master.

195 Q. Then on the same subject, there are those who have been initiated by the Great Master, who see the Great Master's face in the present Master, and therefore they feel that they can engage with that special dhyan.

A. Ultimately it will come to the same thing. Christ said: I have not only to look to my own sheep, but I have also to look to some other sheep,[2] which means the initiates of my own Master. I have also to look after them, those initiated by my predecessor. He is reponsible to look after those sheep also.

Q. In what way, Sir?

A. In every way. But ultimately, he says, there will be one shepherd and one fold, because all Masters are one.

Q. Then in a very subtle way, they can look upon the present Master for getting that devotion and getting that urge for meditation.

A. Actually, even if disciples keep the company of their Master's successor and they love him, automatically that love will generate love in them for their own Master. Automatically the successor will generate love in them for their own Master.

196 Q. Master, you said the other night that once we are initiated and if we come back, we have got to be initiated again. At that time if we reach the Radiant Form, do we see two Masters there?

A. Sister, no. You probably have not followed my point. The Master is only one—Shabd—and whosoever initiates you will project himself from that Shabd, because the Source is one. All Masters are one, which means the Shabd is the Master. That Word, that Spirit, that Holy Ghost is our actual Master, and whosoever initiates, projects himself before us from that Shabd. So the Source of all Masters is the same.

You won't even know who your past Master was until after a very high stage is reached. But sometimes the past associations with the Path and with the Master are so strong that along with your own Master, that previous Master also appears within. Then you will know that you had an association with that past Master, who ultimately merges into your own Master, the present Master, because they're all one.

197 Q. Why does the Radiant form have to be projected out of the Shabd?

A. Otherwise we won't recognize whom we are in touch with.

Q. And this is done consciously by the Master?

A. Yes, that's right, so that the disciple knows where he is and with whom he is dealing. But ultimately the Radiant Form becomes the Shabd and you become pure soul, without form and shape, and the soul just merges into the Shabd.

198 Q. Master, when we're doing dhyan and we get to a point when we do see Light within, Great Master says that we should concentrate on the Light, and the Light, that faculty of seeing, will lead the soul forward.

A. That is right. When you see the Light, then you have something to hold your attention there. Both faculties have to be occupied: thinking and seeing. Now, when you are seeing the Light and the Light is becoming brighter and brighter, your faculty of seeing is being occupied. You may not try to contemplate on the form of the Master then, but automatically you will feel his presence throughout. You will feel the form of the Master in that Light, whether you think about him or not.

199 Q. Maharaj Ji, in meditation, where does dhyan end and nirat begin?

A. With dhyan we try to contemplate on the face of the Master while we do simran. We begin with dhyan, and then nirat means when the third eye opens and we start seeing the Light. Nirat begins when we start seeing the Light. Then it is better to concentrate on the Light, because there is something substantial to catch your attention. The purpose of dhyan is only to hold your attention at the eye centre so that the attention may not drop down. But if you are seeing the Light, if you are enjoying the Light, you can look into the light and do simran, and that will absorb your attention. That is nirat.

200 Q. Master, if during meditation we put a little bit of pressure on the eyes with our hands, not heavy pressure but light pressure, will that cause light to—

A. This is a physical light. You should not put any pressure on the eyes at all.

Q. Shouldn't you touch the eyes?

A. No. When you are sitting in simran, you don't have to put your hands to your face. Even when you are hearing the Sound, you should not touch the eyes at all. Otherwise, just by pressing the eyes, you see some light. This is all physical, of these eyes, but that is not spiritual Light.

One should neither keep the hands on the eyes, nor on the nose, because if you keep the hands on the nose, there's difficulty in breathing. If you keep them on the eyes, you will strain your eyes. And neither should you block your face just in front of your mouth, or you may feel some discomfort in breathing. Your hands must be positioned in such a way that fresh air goes to your eyes and nose, and you breathe freely. Then there'll be no difficulty with your physical breathing.

201 Q. Where does the Light come from?

A. The Light is already inside. It doesn't come from anywhere. Christ said: if thine eye be single, thy whole body shall be filled with Light.[3]

Q. So do we see Light within ourselves or do we see Light outside?

A. We see the Light within ourselves. When we open the third eye, when we become single-eyed, then we see that Light. Now our attention is downward and we don't see the Light. When the attention is downward, the Light is still there. The Light doesn't go anywhere, it is always there; but the mind has to see the Light, and it cannot do so when its tendency is downward towards the senses. When we withdraw all our attention to the eye center, then we see the Light, because it is there.

202 Q. Probably that is the "fire" that Moses saw when he fainted, Sir?

A. I was reading in the Bible—in Matthew—that the disciples of Christ fell flat when they heard the thundering of the clouds and saw the dazzling light.[4] All the disciples fell flat. Actually, this is an inner experience, it's not the outside light. And because they were not prepared, they fainted.

Moses also saw the same thing when that mountain was burning and there was the sound of trumpets and thundering of clouds.[5] Actually, that was all inside. Light was not on the mountain—Light was within him. He saw that reddish Light within himself, which must have been the Light of the second stage, and he heard that Sound which resembled the thundering of clouds. Then he became unconscious. From the worldly point of view, the man had fainted, but he may have been in a trance, in a state of bliss there.

203 Q. Maharaj Ji, is this Light always a white light, or is it sometimes a blue light?

A. Now this depends upon what stage our consciousness is at. Light is always the same, but when you see the Light from a distance, it will appear one way to you. When you go nearer, it will become different to you. When you are in the Light, it will become still different to you. The sun always has the same light, but from different angles and at different distances, it looks different to us. The light of the sun is sometimes reddish and golden, and so many other colors come, but actually the light of the sun is the same always. It never differs.

When we see the inner Light in the beginning, we just see flashes. It comes and goes; but actually the Light doesn't come and go. It is the attention which falls down and the attention which comes back. When the attention is there, it sees the Light, and when it drops down, it sees the darkness, so we think flashes of light are coming. Actually the attention is coming and going. And then we see shimmering types of light. It is the mind that is not steady, but we think the Light is not steady, that the Light is shaking. It is the mind which is shaky, so we get a shimmering effect of that Light. Therefore, what we see all depends on the stage of concentration of the mind.

204 Q. When the consciousness is withdrawn from the body and the disciple is perhaps seeing things like the starry skies inside, when does the disciple stop doing simran and dhyan and start attending to those things?

A. You should continue doing simran until you reach the second stage.

Q. And dhyan?

A. Dhyan automatically will be there when you will see the Radiant Form of the Master within. You can't get rid of that. When you reach to that level of consciousness, dhyan is bound to be there because you see the Radiant Form of the Master.

Q. So then you should never really attend to those inner experiences? You should always keep your attention in simran and dhyan?

A. What do you mean by attending to the experiences? They will be there. You will go on looking at them, but you will keep your mind in simran.

Q. And dhyan?

A. Of course, automatically it has to be there. Dhyan means you are seeing those objects, you are seeing those things. That is dhyan.

Q. Dhyan of the Master?

A. Certainly. When you see the Radiant Form of the Master, it will definitely catch your attention. The purpose of seeing the Radiant Form or the purpose of the appearance of the Radiant Form is only this: that we concentrate, that the Radiant Form catches our attention and doesn't let it go to the right or left, because if with our mind we go to the right and left, we can go astray. The Radiant Form so much catches our attention that we are never allowed to go astray. Otherwise you will be lost in those mansions—there are so many attractions, so many attractions.

205 Q. But is there a stage inside where you do not have any experiences of the Radiant Form and you're having other experiences?

A. That you will also have along with the Radiant Form. Before that you will have visions here and there.

You should look at them disinterestedly and keep your mind in simran. For example, you see light or color or other things, views or scenery. Look at them but keep your mind in simran.

206 Q. Is it correct to see colors, very nice colors, while we are meditating, or should we stop seeing colors? I have been told we have to stop seeing the colors.

A. You will see many types of colors inside. You just look at them, but keep your mind in simran. They will come and fade out They will automatically be left behind. You can't close your eyes to them because they are there. You can look at them, you can see them, but keep your mind in simran, and you will gradually pass them by.

207 Q. Maharaji Ji, in *Divine Light* you have written that we should not pay too much attention to the Light that we see, but we should keep the attention at the eye center. And at other places you have written that we should put all the attention into the Light and pierce that Light.

A. My letters are always in reference to the particular person who's writing me. There must be some particular problem which I'm answering. The writer may be confused with the Light, or there may be flashes of Light, or some Light may be disturbing him too much in the eyes. I don't know what his problem is unless his letter is before me. You can't always generalize my answers, but there's no contradiction, because everybody has an individual problem in meditation.

Q. My question is, when does a person know when to concentrate on that Light, or not?

A. The Light will automatically catch your attention. When you see the Light, it will catch your attention and it won't let your attention go out. It's so blissful and peaceful and enchanting and pulling that it will automatically hold your attention. You can't help looking at that Light and eventually penetrating it.

208 Q. Maharaj Ji, in the inner regions, is the Radiant Form of the Satguru always visible to the diciple, or are there times when he just does not see his Satguru before him?

A. Generally it is, but sometimes it's not. After the second stage it is always visible but till the second stage, sometimes it is and sometimes it may not be visible to you.

209 Q. Maharaj Ji, when we reach the Master inside, are there big groups of souls with the Master?

A. Do you want to be with people there? If your way of thinking is in that state, you will never see the Radiant Form of the Master. You will see the Radiant Form of the Master when you are concerned only with yourself and with the Master, and with nobody else in the world.

When you see the Master within, the whole creation ceases to exist for you. You exist and the Master exists. You're not aware of anyone else. You're so much in love that you're not aware of anyone else around you. You have seen moths. The moth is in love with the light, and there are a thousand moths on that light. Ask that moth if he knows any other moth there. He knows only one thing: the light he's in love with. He's not conscious of any other moth—and if he's conscious of the other moths, he is not a moth at all.

BHAJAN—LISTENING TO THE DIVINE SOUND

210 Q. Before you come to the eye center, you haven't heard the Shabd. You've just heard the local sound or something, and—

A. You hear the Shabd, but it will not pull you upward. You enjoy it, you hear it, you feel its bliss and peace, but it will not pull your consciousness upward unless you're able to concentrate here at the eye center.

Q. Then it's the simran that will make you go up there.

A. That's right.

Q. Well then, isn't it a waste of time listening to that Sound?

A. It's not a waste of time because we also have to inculcate the habit of listening to the Sound. Even if we don't hear anything, we must devote time to listening for the Sound, to create a habit in us to be attentive to that Sound which is within every one of us. Both simran and bhajan are essential. You can't do one at the cost of the other.

211 Q. In the beginning when you're devoting most of your time to simran, is it necessary in every sitting to devote at least some time to bhajan no matter what may be heard or not heard?

A. When you give the proper time for sitting, then it is always better to start with simran and to end with bhajan. You may give more time to simran and less time to hearing of the Sound, but it's always better to attend to both of them in the same sitting. But sometimes if you can't do both and you just want to do simran, it is all right. There is nothing wrong with this. Sometimes if you feel like just attending to the Sound, just attend to the Sound.

212 Q. Master, if when you switch from simran to bhajan you should not catch hold of the Sound, your attention will come out of the eye center very fast. You advise in initiation that we spend approximately three-quarters of the time in simran and one-quarter in bhajan, but that must be about an hour of bhajan. If the disciple finds that his consciousness goes out very fast, would it be more advisable to spend ninety, ninety-five per cent of the time in simran?

A. Even a hundred per cent I don't mind. Sometimes when you are not very attentive to the Sound and your mind is running out, you can switch onto the simran again. There is no hard and fast rule, that this much time must be given to simran or this much time to Sound. It is a general division so that we get into the habit of listening for the Sound and not only attending to simran. It's always better to attend to both, a little to the Sound and more to simran to begin with, but if sometimes the mind is very rebellious, you can give more time to simran. You can give even one hundred per cent of the time to simran. We are not very rigid about these things.

At times the Sound is really pulling you and you are being attracted towards the Sound, then you can get out of simran and attend to the Sound. It's all right. There's no hard and fast rule, but generally we should attend to both.

213 Q. After we change positions and start listening to the Sound, for the first few minutes of bhajan should we continue doing simran to make the changeover gradual?

A. No. First you should attend to simran; then you should switch on to the sound.

214 Q. When a person is doing simran during the time of meditation, what happens if the soul has gone up but still not to the eye center? Is it possible to hear the Sound before the soul has been withdrawn to the eye center?

A. Yes, without proper concentration, proper withdrawal, you do hear the Sound, but that Sound won't pull you much. You will enjoy the Sound, you will hear the Sound, you will relish it, and your mind will be absorbed in it. You will be very happy and feel quite peaceful and blissful, but it won't pull you much without proper concentration.

215 Q. It is said that the Sound that one is supposed to hear in the beginning stages does not have much of a withdrawal effect. But does it have a purifying effect?

A. Yes, Any Sound that you hear in the beginning always has a purifying effect on the soul. Even the echo of the Sound has a purifying effect on the soul. Every internal Sound of *any* stage has a purifying effect on the soul.

216 Q. Is there any Sound that we might hear before reaching the Radiant Form? I understood these would not have any real pulling power.

A. No, any Sound which you hear within yourself has some pulling power, but its pulling power increases with the help of concentration. The pulling power is always there because the Sound holds our attention, it catches our attention, whatever Sound we may hear. But when the Sound becomes very distinct and clear, then it pulls us more and more, and we are able to attach ourselves to it more and more.

217 Q. Does listening to the Sound help the concentration, though, before the attention has gone up?

A. You mean when we hear the Sound, will it help concentration? That's also right, because when you are fully concentrated, when you have fully attached yourself to the Sound and you've eliminated all other thoughts from your mind, that helps concentration also. But simran helps concentration more. With the help of simran, other sounds fade out; only the real Sound stays. Your mind is taken out from the other sounds which are distracting you, they fade away, and the real Sound becomes distinct and clear.

218 Q. I think it is said that there are ten sounds at the third eye, and we're told to listen to either of three, and—

A. No, I've never confused anybody by saying that there are ten sounds and you have to listen to only three. Whatever sound you hear can be compared to about ten examples of sounds, not that .there are exactly ten sounds. So, listen to whatever sound you hear. With the help of simran and concentration, other sounds will fade out, and the real Sound will become distinct and clear, and will start pulling you and catching your attention.

Don't try to differentiate one sound from another. Then you will be lost in deciding which sound you should hear and which you should not hear, and your mind will run away because it becomes difficult for you to discriminate one sound from another. It is always better and more practical just to give your attention to the sound, whatever sound you are hearing. With the help of simran, the real Sound will become more distinct and clear, and other sounds will fade out. Automatically you will be in touch with that real Sound.

219 Q. Very much importance is put upon stilling the body for meditation to begin with.

A. Stilling the mind. The body automatically becomes still. The effect of meditation will be that the body becomes numb to some extent, but the purpose is to still the mind, not the body.

Q. My question is, why do you reactivate the body for bhajan? Why is the body moved, restimulated, for bhajan from simran?

A. By changing the position, you don't lose anything. We change the position because it would be difficult to stay in the bhajan posture for the entire sitting; it wouldn't be practical, and in order to hear the Sound we want the bhajan posture. But even if you're not in the bhajan posture and you're hearing the Sound, you can continue in the same posture. It's not essential to change to the bhajan posture.

If by doing simran your concentration is fair and your mind is still and you are in touch with the Sound, then you can listen to the Sound right in the same posture for simran; you can be one with the Sound. People do that. But even if you change the posture, your concentration is not scattered. Concentration is of the mind, not of the body.

220 Q. Is it necessary, Maharaj Ji, to do bhajan with your hands up to your ears? What if you just can't quite get to it?

A. I think that to begin with, it is very essential. It is always better to use the hands, but when the Sound is very audible, distinct and clear, and it is pulling you upwards the moment you are able to concentrate here at the eye center, then you don't have to use your hands.

Q. In the plugging of the ears, must this be done manually or can ear plugs be used?

A. I think we should try to avoid ear plugs, artificial things. The Lord has given us beautiful hands, and let us make use of them.

221 Q. Maharaj Ji, is the purpose of putting the thumbs in the ears to exclude the noise of any other person?

A. Well, brother, there are two reasons: one is to exclude the outside noise, and another is, we have to become conscious of hearing the Sound from the right side. That is why it's always the right side that's closed, because we are to become conscious of the right side, of the Sound coming from the right side.

222 Q. Master, if you're living in a very quiet place where nothing will disturb you, is it still then necessary to put your thumbs in the ears? Even if there is no sound outside?

A. Yes, even if there is no sound outside, you should sit in the posture.

223 Q. Master, should both the ears be closed when you're listening to the Sound? I saw in one of your letters that you advised someone to take the thumb out of the left ear.

A. Actually, the Sound that we hear has nothing to do with the ears at all. These ears don't hear that Sound—our consciousness must be at that particular spot (the eye center) to hear the Sound. Whether we have ears or not is immaterial in hearing the inner Sound, but we are so used to hearing sounds through the ears that in the early stages we try to hear the inner Sound also with the help of the ears.

And why do we close the right side and not the left side? It's just to get into the habit of giving a little attention to the right side, because ultimately we have to catch the Sound coming from the right side and not the left. Eventually, when the Sound becomes distinct and clear with the help of simran, you will know whether the Sound is coming from the right or the left, and then, since you'll be conscious of the Sound from the right side, you'll be attached to the Sound at once. But before you are sure whether the Sound is coming from the right or from the left, you can listen to whatever Sound is coming from within.

When the Sound becomes distinct and clear, you don't need the hand or ears at all. Then the moment you close your eyes and you draw your attention up to the eye center, automatically you will be in touch with the Sound.

224 Q. So that's why you hear it sometimes when you're just concentrated or quiet?

A. That's right. Sometimes you're studying or you're thinking deeply about some problem and you start hearing the Sound, because concentration comes with deep thinking.

225 Q. I've heard that people- non-satsangi people— have mentioned at the time of their death, perhaps in the semi-conscious state, that they can hear music. Could this be the Sound?

A. Not only at the time of death, but even while living they may hear the Music. The moment they concentrate at the eye center, to whatever little extent it may be, they at once hear the Sound. Sometimes if someone is reading a book in a quiet place and he is absolutely concentrated in reading, he may start hearing all these Sounds. He probably thinks some music is going on in the room and he doesn't know what it is. It happens with people—even non-satsangis. But they're not conscious of that Music, so they don't pay much attention to it. Some even run to the doctors, thinking that there is something wrong with their ears.

With a little attention at the eye center, you hear that Music, so naturally when the soul withdraws at the time of death, concentration is there, and some people definitely hear it. It's of no use to them, however; that Sound won't pull them upwards. The Sound is always at the eye center, but since they are not connected with it, they are not initiated, the Sound won't pull them up.

226 Q. Let us say a person is moving about in a crowd or you are at odd places where you haven't the least idea of the Sound and you're not doing simran and you're not doing bhajan and you're not at all thinking of hearing the Sound. Is it possible to hear the Sound on such occasions, or is it just during meditation?

A. It's certainly possible, and rather sometimes at very odd places you hear it quite plainly. That Sound is sometimes a warning to you also, and also the Lord's grace to keep you away from something negative so that you may attend to the Sound and can escape from that negative atmosphere.

227 Q. Maharaj Ji, in *Divine Light* there was a letter from you to a lady, and she heard the bell Sound and thought that was encouragement to go along with a certain action, and in your reply you said that wasn't encouragement, it was a warning not to do that action,[1] and I was wondering—

A. Sister, it may be in reference to her letter. You don't know what else she has written. These letters are always in reference to their questions, their problems, so you can't generalize them.

Q. But would it be possible for you to talk about what happens if a disciple hears the preparatory sounds before the bell Sound in some situation or talking to certain people? Is it possible to use that as a way of discriminating between a good action or a bad action?

A. You can't analyze these things. Even if you hear a Sound, you can't confirm your action, neither can you disapprove your action. You can't analyze or judge that since I'm hearing the Sound, whatever I am going to do is perfectly all right. You shouldn't think like that. Just use your own conscience, which always becomes better and better, finer and finer, with the help of meditation. You get right answers from your own conscience if you continue meditation and attend to the Sound. The Sound is meant to be heard. But if we try to analyze the meaning of the Sound at a particular time, we can be misled, we can be wrong. Then we start justifying actions which may not be right.

228 Q. Christ has said that the wind bloweth, but you cannot tell where the Sound comes from.* Could you discuss that, please?

A. Christ meant that the Sound can be compared to the noise of the wind. If you are inside a room and you are hearing the sound of the wind blowing outside, you don't know from which direction it is coming, nor where it is going. Similarly, when you go within you hear that Sound, but you don't know its

---

* John 3:8—The wind bloweth where it listeth, and thou hearest the sound thereof, but canst not tell whence it cometh, and whither it goeth: so is every one that is born of the Spirit.

Source, from where it is coming. You have never been to its Source. Christ says that you will hear the Sound without knowing its Source, without knowing whether it is coming from below or above or the right or the left. You will just be hearing the Sound.

Christ compared the inner Sound only to the rushing of the wind, but we compare it with so many other sounds also, like the humming noise in a telephone post, the sound of a train passing over a bridge, or dry leaves rustling in the autumn season. Christ was just giving an example to explain about that Sound.

229 Q. What should one do to prevent the sound coming from the left ear?

A. You can't do anything at all. We are unnecessarily confused with the sound of the left. Normally, we are not allowed to go to the left. The left sound is explained only so that we know that there is also a deceptive sound which can mislead us, but Master generally does not allow you to go to the left side at all.

In the beginning we can never be sure whether the sound is coming from the right or the left. Sometimes we feel that it is coming from the left, sometimes we feel that it is coming from the right, and sometimes we feel that perhaps it is in the center. It is always best to keep our attention in the center and to hear that Sound from whichever direction it may be coming. With the help of concentration it will become distinct and clear, and then you will know whether it is coming from the right or the left—not before that. And then if at all it comes from the left, you can ignore it; you can attend to simran.

230 Q. When the Sound is very fickle or it's not very well marked, then along with listening to the Sound, should one also try to inwardly pray to the Master?

A. No thoughts should come when you're trying to hear the Sound. Your whole attention should be in the Sound. It should not be that you're talking to your mind, for then the mind will start thinking of a hundred and one things. You have to still your mind and try to be attentive to the Sound.

Whatever time you're devoting to meditation is in itself a prayer. Rather than shouting, whatever knocks you are giving on the door are a sufficient invitation for the person within to open the door. Whatever time we're devoting to simran and to hearing of the Sound itself is a prayer; we are knocking on that door. So we shouldn't try to pray along with hearing the Sound.

231 Q. Should we do dhyan also while listening to the Sound?

A. To begin with you shouldn't, but when you see the Light or the Radiant Form of the Master, then you will see that while also hearing the Sound. But to begin with, dhyan should be done only when you are doing simran.

Simran takes us up only to some extent. Ultimately you have to leave the simran. When you see the Radiant Form of the Master, you start merging into the Master and you lose the simran. Then you don't do simran because you're not conscious of anything except the Master, who is all Sound and Light. You forget simran, you are not bothered with it, and there is no necessity for it. But to begin with, to reach to that stage, we have to do simran along with dhyan.

At the time of hearing the Sound we shouldn't worry about simran and dhyan, because if we try to think about the Master, then we are not concentrated enough to be one with the Sound. When we try to contemplate on the form of the Master, the tendency of the mind is to run out, sometimes thinking of him sitting in satsang, sitting in seva, walking, talking, meeting, and then you become unconcerned with the Sound. Just be here, at the eye center, and try to hear whatever Sound you are able to hear.

232 Q. Master, the Great Master in *Spiritual Gems* says that we can go on hearing the Sound all our lives, but this won't help unless we develop the nirat.[2]

A. Our soul has two faculties: the faculty to hear and the faculty to see—the power to hear and the power to see. The power to see is nirat; the power to hear is surat. Surat will hear the Sound and nirat will see the Light, but both come from the same Source. The Light comes from the Sound, and the Sound comes from the Light. Ultimately they become one. We know the direction of our home with the help of that Sound and we follow the spiritual Path within through the help of that Light. Both have to go side by side.

Q. What does he mean by saying to develop the nirat?

A. To develop the nirat means to give more time to concentration, more time to simran. Generally, we give more attention to the Sound, to hearing the

Shabd, because we enjoy the Sound. But when we ignore the simran side, nirat is not awakened and concentration is not complete.

The moment concentration is complete, the Light is there, nirat is there, and the Sound is very pulling. If you don't try to awaken nirat, which means that you don't try to concentrate with the help of simran, then you will hear the Sound, but it will not pull you. The Sound will pull you only when the concentration is complete, and the moment concentration is complete, you will also see the Light.

233 Q. Maharaj Ji, in *Spiritual Letters* I read that Baba Ji said that when listening to the Sound, the nirat should be concentrated upwards.[3] What does this mean?

A. The faculty to hear is to catch the Sound; the faculty to see is to be one with the Light. When you are seeing the Light and also hearing the Sound, then you should try to keep your nirat upwards along with that Sound. Don't hold your attention in that Light without trying to go along with the Sound, upwards. You should keep your nirat upwards, which means to go along with the Light and also hear the Sound. Sometimes one is absorbed too much in the Light and doesn't want to follow the Sound, but we have to follow both the Sound and the Light.

234 Q. Some yogis who do yoga exercises make all the chakras work, and they know about Nam, but they can't get there.

A. As you have read in the life history of many yogis, they see the Light, they believe in the Light, they try to travel by the Light, but they think that the Sound is disturbing them. They don't understand the Sound and they think that the Sound is taking them astray from the Light. Actually, they have to go up by the Sound. The Light is coming from the Sound and from nowhere else, but they know only about the Light and not about the Sound. So they try to withhold themselves from the Sound, they don't try to become receptive to it, because they think the Sound will not let them make progress.

INNER GUIDANCE

235 Q. Master, I have a question about inner guidance, Master's guidance. When we're trying to make a decision or arrive at a decision, we try to listen inside for Master's voice, but sometimes it seems to be very faint. Should we try to do our best to listen to the Master's voice inside of us in making a decision, or should we just try to use our reason and intellect to the best of our ability?

A. Whenever we make a decision, we should keep the teachings in view and our Master in view, and by meditation our level of consciousness is also developed to the extent that we make the decision. Still it can happen otherwise, but then we have to go through our fate karma too. So we should try to do our best.

236 Q. Should we consciously seek Master's guidance in making our decisions or just do our best?

A. Do your best. How can you seek Master's guidance? Unless you come face to face and talk to him and tell him the problem within, how would you get the right guidance? You have to do your best, until you reach to that level of consciousness where you can put your problem to the Master and get the solution. But merely hearing certain voices can be deceptive also.

237 Q. Master, is it true that the Master will never give advice through only a voice, that he will come before the disciple inside?

A. I say that by meditation your consciousness is developed to the extent that you can make your own decision rightly. Whether you hear a voice or not is immaterial. A voice can even be deceptive. You can hear the voice without seeing the Master, but then how can you be sure that it is the Master's voice?

You may get the right solution in the beginning. Your mind may win your confidence in this way, and then it may deceive you later on. One or two problems it will rightly analyze and give you the right advice. After having won your confidence, the mind can misguide you.

So we shouldn't give any thought to the voices within at all unless the Radiant Form of the Master is before us and we know it is the Radiant Form and we can have communication with the Master. Then only can we depend on that voice. Otherwise, we can't depend upon these voices, glimpses or visions. We can't make an analysis of all these things—"This could mean this, this could mean that." You can only do your best to make your own decisions.

238 Q. Isn't that what simran is for, to help us decide whether the voices are true or the vision is true?

A. Well, a vision still can stay for some time even in spite of your simran because your simran may not be concentrated much. Concentration may not be there, simran may be mechanical. You shouldn't rely on those visions unless you see the Radiant Form of the Master and you are sure that it is the Radiant Form of the Master. Then you can put your problem to him and get the decision. That will be foolproof. Otherwise, there can be a mistake.

Q. I always thought that the simran we have to repeat was more or less our guarantee.

A. Yes, simran is the guarantee to know whether what we see is the Radiant Form of the Master or not. That is the guarantee.

Q. So it doesn't apply to voices?

A. Unless someone is before you, you should not give any attention to voices at all. You are never instructed at the time of initiation that you have to check the voices by simran. You should only test the form of the Master by simran, but not the voices.

Master never hides his face and talks to you. Whenever he wants to say anything, he comes face to face. He must come face to face, for only then will you be sure that he is the Master. Voices can be deceptive. Sometimes our own mind starts speaking to us, and a lot of other things also come from our own mind. We see our own face within ourselves and we start thinking, "I am God. I am seeing my own self. There is nobody else in the world besides me." These are all deceptions of the mind.

And then we always try to interpret these visions and voices according to our own way of thinking. We interpret these things according to what we want, because our mind is already conditioned by what we want. It's always better not to give much attention to these things and not to analyze these visions or these voices. Instead, reach the Radiant Form of the Master and be sure that it is the Radiant Form of the Master. Then you can put your problem to him and you can have direct communication, and there's no deception in that.

239 Q. Master, can fear hinder one's progress in meditation?

A. Fear of what?

Q. Fear of possibly being led astray before we meet the Radiant Form.

A. In our subconscious, we have so many hidden fears. They are all our past associations, our past attachments, our past suppressions, not only of this birth but even of previous births. Those fears are suppressed within us, and they appear before us at the time of meditation. We shouldn't try to analyze them or give much importance to these things. With the help of meditation you are able to rise above these fears and you are able to shed them all. Otherwise, in one way or another you are always frightened of something or other.

We must attend to our meditation, and slowly and slowly we are able to shed all those fears, and we become fearless. Then we're not frightened of anything, whatever may happen in this creation. Meditation makes us fearless, and it is the only remedy for fear.

Christ has said in the Bible: at the most they can kill your body, but they cannot kill your soul.[1] The worst fear is that you will be deprived of this body. He says, then what? They can't kill your soul. You are concerned with your soul more than with your body, and we should feel more concerned with the development of the soul rather than being concerned with fears.

240 Q. If you experience any form, whether the Master's or the Negative Power's, and you feel fear and not love, what does this mean?

A. You mean when you see some form of the Master, you feel frightened? Frightened of what?

Do you feel frightened when you look at the face of a person with whom you are in love? You are not in love if you are always frightened to look at him. When love is there, the question of being frightened doesn't arise. You're happy.

One should never feel frightened. There is nothing to fear, nothing to lose. It's only the mind that creates such feelings in us. It tries to deceive us by such concepts. There's nothing to feel frightened of at all.

Sometimes people get frightened when they see the Light. They see flashes of Light and they get frightened, and they don't sit in meditation. For what are they giving their time? If they don't want to see that Light, why do they sit in meditation? This is a weakness of the mind. There's nothing wrong with it. You'll be able to overcome it.

Some people do feel fear. They are a little scared because their background is such that there is something in their subconscious which comes to the surface sometimes, and they start feeling frightened of these things. They have some sort of guilty conscience or something weighing on their heart. They feel frightened even to face the Master outside, and then the same feeling they carry within. We should not feel frightened even outside, with all our guilt in the mind. Then that feeling of fear will not come inside either.

241 **Q.** Can't someone be frightened to venture into some unknown place, because I've heard that before we come to the Radiant Form of the Master, we have to cross the stars and moon.

A. That's right.

Q. I mean, there we have nobody with us until we reach the Radiant Form of the Master. Can that sort of hold a person from being pulled by the Sound, when a person's frightened to allow his—

A. Whenever a disciple sits in meditation, he's never alone. He's *never* alone, and he's never allowed to go astray within. There is always a guiding hand, a guiding force, to lead the disciple within. There is no danger of the disciple going astray, so one should have absolutely no fear. The one for whom we are meditating is always there with us to guide us, and we shouldn't ever worry or feel fear at all.

242 **Q.** Does the Master protect the disciple from falling for temptations inside?

A. The greatest protection the Master has given us to save ourselves from these temptations is meditation, and we should try to make use of it. If you have to fight an enemy, and you have been given a sword or pistol but you don't use it, then it is your fault. The Master has armed you with a "sword" and a "pistol" (meditation) to face the enemy, and now you should be prepared to face the enemy with these weapons.

Attend to your meditation and you will be able to face these enemies.

243 Q. I was once told by someone that there are times when an evil form appearing inside will not leave when the five names are said. Are there exceptions to the five names making anything negative run away?

A. No evil entity can come near the disciple. Christ said: when I whistle, my sheep recognize my voice, because they know me and I know them, and robbers and thieves will run away. Robbers and thieves cannot deceive the disciple.[2] If anybody appears to you inside except your Master, it is nothing but a robber and a thief, which means that his purpose is to destroy you or to lead you astray. If you are doing simran and you are in touch with the Sound, no robber or thief will come near you. You're always protected, and Master is always there. Whether you're conscious inside and you see him or not, he's always there. He's always there to protect you, and nobody can harm or misguide you.

244 Q. Master, why are some people troubled by spirits? Can't anything be done about it?

A. Sister, it is their association with those spirits in past lives. Their unconscious attachments still exist with those particular spirits, and sometimes people are troubled, definitely. Continue meditate; they won't bother you then. No spirit comes near meditation. If you meditate, you won't be affected by them or bothered by them, and you will just forget about them. They can do no harm in any way.

245 **Q.** Maharaj Ji, if we ever see frightening or evil faces inside, are these purely projections of our own individual mind, or are they actually spirits?

A. Well, brother, there can be many reasons for it. It can be something in your subconscious mind. The mind starts projecting all those things. It can be certain entities which are trying to lead you astray. Whatever it is, keep your attention in simran and don't give any attention to anything.

246 **Q.** I had also heard that sometimes the form of a certain individual will appear, and it will not leave until our karma with that individual is over.

A. Karma of what type? No, this is not like karma. Sometimes we have very strong attachments, past strong attachments with certain people, and our own mind projects their forms before us. They are our past associations, our past relations, our past attachments. If you give too much attention to them, there is always a danger of reviving those attachments and of your attention, your consciousness, falling down.

But if you keep to simran, if you keep your whole attention in your meditation, those forms will automatically fade out. You will just rise above them and they will disappear forever. That is why it is explained at the time of initiation that many forms may appear before us. Even if you are doing simran, they may appear before you for some time.

You are not to give any attention to anyone within except to your own Master. Even if you're interested in the past Mystics, you should not give any recognition to them unless they are being accompanied by your own Master. Your Master is the real guide within. You have not to give any recognition to anyone else.

247 Q. I remember reading a letter in, I think, *Spiritual Gems*, in which the Great Master told a disciple that they had done very well to go so far in that they had made contact with Christ, with Jesus, and that they should go in again and go further and do better than that.[3] What did he mean? How could he do better if Christ, indeed, according to Saint John, is a Master?

A. The question is whether the disciple actually saw Christ or he saw only his own conception of Christ. Master will not discourage you on the Path. It is just possible that the disciple was so much attached to Christ, through his religious background before coming to the Path, that he wanted to follow the Path only from one point of view: to see Christ. The disciple may have seen only his own mental concept of Christ. He may have been at a much lower stage, and he may not have actually seen Christ at all. Yet that idea, that mental attachment for Christ, may have gone out of him after he had "seen Christ" inside. Even if you want to see previous Saints, your Master *must* come with the other Saints and introduce you. Otherwise you're liable to be deceived or misled. For you don't know who Christ is, you have not seen him in this life.

I often receive letters of that type. You may not like to discourage the disciple from meditation by telling him that what he has seen is not the Christ, because that vision creates longing in him to go ahead with his meditation. Gradually, he himself will grow spiritually to know where he was and where he is supposed to go.

248 **Q.** Maharaj Ji, I'm afraid there's something I didn't quite understand. I was told at initiation that when one does meet other souls inside and one continues doing the simran, then if these beings remain, one can talk to these beings. But you have said that one wouldn't be interested in doing that. Could you just clarify that? That's what I was told at initiation.

A. What is explained at the time of initiation is that if we are interested in anybody else besides our Master, then our own Master will bring those souls along with him, so that desire will no longer be a hindrance to us. Then we can talk. But who would like to talk to anybody else in the presence of the Master? I don't understand. Except for the Master, we should not recognize anybody within. If we are interested in the past Masters or anybody else, our own Master will bring them and then we can talk to them—but nobody would be interested in that.

249 **Q.** Speaking about the Radiant Form of the Master, I've heard that the Negative Power can take on the form of the Master's face—

A. That's right.

Q. —but not the feet of the Master.

A. Why should you look at the feet of the Master?

Q. I've heard this.

A. Did you read this anywhere in the Sant Mat books?

Q. No, I didn't read it.

A. Don't listen to gossip. Always depend upon the books, and you can point out anything questionable in them to me. Never listen to people's gossip. That is why so many books have been printed, just to give authentic information.

250 Q. Sir, if the sound from the left side persists loudly and it doesn't stop, how can one cure it?

A. More simran. More simran. With the help of simran we are able to eliminate the sound from the left.

We should give more attention to simran. Generally we are not allowed to go to the left side. The left side is just a reflection of whatever we have to the right side, a deception by Kal so that the soul may not be able to escape from his clutches. But the Master is always there to guide the disciple to the right side. At the time of initiation, the left sound is explained so that the disciple may know about it, but it's very rare indeed that an initiate will go to the left side.

251 Q. Master, does the form of the Master stay with the disciple all the way back Home?

A. Absolutely. Without that form, no soul can go back to the Father. As you have read in the Bible, Christ said: I am going to prepare a place for you according to your spiritual development, and there are many mansions in my Lord's house. Then after that he says: you will merge into me, and you will become me and I will become you.[4] You will merge into me and I will merge into you, and only then can you merge into the Father. When we lose our own identity, we become the Master, we merge into the Master, and then through the Master we merge into the Father. It is the same thing. There's no difference. With the heat, water evaporates from the mud. It merges into the clouds, and through the clouds it merges into the sea. There's no difference between the water in the dirt and the water in the clouds and the water in the sea.

252 Q. Master, aside from meditation, it seems that sometimes when we're with you and you leave, it's like taking a fish out of water for us. It's the feeling of this love that it seems that the Master's putting within us, it is sometimes so painful, and just when you walk away—

A. You mean to suggest that Master should always take all the disciples with him everywhere he goes? They'll all become miserable. They also want rest, they also want to relax. The sun comes and the light is there, the light shines, but then night is also required for sleep and rest. We say the sun has set—the sun never sets; it is always there, giving light somewhere. But we need the night to rest and sleep. When night is here now and we are sleeping and resting, the sun is still there. The sun doesn't go anywhere. Master is always with us. He doesn't go anywhere at all, but probably we need the night, to rest and sleep and relax.

THE EFFECT OF MEDITATION

Meditation is a way of life. You do not merely close yourself in a room for a few hours, then forget about meditation for the rest of the day. It must take on a practical form, reflecting in every daily action and in your whole routine. That itself is an effect of meditation. To live in the teachings, to live in that atmosphere is itself a meditation. You are building that atmosphere every moment for your daily meditation. Everything you do must consciously prepare you for the next meditation. So meditation becomes a way of life, as we live in the atmosphere we build with meditation.

To live in that atmosphere is to live a simple, happy and relaxed life. The effect of that peace and bliss of meditation enables you to adjust according to the weather of life while retaining your equanimity and balance. You contentedly face your karmas, both good and bad, by continually adjusting to their ever-changing pattern. You can't change the course of events dictated by your destiny. But by obedience to the Master and by attending to meditation you remain happy and relaxed as you go through it. You accept whatever comes your way as the grace of the Master. He is the helmsman of your life now, and he has only your happiness and best interest at heart. By his mercy, he is bringing you to Him as swiftly as possible to give you all He has. So worry has no place in a disciple's heart.

Through meditation we fulfil the very purpose of human life. Meditation is the only worship that pleases the Father. Through meditation we become worthy of His grace and receptive to His love. We build and grow the love and devotion which He gives us to carry us speedily towards our goal. So attending to meditation is submitting to the Will of the Father, it is being obedient to our Lord and Master. It is through meditation, by His grace, that we develop an intense longing to return to our Source. The effect is truly a miracle! We turn from the world, and with the same intensity that we once ran towards it, we now run towards the Father. We experience that bliss and joy of real love and real devotion, as we ultimately merge with our Master to be transformed from the drop into the Divine Ocean itself.

253 Q. Maharaj Ji, in *Science of the Soul* it says that if you want results, you must put in two and a half hours of meditation daily. Then at another place it says that with only three hours of bhajan, the scale will always weigh heavily on the worldly side.

A. This is just a way of explaining. Sardar Bahadur Ji* may have explained to some other people in a different way, but the main thing is not whether we attend to our meditation for two and a half hours or three hours. That is meditation, no doubt, but real meditation means living the way of life throughout the day.

We live in the atmosphere which we build by meditation for the whole day. We don't forget meditation even in a dream, even in our worldly activities, and we try to deal with people in the light

* Maharaj Jagat Singh.

of that meditation. Our dealings should be straight, in fact our whole way of life should be straight. That is real meditation. Merely closing ourselves in a room for a couple of hours and then forgetting the Path for the rest of the day is not real meditation. Its effect should be with us all the time. It is a very hard struggle, but we have to retain the atmosphere that we build in meditation.

254 **Q.** Maharaj Ji, is it better to do a lot of meditation, or less meditation but better done?

A. You mean should we worry about the quality or the quantity?

You will get quality from quantity. Meditating a lot depends upon the individual circumstances. If one is regular and punctual, then two to three hours is enough. If we have to make up for the past—sometimes we skip meditation, and then suddenly we think of meditation and of making the bank balance complete—then it is different.

The only danger in giving too much time to meditation is that sometimes the mind becomes frustrated, because you expect that when you give four hours or five hours to meditation, you will get something, you will reach somewhere—and when you don't, you feel frustrated. Then you leave meditation, which is wrong. If you continue giving regular, punctual time every day to meditation, fitting it in with your other daily engagements, then you are never frustrated. You enjoy the bliss slowly and slowly and you continue your meditation. But if you suddenly give more time, and then suddenly you leave it, that is not right.

To live the teachings of Sant Mat, to live in that atmosphere, is also meditation. Meditation is not just closing yourself in a room for a couple of hours and forgetting about it. You have to give it a practical shape in your daily routine, in your daily dealings with people. If you just give two to three hours and then forget about it and start cheating people, hurting people, abusing people and trying to be clever with them, black-mailing them, then what is the use of that meditation? Its effect should reflect in all your actions. That is also a part of meditation, because you are building an atmosphere all day for the next meditation. So meditation is a way of life. Of course we have to give proper time to meditation, but it should also be our whole way of life.

255 Q. While having the consciousness of the Lord, one is busy with social obligations and obligations with the family. Now, which takes more priority—the simran or the obligations to your—

A. These are all karmic obligations. We have to discharge all these karmic obligations, but our real obligation is to the Creator, though He has given us all these other obligations. We must reach Him, we must find Him. We cannot discharge these worldly obligations at the cost of that obligation to the Creator. That duty to Him is first and foremost, but Saints don't advise us to run away from worldly obligations. You will be able to discharge them in a much better way if you keep your destination in view. If you travel on the Path, you will be a better husband, a better citizen, a better friend, and a better associate, which means you will be discharging your obligations in a much better way.

256 **Q.** When we are discharging these obligations at home and with friends, and especially when we are with people we work with, should we try to create love for the Lord in them by just being an example of love and understanding, or should we also talk about the Path?

A. Example is always better. You always influence people much more by example. That is, as Christ said, putting a light on a high place, on a rock, and people see the light from a distance.[1] You have to set an example, and then people will naturally want to know how you have changed, what has made you like this. Then if they are sincere seekers, automatically the subject matter will be discussed.

257 **Q.** When a strong desire to do service awakens in a disciple's heart, should he think only of turning that service to simran and bhajan?

A. No, whatever service he's capable of doing he can do. Of course the best service is bhajan, but there are other services also which are strong means leading to bhajan. To train the mind to live in the Will of the Father is also a service.

Q. How do you do that day by day?

A. We have to face situations at every step in this life, and at every step in this life we have to explain to our mind, "You have to accept whatever comes in your fate and accept it smilingly, cheerfully. Why grumble?" It's a constant training of the mind.

This is also doing service, because that will help us in meditation. If we always feel perturbed with every little thing, then how can we concentrate, how can we meditate? If we make every little thing an issue the size of the Himalayas, then how can we concentrate? We have to forget, we have to forgive, we have to train our mind to take things easily, lightly, to laugh them away, ignore them. This is all training the mind.

258 Q. Master, can one be too serious about Sant Mat? I find it difficult at times to laugh at certain things where other people can laugh at them.

A. We should be serious about following Sant Mat, but that doesn't mean that we should disregard the cheerful side of life altogether. Rather, we should feel more relaxed because we are following the Path. Concentration helps you to get rid of your tensions. Meditation helps you to rise above your problems, and when you are able to rise above the problems, naturally you are more relaxed, you're not so tense. Meditation will help you to rise above this feeling of tension or remorse, or any miserable feeling.

259 Q. Maharaj Ji, could you speak to us about the need to lead a more relaxed life, not to take ourselves and others so seriously—the idea that we say, sometimes, to "just take it easy"?

A. Meditation is the only factor which can make you relaxed, actually. When something happens against our wishes, against our desires, we become tense, and when something happens according to our wishes or we adjust according to the situation, we are relaxed. Therefore, Mystics say that we should always try to adjust to the situation. The situation will never adjust to us, so there is no sense in becoming tense. We should adjust to the situation; happiness lies in that.

Even if we say winter should not come, winter will come, it has to come. By preparing ourselves to face the winter, we are not changing the course of winter. Winter has to come, but we can prepare ourselves to face the winter. If we have warm clothes, we have a heater, we are happy in that winter. If we don't prepare ourselves to adjust to the cold, we will be miserable. But if we adjust, then we are happy. Similarly, when summer comes, if you insist that summer should not come, you are not going to change the course of summer, for summer must come. But if you adjust to the summer—you have light clothes, you have an air conditioner, a fan, shade, cool water—then you are happy, because you have adjusted to the situation.

In the same way, we have to face in this body the "weather" of life, the effect of good karmas and bad karmas. We can't always have the effect of good karmas, nor do we always have the effect of bad karmas. We have to change according to the effect of those karmas, and then we are happy, then we are relaxed. But if you say, "The tragedy should not happen in my house," that person still has to die, and he will die. If you adjust according to the situation, you will be happy. If you refuse to adjust to that tragedy, you will be miserable—but he still has to go. Happiness or relaxation lies in adjusting according to the situation. If we refuse to adjust to the situation, we are miserable. That is why I say that we should take it easy, we should try to feel relaxed and adjust to situations.

260 **Q.** Could you explain a little bit how we can learn to carry that atmosphere of our meditation with us through the day?

A. By attending to meditation. If you attend to meditation, you will naturally build a certain atmosphere around you, and you will build that bliss and peace within you. In our daily lives, in our daily activities, in our daily dealings with people, we should try to live within that atmosphere of peace and bliss, by always remembering the principles of Sant Mat, the teachings, the meditation, the whole pattern of our life. This is how we can carry the atmosphere of meditation with us.

Q. If it isn't happening, does it mean perhaps you're doing something wrong in meditation?

A. There's nothing wrong with meditation; there is something wrong with our karmas. Meditation will help you to deal with the karmas and to build that atmosphere of peace and bliss, but if we are not happy, it means there is something wrong with our karmas, our approach to life.

261 **Q.** Even if we might not see anything in meditation, do we get to know its result through our everyday life? Through someone's contact or during satsang—

A. I follow your question. You will experience the effect of meditation. You may not have experiences within, but definitely you will feel the effect of meditation. You will enjoy that bliss and happiness and contentment within yourself, and your whole attitude towards life will change. That effect of meditation will be there always whether you experience anything or not.

Q. The sword thrust will become a pinprick—is that what is meant?

A. No, he means to say that if we don't experience anything within, if we don't know what we experience within, then what other advantage do we get from meditation. I said the effect of meditation will be there: you will feel contented and happy within youself; you will feel that peace and bliss, and your attitude towards people and towards life will change. You are becoming a better person. That effect will be there.

262 Q. Master, if we have circumstances which make meditation difficult, an environment or responsibilities which make it hard to find time, and we really want to meditate, then will Master fix it so the circumstances and the environment change so that we can?

A. It's not that the environments change, but you will not be affected by those environments if you attend to meditation. You can't change the environments, you can't change the course of events, you can't change the situations. Your destiny has brought you into a certain atmosphere, into a certain situation, and you have to face all that. But you are given strength so as not to be affected by all those situations, you won't be bothered by them. Just attend to your meditation.

263 Q. Maharaj Ji, will you please put these two points of view in perspective for me: we have the saying that it is a satsangi's duty to be happy under all circumstances. I've also heard it said that in the world, a satsangi cannot find the Lord while he is happy or joyful.

A. Both things look contradictory, but they are the same thing. We should be happy under all circumstances, means if you adjust to a situation, you will be happy whatever the circumstances. If you adjust to the winter when it comes, you are happy. If when summer comes you adjust to the climate, you are happy. In this way under all circumstances you are happy.

The other means that if you give yourself to merry-making and try to enjoy the sensual pleasures, but you also want to meet God the two things are not possible. That second type of happiness is very different from the first type. If you are lost in the senses and also want to go back to God, the two things you can't do. You have to rise above sensual pleasures, and only then you can go back to the Father. So they are not contradictory points of view.

264 Q. In *The Book of Mirdad* it says either every thought or every word should be a prayer, and every deed should be a sacrifice, and I would like to understand what is meant by that—every deed should be a sacrifice.

A. Actually, what Mirdad means is that our whole living should be a prayer. There's no question of devoting half an hour or an hour of praying to the Lord—our whole day should be passed in prayer, in devotion and love for the Father. Prayer means just to live in love and devotion for the Father. That's constant prayer. No particular words are required, no set prayers are required to be repeated. It should be a prayer from the heart.

We should also live a life of sacrifice. We should abstain from those things which do not please the Lord and try to follow the Path which pleases Him. That's a life of sacrifice. Sacrifice doesn't mean that you have to leave your children and family members and run to the forest. Sacrifice is to detach yourself from everything and to live with people without being attached to them. That is what Mirdad means by a life of sacrifice.

265 Q. Maharaj Ji, you have said that Sardar Bahadur Ji always lived at the eye center, and I wondered if you could comment on this. I guess a satsangi can reach the stage where he is always at the eye center, even when he's walking around during the day?

A. What is meant by being at the eye center? It means you don't let your mind scatter into the world. You don't lose your balance. Your mind is absolutely still, and you're always contented and feel happiness, and radiate happiness. That will be the effect of stilling the mind: you're always happy, nothing bothers you.

Q. Master, does that effect come from the concentration which we develop from just coming to the eye center, or is that from the meditation itself?

A. Meditation is all one thing. You may split it in any way, but meditation means meditation.

LOVE AND DEVOTION

266 Q. Maharaj Ji, would you tell us what is love?

A. Love is losing your own identity and becoming another person. That is love. There's no ego left. To become another being and to just lose your own identity, you don't exist, only the other being exists. That craving to become another one and lose your own identity, to eliminate your ego and be in the will of another being, that is love. But how far we succeed is something different.

267 Q. Master, wanting to love the Master, is that beginning to love him?

A. I don't know what the difference is. How can you intellectually want to love?

Unless there is a feeling of love for the Master, the question of wanting to love doesn't arise. You will not want to love unless there is love for the Master. You can say that you want to grow that love, but the seed is already there, otherwise you wouldn't be wanting to grow the seed. Without having a seed, you can't grow it. The seed is there. What you want is only to grow it, more and more. The more you love, the more it grows, and the more you want more. But for that seed, you wouldn't have that feeling. So wanting to love can't come without love.

Q. Then we do have a tiny, little bit of love?

A. Yes, we have a little bit of love, no doubt. Otherwise, why should we think about the Father and meditate and try to conquer our senses if He has not given us that instinct of love. The fact that we are fighting to overcome our senses is a proof that He has given us the instinct of love. But we should be more receptive to what He is giving us.

268 Q. Maharaj Ji, is love for the Master something that grows slowly and slowly as you do your bhajan and simran, or is love for the Master something that comes suddenly when you reach a certain stage, say when you see the Radiant Form of the Master within?

A. Well, brother, both ways can be right. Love can grow slowly and slowly, and you can also have it suddenly. You can't differentiate between the two of them, they are practically the same thing. When you say you get love suddenly, you don't know when it started. It may have been growing in you since long ago and now you suddenly realize it.

"A needle" has a natural pull towards the magnet. But if we put some weight over the needle, it will not be able to move towards the magnet. There is a natural pull, natural love in the soul towards the Lord. But it is weighed down by the heavy load of karmas, and is, therefore, unable to experience that love. Meditation gradually removes this weight of karmas. When the weight begins to reduce, the soul gradually experiences that love, that pull from within. Although that love is always there, we have to experience and develop it through regular meditation.

269 Q. Maharaj Ji, doesn't that love first come through attachment? First we become attached to the Master?

A. Call it anything, but our general concept of love is that another person should lose his identity and become us. We always want another person to lose his own identity and dance to our tune and become one with us. That is not love at all. To lose our own identity and become another being is love. There's no instinct of possessiveness in love, it is the instinct of surrender.

270 Q. How can we love everybody?

A. Loving everybody means loving the One who is in everybody, but not being attached to any particular person. And we can only love that One after we have merged our identity into His. Through meditation, by His grace, we become perfect and pure so that we can merge into the perfect and pure One. Only then do we truly see Him in everybody, only then do we see just the Creator in the whole creation, and only then can we love everybody, because then there is only One in every being, in everyone.

Loving everybody means to have a loving nature, a kind nature, a very kind heart. That is loving everyone. But our modern concept of love is something very different. We think that when we possess someone, we love him. Possession is not love at all.

271 Q. Master, is it possible to learn to love the Lord by trying to love the creation?

A. No. To think that by loving the creation we will

be able to love the Creator would be a negative approach. You may become so much involved in the creation and its attachments that you may absolutely forget the Creator. That concept has come in many organized religions—to serve humanity, while forgetting the Lord.

To serve humanity is a good thing, you are cleaning the "vessel." But our approach is that if you love the Lord, all good qualities come in you like cream upon milk. If you love the Lord, you become kind, loving, generous and helpful to all humanity. But if you eliminate the Lord and try to help the creation, then you just involve yourself and become attached to the creation, which does not help you love the Creator at all.

272 Q. I think it's possible to be loving or to act loving without feeling loving. And sometimes I'm not sure where it's coming from, whether it's a real loving feeling or not.

A. At least behave in a loving way, and then you may also feel the love within. If you try to develop the habit of acting lovingly, then you may also begin to have a genuine loving feeling for others. At least start by behaving like that.

273 Q. Maharaj Ji, you were saying that love exists only when you give up your ego. Does that mean we feel no love while we're still below the second region? No love at all?

A. No, the ego starts lessening right from the third eye. I didn't mean that the ego leaves us only at the second stage. We start losing the ego right from the beginning, even with our emotion and devotion. Ego is a very big load!

274 **Q.** I was just reading that in order to go through your karmas cheerfully you need love and devotion, and it also said in the same spot that we don't get this love and devotion until after we're in touch with the Sound. We get the love and devotion only after we reach the eye center.

A. The more you attend to meditation, the more this love and devotion grows. You start with love and devotion, and then with the help of meditation, it grows and grows. The more you give, the more it grows.

275 **Q.** Maharaj Ji, there's something I don't understand. I've read in Sant Mat literature that you can do meditation, and if you're void of love and devotion, you will get no fruit. But I've also heard it said that the only way to get love and devotion is through meditation, and it seems to be a bit of a paradox, and I was wondering if you would explain it.

A. There's no paradox here. Attending to meditation will automatically generate love and devotion in you, and when you attend to your meditation with that love and devotion, naturally you will get results.

276 **Q.** Master, what does one have to do to try and get over the frustration that one feels of wanting to make more progress than one actually feels one is making?

A. We should never attend to our meditation with frustration or with any excitement. We should just attend to it as our duty, and when results have to come, they just come. Meditation is a lifelong struggle, it's a way of life which we're trying to mold, which we're trying to live. The question of frustration shouldn't arise, one shouldn't feel that. There's a difference between frustration and *bireh*—that feeling of separation and longing. There can be a deep longing in our mind to achieve that Object, and that longing should be there always, but frustration is something different.

Q. Would frustration come from that deep longing?

A. It shouldn't. If there's really a deep longing, then frustration has no place. Frustration comes when we expect too much and we don't get it. Then naturally threre is frustration.

277 **Q.** What can one expect? We know we are nothing and we shouldn't expect anything, but—

A. Just give yourself to Him. To love somebody means to give yourself without expecting anything in return. To give yourself, to submit yourself, to resign to Him is all meditation. We are losing our own identity and our individuality and just merging into another Being. We have no expectation then. Expectation comes only when there is 'I-ness', that I exist and I want this. When I don't exist, what do I want? In love you don't exist. You just lose yourself, you just submit yourself, you just resign to His Will. There's no question of expectation or frustration. The more we give, the more it grows, the more we lose ourselves, the more we become another Being.

278 Q. Does the concept of surrender involve giving up even the wish to go within?

A. You can't surrender without going in. You can't surrender your ego without meditation. These are all intellectual surrenderings. "I have given my ego to you; I have surrenderd my mind to you; I live in the Will of the Father; I don't do anything without Master's permission"—and the next moment you will dance to the tune of the mind. This is no surrender. It may be good to think like that, but real surrender comes only by meditation.

Resignation or surrender or living in His Will—they are practically one and the same—you can achieve only when you go beyond Trikuti. As long as the mind is dominant there's no surrender there's no living in the Will of the Father, there's no elimination of the ego. You can achieve real surrender only when all coverings are removed from the soul. Then the soul shines, it becomes perfect, and then it is capable of merging into the Perfect Being. That is real surrender, that is real love, that is real devotion.

279 Q. Maharaj Ji, one thing I wondered about—they say that when a person is meditating and growing on the Path, I guess you could say there seem to be two different attitudes one develops: one is, he develops an intense longing or yearning to go Home, and the other is, he attains a sense of bliss and peace within. Those two seem to be kind of contradictory.

A. No, they're both the same. What is the difference between longing to go back to the Father and having that peace and bliss within yourself?

Those who are filled with love and devotion for

the Father are in great agony, no doubt, but they would not like to exchange that agony for anything else in the world. They would rather live with that agony than have the whole world at their disposal. They don't want to part with that feeling of separation from the Father, of longing and devotion for the Father. They want to live in that love, whatever sacrifice they may have to make.

It means that there is some peace, some solace, some happiness, even in that pain of longing and devotion, which they don't want to part with at any cost. If you are in love with a girl and someone says, "I will give you anything if you will forget her," you still don't want to forget her. Even though you never see her or meet her, you are happy in your love. Though you feel tortured in separation, you still don't want to forget her. Something is in that love which you can't part with. That is why the Saints chose to be crucified, to sit on hot plates, and to sacrifice their lives, instead of leaving their love and devotion for the Father. They were happy; even in persecution they were happy.

280 Q. Master, even though we sometimes try to have this kind of devotion and love, all that we seem to be able to bring to you is our failures. When we're in your physical presence it's easy to be happy, but being away sometimes makes us discouraged and unhappy. Sometimes there seems to be no happiness on this Path of meditation. We read Kabir, we read Mira Bai, They say it is a path of tears and sleeplessness. It's not a path of happiness. But I know we should try to be happy. Can you talk about being happy on this Path before being able to bring any successes to you?

A. Christ gives a very beautiful example of this pain

and pleasure. He gives the example of the birth of a child.* If the woman is frightened of the pain of childbirth, she can never have the pleasure of delivering a child, because that pain carries that pleasure. Without that pain she can never be happy. So there is a hidden pleasure in her pain, for she's the happiest person in the world when she delivers a child—but she must first pass through all that agony.

And it is the same way with us. We have to pass through that agony of separation from the Father before we can achieve the happiness of union. But there is a pleasure in this pain. If you tell a lover or a devotee, "I would like to take this love away from you," he will never let you take it away. If it is so painful, why don't they leave it? But they can't. They don't. They find pleasure in that pain. Call it pleasure, call it pain—it is very difficult to describe all these things. The lover will never like to leave that pain. He wants to be part of that pain, finds pleasure in that pain. It's just a way of expressing their love for the Father.

281 Q. Maharaj Ji, do we all eventually, before merging back to the Father, have this sort of intense longing like Mira Bai† and the other Saints?

A. Whenever you lift a weight from a needle, the needle will automatically be drawn to the magnet.

---

* John 16:21-22—A woman when she is in travail hath sorrow, because her hour is come: but as soon as she is delivered of the child, she remembereth no more the anguish, for joy that a man is born into the world.

And ye now therefore have sorrow: but I will see you again, and your heart shall rejoice, and your joy no man taketh from you.

† Mira Bai is a sixteenth-century woman Saint born in Rajasthan. She is well known for her songs of devotion, which are still sung today.

Whether there are one thousand needles or there is one needle, they all have the same tendency to go to the magnet. That longing is bound to be in every soul that shines or becomes whole and rises above the load of karma, the effect of karma. It is bound to be in every soul, whether it is Mira Bai or anybody else. We know about Mira Bai because she has expressed herself. Others may not be able to express that longing, but every soul definitely feels the same longing at that level of consciousness.

> **Q.** Maharaj Ji, to continue with that, once the needle has reached the magnet there is no longer any longing. So how long is that period in between its reaching the magnet and its wanting to reach the magnet, after its load has been taken off? In other words, does every soul have to go through a period of intense longing before it reaches the Father?

A. It's not a question of having to—that feeling is always there. The soul is always yearning to go back to its own Source, to the Father. But we don't feel that longing now due to our load of karmas and our tendency towards the senses.

Take, for example, a one thousand-candle bulb—whether there is one or there are a thousand bulbs, they each have the same light. On one bulb you have thirty or forty black wrappings, so you don't see the light and you can't make use of it. If you go on removing the coverings, the light will start penetrating and ultimately you will see the full light. The light was always there—to give light is the characteristic of an electric bulb—but we could not make use of the light due to the black wrappings. Similarly, every soul, one and all, is yearning to go back to the Father, but due to the wrappings of karmas, of the mind, of the sensual pleasures, of all these worldly attachments and entanglements, we don't feel that longing. The more we remove those wrappings, the more we start feeling that longing, and ultimately the soul shines and goes back to the Father.

282 Q. Then what about this longing that we think we feel at this level?

A. This intellectual longing develops into the real longing. What we call intellectual longing is the longing of the mind. The intellect is connected with the mind, and devotion is also a part of the mind. To begin with, the mind is filled with devotion and longing, but the real longing that the Mystics talk about comes after you go to Trikuti. That longing is in the soul. The mind's longing is only for its own origin, Trikuti, but the real longing is the longing of the soul for its own Origin with the Father, which we call everlasting life. The real longing starts with the soul, but the soul cannot have that real longing unless the mind develops longing for its own place. So we begin with the longing of the mind, and naturally we end with the longing of the soul.

283 Q. Master, you said, "Is there anything beyond longing?" Please could you explain?

A. What I meant to say was, does a seeker need anything else besides longing? If he has a longing or desire to go back to the Father, love for the Father, yearning for the Father, then is there anything else to be done? But we have only an intellectual longing. Actually, our longing is for worldly possessions, worldly things, worldly achievements. We are desiring worldly things, and we think that we are longing for the Father. We don't have any longing for the Father at all. If we had longing for the Father, then we could have no longing for anything of the world. For when we are attached to Him, then we are not attached to this creation. That is what was meant when I said, "Is there anything beyond longing?"

Is there anything else for a seeker to do if he gets that bliss, that boon from the Father—that longing to become one with Him. Then all desires leave you, and your mind is no longer attached to the creation. That is why Christ said: "Blessed are they that mourn, for they shall be comforted."[1] Those who feel the separation from the Father, those who have longing and intense desire to become one with Him are the blessed ones, the fortunate ones, because they will ultimately get rest in His lap. Longing will eliminate ego and will make you merge into the Being. You will lose your identity and become one with the Father by longing. But this longing, this intense longing, doesn't come without Shabd, because the mind refuses to leave the sensual pleasures until it tastes something better.

284 Q. I was reading in Baba Ji's letters* that Huzur Maharaj Ji had a longing for darshan, and then Baba Ji said because of that longing you received the merit of darshan. I was just wondering, was that just for the Great Master?

A. Definitely it was for the Great Master, and we can generalize it also to some extent. If we have so

* *Spiritual Letters.*

much longing and desire for the darshan of the Master, we are having its benefit. Where will that desire and longing lead us? To meditation, where the Master always is. When you won't be able to find the Master outside, what will you do to find him? You will try to find him within. That love and desire for darshan should lead us on the Path within and bring us to that level of consciousness where our Master is always with us. That is how we get the benefit of longing for darshan.

Those letters were written to Maharaj Ji, and Baba Ji Maharaj knew the intensity and love of Maharaj Ji. This is a particular letter to a particular person, keeping in view the desire, the longing of the Great Master for Baba Ji Maharaj. So you and I can't generalize these letters entirely. We can only try to take advantage of them. We also want to become like that, no doubt, but then their relationship was something very different. One Master was preparing another Master.

285 Q. Would you agree that while we are sitting for meditation, that perhaps the strongest motivation we should have is that of longing for darshan while we're sitting?

A. It's not a question of what we should have. "Should" doesn't come in love. Love is something which you can't help, it is just there. It's not something which you are calculating to have or you are contemplating or you are trying to have. It's something which makes you helpless, and if that helplessness is already there at the time of meditation, it helps.

If love is there, it is there. If it comes, it just

comes. But by meditation everybody can grow that love. If the Lord has given certain grace to somebody, that's a different thing. That may be for a rare few. If somebody inherits riches, that is the grace of the donor, but everybody can become rich by hard work. Everybody can grow that feeling, that love, that intensity, by meditation.

286 Q. Master, would you explain what this means from *Spiritual Letters*: "Longing for Master's darshan is equal to or better than just doing bhajan" [meditation].

A. Longing for darshan is equal to meditation? But how can you have darshan without meditation? By darshan Baba Ji Maharaj meant the inner darshan of the Radiant Form of the Master.

But longing to be one with the Radiant Form of the Master you can't obtain without meditation. The purpose of physical darshan is to create longing for that inner darshan, and then meditation naturally takes us to that level of consciousness where we can see the Radiant Form of the Master. Then the purpose of darshan and of meditation is achieved.

287 Q. Master, would you tell us the meaning of outer darshan and the meaning of inner darshan?

A. Outer darshan is when you see the Master outside; inner darshan is when you see the Master inside. But you can't have inner darshan without the outside love and faith and practice, for they lead to that inner darshan.

288 Q. The tears that satsangis experience when being aware of the presence of Master inside would appear not to be a perception of love, Maharj Ji, because love, I take it, would be a joyous experience. Would it be a sense of realization of one's separation from the Lord that brings the tears?

A. No, there can be tears of love. Why not? When you meet a friend after some time and you're happy to see him, naturally tears flow. Tears can be of happiness and joy. A tear is not always of sadness.

289 Q. Maharaj Ji, there are two quotations from letter 18 in *Spiritual Letters* that I would like to ask about. The first is, "True longing for darshan is the principle means of God-realization," and the next: "Even after one hundred years of bhajan one does not get so purified as by an intense longing for darshan, provided that longing is real and true. "My question is, does this mean inner darshan or outer, physical darshan, and how is this true longing engendered?

A. It means longing to merge back into the Father, longing for the inner darshan of the Master. But you will get the inner darshan only when you have longing for the outer darshan. The outer darshan is a means to an end, because longing for the outer darshan will lead you to longing for the inner darshan. Christ says that they are the blessed ones who mourn, they will be comforted[2]—which is exactly what you have asked about. We mourn when we can't bear the separation from the beloved. They are the fortunate ones or blessed ones who mourn, who feel the separation from the Father, and who have that real longing to go back to the Father: they will be comforted. Ultimately, they will be able to reach back to the Father.

Christ referred to the inner and outer darshan in

an indirect way when he said: it is expedient, it is in your interest, that I leave you now, for then I'll be able to send you the Comforter.[3] How can it be in the interest of a disciple for the Master to leave him physically? The Master, by his physical presence, creates love and devotion in the heart of the disciple, but the Master cannot stay physically with the disciple forever. He eventually separates himself from the disciple, who then has no option but to seek his Master within.

In separation, the disciple will direct all his devotion and longing within to find the Master, and ultimately he will find the Comforter. That is why it is in the interest of the disciple for the Master to leave him. No doubt the disciples are in love with the Master's physical form, they are running after him—but how long can the disciples be with the physical form of the Master? When the Master leaves the disciples and they want to be with the Master, they have no option but to turn within to find him. The purpose of the physical presence of the Master is to create that love and devotion in us, and ultimately to convert it into the real inner darshan, which is the end, which is the real love, the real devotion.

290 Q. Maharaj Ji, regarding the outer darshan, we are told what we should look at the physical Master with the physical eyes and the mind.

A. Do the eyes see without the mind? When do we really look at somebody? When the mind is there, when emotions are there, when devotion is there, when love is there, then we can't help looking. So the mind is playing its own part and the eyes are only an instrument. Actually, the mind wants to look because the mind is filled with love and devotion for its object of love. Eyes are mere instruments through which the mind works. Otherwise it's just looking without seeing, when the mind is not there. Whenever you look at anybody you like, you don't look without the mind, naturally, because your mind is full with devotion and emotions for that person. So you want to look, you can't help looking.

291 Q. Then can this be explained by saying you look with the mind while having the attention here, at the eye center?

A. That is for within—that is in meditation. How can you have the attention here? Either you have your attention on the Master or your attention at the eye center. If physically you look at your object of love, then your whole concentration should be on the object, not on anything else. "With the mind" means that your attention is concentrated towards your object.

292 Q. Then you don't do simran while looking at the Master's physical form?

A. Well, do it if you feel like, if you are still there. But if your mind is so absorbed and occupied, then who will do simran? If your mind is still running out then definitely it is better to do simran. But if it is no longer there, then who will do simran?

293 Q. Sometimes when we're looking at you, we feel automatically attracted and we feel this something pullling, and yet we feel so far at the same time. We feel close to you, but yet so far.

A. When we look at the one with whom we are in love, we are never far. We are always near him. Far in what sense? We're not far away from our own love. Our love is within us, we're carrying it with us. So from where are we far?

> **Q.** Well, I don't know. Our thoughts seem to wander, and it's painful because we know where they should be, and we know we should be steeped in that love and devotion, but sometimes the mind just seems to drift... and drift... and drift.

A. So you have to pull it back, pull it back, and pull it back. That's the only way. If there's real love and devotion, the mind doesn't drift. Love doesn't let it drift.

294 **Q.** What if we as satsangis reach a point where we actually deny the Master? Can that evoke a punishment? Does the Master punish us for that?

A. Master doesn't ever turn his back on us. We are punished only if Master turns his back to us but he doesn't show his back to us. If a child disobeys his father, is rude to the father, or hurts the father, he will set the child right, he will discipline the child to make him a loving, obedient son and a good citizen. But he will never hand over the child to the police, he will never send him to jail, because he loves the child.

In the same way, the Master is constantly helping us to rise above the weaknesses which are torturing us and making us miserable in this world. The Master does not punish us, it is our own karmas that punish us. Christ said: I have not come to condemn you, I have come to save you.[4] Masters come only to save us, they don't come to punish us. If *they* start punishing us, then we have no escape at all.

We should attend to meditation not from any fear of the Father, but with love for the Father. We should base our meditation on love, not fear. And when that love is there, then we don't worry about punishments and we are not bothered by anything. Also, when we have love for the Father, we don't carry much of a sense of guilt if we fall here and there. But our approach should be that of love: we must base our meditation on love for the Father, and not on the fear that, "If I don't sit in meditation, I'll be punished." The basis of religion is love, not fear.

295 Q. While looking at the Master, I often feel frightened. How should one look at the physical form of the Master?

A. Is Master so frightening? Why should we fear him with whom we are going to stay forever and from whom we will never separate? Why fear him? Why not love him!

We fear our own self actually, we don't fear the Master. We fear our own shortcomings, our own conscious guilts. There is nothing to fear in the Master. There is no punishment in the love of the Master, so that fear should not be there at all. But we should be concerned whether we are on the Path, whether we are steadfast or not, whether we are attending to our meditation or not. Our own guilty conscience frightens us. Master doesn't frighten us.

296 Q. Maharaj Ji, how can love be described in words? Doesn't it have to be felt and experienced?

A. Love is to be experienced. Great Master used to give a very beautiful example: if a dumb person eats candy, how will he describe it if you ask him, "What is the taste of the candy?" He will just smile he won't be able to say anything at all. Words can't describe love. Love is to be experienced, love is to be gone through, and language is a very poor expression of love.

DIVINE GRACE

Only those who reach their True Home obtain everlasting joy and peace. They break out of the cycle of birth and death forever and return at last to the Father, thereby escaping the repeated tortures of the messengers of Death.

With whose grace do we gain admission to the Court of the Lord? Surely not by our own efforts. Alone, we can do nothing. We can never, by ourselves, traverse the uncharted terrain of the inner Path. We owe everything to the immeasurable grace of the Master. He showers his blessings on us by joining us with the Shabd and Nam, removing all our doubts, and pulling us out of this quagmire of illusion. It is our Master who puts us on the right Path and awakens in our mind abiding love and devotion for the Lord. Blessed with His infinite grace, through meditation, we seek the door, we find it, and we knock.

All beings in the world are helpless puppets in the hands of destiny. There is nothing that they can accomplish by their own efforts. Those on whom the Lord wishes to shower His mercy and grace are given the gift of the human form. Out of these fortunate souls, He draws the attention of the marked ones to Himself. These are the souls whom He, in His supreme bounty, wishes to deliver from doubt and delusion, whom He wishes to call back to His Mansion by joining them with the Light and Sound.

It is the Lord's Will which is supreme. It is His Will that is "done on earth as it is in heaven." Man is helpless. Not till He Himself showers His blessings, are we put on this Path. Not till He Himself wants to lift us out of the mire of doubts, are our minds made pure and clean. Not till He Himself takes us into His fold, are we redeemed through the Master's grace. And that grace is showered on us through His gift of devotion and love, which eventually tunes us to Him and draws us to our Home to merge with the Lord forever.

297 **Q.** Maharaj Ji, is there a difficult way—not a short cut—besides meditation to achieve your goal?

A. Meditation is itself a difficult way. I don't think there is anything more difficult than meditation. Meditation is the most difficult. It looks simple, and yet it is so difficult to attend to it. It's easy to understand Sant Mat because the whole philosophy is very simple, but when we put it into practice, many obstacles come in the way. To live Sant Mat, to live the teachings, means a constant struggle with the mind.

Q. Then a short cut may lead you to the wrong direction?

A. There's no short cut at all. In this modern age, we are so used to saving time by trying to find short cuts, trying to save money and energy by putting in less money and less time and getting better results and more achievements. But no, not in Sant Mat.

298 **Q.** Master, what is meant when people say that Sant Mat is like walking on the edge of a sword?

A. It means it is not easy to follow this Path. One has to sacrifice a lot in life to achieve the end. You constantly have to be alert with your mind as if you were on a razor's edge. Christ himself has said: it is easy to fall, and the road to destruction is wide, but strait and narrow is the way to everlasting life.[1]

Sant Mat teaching is very simple, but to follow it is much more difficult than it looks. It's a constant struggle with the mind, and one has to change one's entire way of life and one's attitude towards life. To follow Sant Mat requires a complete transformation, so it's not easy. One has to sacrifice a lot in life.

And then to be filled with love and devotion and to yearn to become one with the Being is not a very pleasant feeling. You always live in the agony of separation because you're filled so much with love and devotion. But you love that agony. You don't want to part with it. Still, it's not a very pleasant feeling.

299 **Q.** I've heard often that there is no gain without pain.

A. Pain means sacrifice. Read the Bible—Christ's teachings are filled with that. He says, unless you are prepared to face hardhips for my sake, unless you are prepared to sacrifice the sensual pleasures for my sake, to detach yourself from worldly possessions for my sake, you will not reach back to the Father.* That's pain. To ask someone to leave the temptations

---

* Matt. 16:24—Then said Jesus unto his disciples, if any man will come after me, let him deny himself, and take up his cross, and follow me.

of the senses, to sacrifice all these worldly pleasures and worldly ambitions for my sake, is a pain to one who is a slave of the senses. That doesn't mean there has to be physical pain. It's a mental pain. Christ told that rich person: go and give away your wealth if you want to follow my teachings, and the rich man wasn't happy to hear that. It was mentally painful to him.[2]

300 Q. At Dera we're living a very sheltered life in which our whole object is, of course, the Path. For those of us who are visiting here for the first time, what would your advice be to us when we go back to our normal, everyday lives? I'm thinking now of our communal life, not our meditation. What sort of mental approach?

A. I have not followed your question exactly. You mean how should we conduct ourselves in the world?

Q. To just fit into our normal lives when we go back, because for many of us, or myself at any rate, the visit here has been a complete sort of rebirth, and when we go back to our homes and our normal surroundings—

A. Live in this atmosphere which you have built within yourself. That struggle with the mind is always there with everyone. And we must struggle. We should be bold enough to struggle and try to keep up that atmosphere in which we have to live. We must build up that atmosphere of love and devotion and live in that. We have to struggle to live in that, no doubt. It's not so easy. It's difficult, I know.

But we can read the books, we can mix with good satsangis, we can attend group meetings. We should try to keep that atmosphere of love and devotion around us, in which we have to live. If we go away from this atmosphere, then the mind pulls us back to worldly thoughts. To build that atmosphere is essential for meditation. Great Master used to call this atmosphere of meditation a fence around the crop. Crops can grow without a fence, but there is always a danger of somebody ruining your crop if it has no protection. So we need to protect whatever meditation we do by keeping up that atmosphere of love and devotion around us. It's not so easy, I know. It can be a struggle for a lifetime.

301 Q. But Master, can't the mental atmosphere of the world outside be so strong that it would make us do things that we would not dream of doing in our normal daily lives?

A. The worldly atmosphere may not be that strong, but we are so weak that we are easily influenced by it. We should be so strong within ourselves that no atmosphere can influence us. We have to be strong within ourselves and not be led away by anyone.

Q. In the meantime?

A. In the meantime, try to be strong.

302 Q. Maharaj Ji, it says often in the writings that the Shabd will eliminate the negative tendencies, and my understanding is that you have to eliminate the negative tendencies before you can hear the Shabd.

A. Both are right. To some extent you have to abstain from these negative things in order to withdraw to the eye center, but you can escape from them permanently only when your mind is attached to the Shabd and Nam within and the Shabd pulls you upwards. But you have to fight before that, to some extent, in order to withdraw your consciousness to the eye center—with the help of simran and dhyan, and by abstaining from these negative tendencies. But that is not a permanent cure. Again your mind will come back to the senses. When the mind is attached to a better pleasure than the sensual pleasures, only then is it permanently detached from the senses.

Let me give you an example: if you put a dam across a flowing river, you will be able to hold the water for some time, but not permanently. When the water rises too high in the catchment area, it will break the dam and overflow the banks. But if you make another channel for the river to flow in a different direction, the dam will stay there permanently and the river will also start flowing in a different direction. Without the second channel, the dam could hold the water for some time, but not forever.

Similarly, mere simran and dhyan is holding your attention at the eye center, which is suppressing your instincts, and that even makes you wild sometimes. But if you are able to attach the attention to the Shabd, the whole direction of our attention is changed, and the "dam" is permanent.

Though we have to fight with the negative tendencies for some time in order to withdraw the consciousness to the eye center, that's not a permanent cure. When there is too much suppression, the mind will again make you dance to its tune. But when by withdrawing to the eye center, the mind is attached to the Sound and Light within, it is permanently cured, because then the mind is diverted and it flows in a new channel, upwards. And as long as the tendency of the mind is not upward towards that Sound or Spirit and Light, it refuses to abstain permanently from the lower senses.

303 Q. Master, is there apt to be any trouble with withdrawal of soul currents from the body if during our life our concentration has been at the lower centers?

A. I don't know what you mean by concentration centered at the lower centers. The mind is always running towards the lower centers. One person may have one weakness, someone else may have another weakness. The mind is always running outside through these nine apertures, hence we always remain slaves of the senses. So when you try to withdraw your consciousness from any of these sense pleasures, there's always trouble, there's always a fight, and we have to fight for that.

304 Q. If the lower chakras are developed, is that good?

A. If you try to withdraw from the lower chakras, sometimes they become very active. When the candle is going to be extinguished, it at once burns brighter and creates more light. Similarly, when you begin to withdraw from those lower chakras, sometimes they become very active.

305 Q. The struggle from here to Sach Khand—is the worst part of it while we're living on this plane at this level?

A. That's right. The most difficult part of our

struggle is to withdraw the consciousness to the eye center and to hold the attention there. That's the most difficult part of our struggle.

Q. And then once inside is it easier?

A. Then it becomes easier. We have all sorts of obstacles and difficulties inside, but they are easier to overcome.

306 Q. Why is it difficult for some of us to contemplate on your physical form when we're meditating?

A. Well, brother, the whole of meditation is very difficult. The mind is in the habit of wandering out so much, it's very diffcult to still the mind. I have read from the Bible that wide is the road to failure, and very narrow and strait is the road to success.[3] That's what Christ was trying to prepare us for. The way to destruction is easy, but the way to go up, to have spiritual uplift, is very difficult.

307 Q. Maharaj Ji, what can we do to increase the desire for meditation? Say, if we're having trouble meditating or wanting to meditate. What can we do to increase that desire?

A. We have to fight with the mind to attend to meditation. We have to force the mind to attend to meditation, and meditation will automatically create the desire in us to increase our meditation, to improve our meditation. The mind always rebels, it doesn't want to sit in meditation. But we have to fight with it. That's the only way. Also, we are generally influenced by good company, meeting, satsangs, by good Sant

Mat books. These also create the atmosphere in which we feel like sitting in meditation, so they are a great help.

308 Q. Master, what is the remedy when the mind rebels too much against meditation?

A. The remedy is only one: to attend to meditation again, to persist and not to give up. There's no other remedy. Only the medicine eliminates a disease from the body, but what use is the remedy if we don't take that medicine? The doctor has to force that medicine down us. You force a tablet into a child's mouth if he doesn't take that medicine because you know that unless the medicine gets in, the disease won't go. You have to force yourself to take that medicine, then automatically this disease of ego will go. If the mind takes it willingly, it's good. Otherwise, you have to force it.

309 Q. Master, will this forced meditation bring about good meditation?

A. Yes, naturally. When one is not in the habit of sitting at all, the first step is that one has to force oneself to sit at least. To sit still is a great credit, and when you learn to sit still, then you learn also to still your mind. The first problem is to still the body. It doesn't want to sit in one place even for twenty minutes. So first you get into the habit of stilling the body, then you get into the habit of stilling the mind.

310 Q. I just think we all are able to still our body a little bit, and then instead of doing the next step of stilling the mind, we want to jump ahead and start stilling our body for more hours. But the stilling of the mind never takes place in the first instance, so we're worried about six or seven hours of sitting still and our mind never learns to still itself.

A. It will learn, gradually. What will the mind do when it knows it will not be permitted to go out of the room, and that the body will not move out of the room? Slowly and slowly, it will start concentrating at the time of meditation. But at first, the mind runs out towards worldly pleasures and activities, and you have to deprive yourself of these by force. You have to tell your mind, "I will not let you go," and ultimately, the mind will turn to meditation. If you yield, then you have lost. If you fight with the mind, slowly and slowly you may be able to win.

311 Q. One level of the mind is repeating the names, and another level of the mind is thinking about satsangis that we have met during the day or all kinds of things.

A. You know your mind is very faithful to its own master, to Kal, the Negative Power. The mind is always running out. It is a constant struggle with the mind to bring it to the eye center. The mind will run away, again you have to bring it back; it will run away, again you have to bring it back. In the same way that we form habits in this world by repeating something again and again, we also have to create a habit of concentration with the mind by regularly and constantly and punctually attending to meditation. We have to create in our mind the habit of concentrating, and slowly and slowly, we will succeed. Of course it's very difficult. It's a struggle for a whole lifetime, not just for a day or two. It's a constant struggle with the mind—but it's worth it.

312 **Q.** Maharj Ji, during the course of simran, is it better to try and fight the mind and keep bringing it back to the center, or to not fight the mind and just continue with simran and try not to fight with the mind?

A. What is the difference? When you're continuing in simran, you're fighting the mind. You've not to physically fight with it. You're mentally fighting the mind because the mind wants to start thinking of something else, and you're trying to keep the mind in simran. While doing simran, you forget simran and you start thinking about worldly things. Then again you bring your mind in simran, again you bring your mind in simran. It's a constant struggle with the mind.

313 **Q.** Master, is the very moment we're supposed to go inside destined?

A. Do you want to wait for that moment without doing anything? It may also be destined for you to work hard for that moment, so one shouldn't try to find excuses. You're worried only about the coming of that moment; you're not worried about the destiny of working hard.

314 **Q.** When a person has been initiated, does he have essentially so long, so much time in meditation to work and to live in the world before it is possible for him to see the Radiant Form?

A. Well, brother there is no difference between what we are doing and what is destined, because everybody is born with karmas. Without karmas we won't be here, and we have to clear certain layers of karmas before we can reach the Radiant Form of the Master.

Everybody has an individual load of karma, and that is why no time limit can be fixed for how long it will take. If the load of karma is the same for everybody, then you can fix a time limit that, "You can clear this much load in this length of time." But you can't say how much time it will take you to reach that level of consciousness, because everybody has a different load of karmas.

And then the length of time depends upon how much karma you burn. The time it takes to burn a big heap of rubbish depends upon whether it is wet or dry, whether, while you are burning it, the rain is falling. So to burn that heap of rubbish depends upon many things.

315 Q. When an individual is initiated, could it be said that it must take him a certain amount of time to burn this rubbish?

A. It depends upon how much effort he is putting forth, how much the grace of the Lord is there, and the type of environment he has been brought up in and he is living in. There are so many factors to burning that load of karma. Suppose he has even a small load but doesn't attend to his meditation, then how would he burn it? If he is putting in all his effort to attend to meditation but his environment is such that his mind is not there in meditation, or if he has such worldly activities that he can hardly snatch any time for meditation or he's hardly in a mood to meditate, or if he is a victim of certain weaknesses which he can't get rid of, then how can he burn that karma?

There are many factors which affect the burning of that load. That is why Christ said: the first may be the last and the last may be the first.[4] He said the first may be the last and the last may be the first on the Path to reach back to the Father. It doesn't mean that if one is initiated today, he will go there after others initiated before him. There's no seniority on the Path, because everybody has an individual load of karma, and this load is not simply what we've collected here in this life. This load is mainly our sinchit karmas, the store of karmas from our previous births, which everybody has to burn.

316 Q. Why does meditation have to be so long?

A. Sister, the reason is very clear. Can you know when this creation came into being? Can we calculate when this creation started? Since then, we have been here in this creation. We can't even extend our imagination to grasp how long we have been here in this world and how many karmas we have been collecting in every life and how much of a load of that dirt we have collected—and we want to burn it just in a second, comparatively? Naturally it has to take time. The bigger the heap, the more the time, so that is why meditation takes so long. It is not so easy.

317 Q. Master, throughout our life, although we're on the Path and we're thinking about the Master and doing our meditation, oftentimes a period comes where we can't seem to meditate or we can't seem to think of the Master or it seems like a very dry spot. But then we come back to the Path again. Is this due to our karmas where such a cycle comes not of going astray, but yet not being able to achieve the concentration—

A. As I often say, this is a way of life. It is a

constant struggle with the mind. We are all struggling souls on the Path, and it is a way of life which we have to adopt. Constantly we have to watch our mind.

Q. Well what advice would you give to us, to a satsangi who all of a sudden finds himself in a dry period where he just can't seem to meditate? What should he do?

A. Definitely sometimes we feel that vacuum, that dryness, that loneliness. That often happens with satsangis because the things in life which once interested them no longer interest them. Before they were satsangis they were attached to worldly things. In the morning they would get up and think about their wife and children, their daily work, their wealth and position, and their mind would be happy in all those things. But now those worldly things don't attract them any more, and inside they're not getting what they want, so they feel as though they're stagnating in a vacuum.

That vacuum period definitely comes in everybody's life, and it is to our advantage. It's not that we are not making progress within, but nothing else attracts us in this world. We will get what we want from within, but we have to pass through such periods. The sun is shining, and then a thick, dark layer of cloud comes and you cannot see the sun, but the sun is always there. The cloud passes and again the light starts shining. It happens.

318 Q. What about those periods where you do get attracted to things in the world to the point where you neglect your meditation? Do you have to try to actually subdue your attachment or your desires for these things or—

A. Dark, thick clouds come before you and you are absorbed in that darkness and you don't see the light, but they will pass if you continue meditation. That is why Christ emphasized that to sin against the Holy Ghost cannot be forgiven,[5] meaning that you should not turn your back to meditation. meditation is a "must" and all these periods will pass.

319 Q. Could Master explain why a disciple who is hearing the Sound while meditating can become unable to hear it, despite regularly sitting in meditation? Why do we go through a period of time where we just don't hear the Sound at all?

A. At some other time you were hearing it, and now you don't hear it? The sun is shining every day, but you don't see that light and feel the warmth of the sun every day. Sometimes clouds also come; then you cannot feel the warmth of the sun's heat or even see the light of the sun, at times. We have to pass through so many phases of our karmas. Sometimes layers of strong karmas come in the way and we are absolutely thrown off balance, we feel lost. Then we don't hear anything and we don't even take an interest in meditation, and we may not even feel like sitting in meditation. But again we come back, again we are filled with the same love and devotion, again we start. The Sound is always there. Sometimes we are receptive; sometimes we are not. We pass through so many phases of karma, and sometimes a layer of karma temporarily puts us off the Path, shakes us up.

320 Q. Sir, having seen the Radiant Form of the Master, could there be a pralabdh karma that could cause a person to lose the Radiant Form?

A. One reason can be that a layer of pralabdh karma comes, and then you're also off the track sometimes. But the vision of the Radiant Form will be permanent only when you go beyond the second stage, beyond the realm of Mind and Maya. Before that, many times it will come and many times it will go. But after the second stage, it's constant. Then the effects of karmas are lost, and then the grace is always there. But before that, many times you see the Radiant Form, many times it disappears, many times it's not clear, it's hazy; and there can be many reasons for all that.

Sometimes with the grace of the Lord or the Master we get a glimpse of the Radiant Form even before we have earned it so that we may continue on the Path. This is to give us a little faith here and there, a little encouragement. That does happen. For then it becomes a bit easier for us to put forth an effort. But we have not earned that vision.

321 Q. An initiated soul sees the Master when meditating, and all of a sudden the vision stops, and that soul realizes that it has done something terrible. What should he do then?

A. He should attend to meditation, and naturally if the grace was there before, it will come again. There can be so many factors to darshan being stopped. Sometimes some strong layer of karmas comes; sometimes ego comes in our mind; sometimes attachments come in our mind; sometimes our mind is pulled to the senses. We can be deprived of that privilege due to a hundred and one things. But we should keep on attending to meditation, and again we will have the same grace.

322 Q. I read in *Philosophy of the Masters* that only one in several million might reach that level to drink the Divine Nectar, the Name. What did the Great Master really mean by that?

A. What he meant is that very rare are the people who are able to drink that Nectar.

Q. It's not very comforting.

A. No, no even if it's one in a million, even then it's a good ratio, I must say, compared to the population of the whole world. Very few people are able to go to that stage and drink that Nectar.

Every body has a natural inclination towards devotion for the Lord, but hardly any knows how to really worship. People worship Him according to the dictates of their own mind, which leads them towards external practices. Very rare, fortunate ones seek a Master, obtain Nam from him and engage in devotion to the Father.

People mostly worship the Lord not for His sake, but for the sake of His gifts. They love the world and its objects and want the Lord to fulfill their desires, to give them material benefits. Very few worship the Father with a longing to become one with Him. People think that if they do not worship Him, they would lose in business, litigation or love; or they fear that if they do not worship the Lord they would lose a son or some near and dear one or lose health, fame, honor and wealth. Even Satsangis sometimes worship Him with some worldly desire, or out of fear of punishment. But we should worship the Lord because we love Him, because we long to go back and merge into Him.

I often say, the basis of religion is love, not fear. But out of millions only a rare few worship the Lord for His sake, for the sake of His love.

323 **Q.** When you begin to approach that level and the wrappings of the soul are being removed, how do you feel?

A. When the wrappings are being removed, you first see that Light and all those things inside your own self, and you know that the wrappings are being removed. Then you become nobler, more loving, and more and more devotion for the Father comes in you. When the clouds start disappearing, then the light of the sun starts shining. You always know when the clouds disperse and light comes. Similarly, you also know about yourself. When the mind becomes better or purer or nobler, that Light penetrates you and your whole attitude in life changes, your characteristics and approach to life change.

324 **Q.** When one reaches that vantage point, doesn't one have a clearer insight as to the happenings on this level?

A. When you go within, at the second stage, you can consciously know everything that has happened anywhere in this world. Even at the lower stages, you unconsciously know about coming events, you know what is happening all around. You feel that "this is like this," and often the feeling turns out to be right. But consciously you know everything that is happening in this world and can see it if you reach the second stage. You're not interested in those things, however, because you're so much absorbed in that

Melody and Light that nothing else pleases you. Then there's no curiosity left within you about anything.

325 **Q.** To reach that stage I understand that we must go through the tunnel of Bunk Nal. Is it possible to go through the tunnel without having first seen the Light of the prior stage?

A. No. You have to go stage by stage.

Q. Yes, but is it possible to get there without having seen the Light? Is it possible to have gone through?

A. No, first you will see flashes of Light, then a dazzling Light, and you will also hear the Sound, and slowly and slowly you will make progress. You may have visions here and there, but that is not progress. Progress is something very different. Sometimes we do get visions just to keep us going straight on the Path or to build our faith that we are on the right Path.

Q. So if anything is experienced or seen in the early stages, is this just given to one as a form of inspiration or encouragement?

A. No. When we start with meditation—even otherwise, in the later stages also—sometimes just to keep us going and to encourage us on the Path, we do get experiences. But we have to earn them by meditation; they are only an encouragement.

Q. Nothing is lost?

A. No. nothing is lost. You never lose anything in meditation.

326 Q. Having dreams of Master—is that a sign of encouragement for progressing on the Path?

A. Sister, dreams are just dreams. You can't depend upon those dreams because they're not under your control. Neither can you analyze those dreams nor draw any meaning from them, because they are gone when you get up from sleep—half you remember, half you forget. They may be due to your associations with the Master during the day. We shouldn't give much importance to these dreams. Good dreams are just good dreams, that's all. But the main thing is our own spiritual progress, our meditation, and not just depending upon dreams.

Q. Sometimes they seem more like visions than dreams.

A. They are almost like visions at times. Especially if while sitting in meditation one falls asleep, which often happens. Then those dreams are almost visions.

327 Q. Does the Master ever give a disciple advice in dreams?

A. It is a very risky thing to try to find meanings in those dreams. It's better to ignore them. Happy dreams mean happy dreams. Don't try to give any meaning to them or try to analyze them.

328 Q. The karmas that hold your consciousness down and keep you from progressing or breaking through and reaching the eye center to get the vision of the Radiant Form are sinchit karmas. And we burn these off through meditation. But I've read in the teachings that when you get to the top of Trikuti and contact the real Shabd, you burn off the seeds of the sinchit karmas. So I don't understand what we are burning off of these sinchit karmas at this time in our meditation. Is it the effect of the sinchit karmas?

A. Brother, whatever time we give to meditation, we are burning karmas. When you collect a heap of rubbish and you want to burn it, you need a match stick. You know how much preparation is needed to make a match stick, but when it is ready, it takes just a moment to light it and set the whole pile of rubbish on fire. The preparation to make that match stick is also part of burning the rubbish; in the same way, whatever time we devote to meditation is to our credit. We are burning sinchit karmas, even now.

329 Q. Master, is concentration during meditation the part that's burning off the karma, or is it the fact that we're sitting with the intent of—

A. Any minute we devote to meditation is to our credit, and we definitely have the effect of that meditation in one way or another. For example, when a child starts learning to run, he has to pass through so many stages, but every stage is a step forward in his learning to run. Similarly, every effort that we put in meditation is a step forward. Definitely we get its advantage, and we have its effect. Even if we devote five minutes, it is to our credit.

Q. Master, who is counting the time?

A. Your own mind. Everything is recorded on your mind, impressed on your mind.

330 Q. So your time of meditation is taken into account by your mind like all else is?

A. Yes. Meditation makes a groove on your mind. It makes an impression on your mind which can never go away. There's no register that counts how many hours are to your credit. If you scratch a stone, you make an impression on the stone, howsoever little you may have scratched. And if you scratch steel, howsoever hard the steel may be, you make a groove or an impression on it. So we are rubbing our mind against the Shabd and Nam. We are making an impression on our mind, and that is to our credit, that is "counted," you can say. It's just a way of expression.

331 Q. When we do simran during the day while attending to different things and it becomes sometimes automatic in our head, is that any credit?

A. Yes. Everything is to our credit. Whatever time you give to simran—whether moving, walking, sitting—and whatever books you read on Sant Mat, or satsangs you hear, they are all to your credit. All these are preparations. When you want to fill a vessel with milk, you have to prepare that vessel for keeping the milk. You have to go through so many processes for thoroughly cleaning that vessel. But when you're cleaning it, you're also preparing to fill it—the cleaning is a part of filling the vessel. These preparations strengthen our love and devotion, and create that desire in us for meditation. They are all a means to a certain end, and any means to achieve that end is to our creuit.

332 **Q.** In *Spiritual Gems* it says that grief resulting from failure in bhajan is also a form of bhajan. Would you explain that a little bit?

A. Whatever time you devote to meditation, whether you achieve any results by it or not, is added to your meditation. That's what it means. Even your attempt, your "failures" are added to your credit, because only that man will fall who tries to learn to walk or run. There's no chance of falling for someone who doesn't try to run, so failures will come only when we are trying to meditate. That is "failure in bhajan." We are trying to attend to meditation, but we're not achieving any results within, so we are failing in our meditation—that's what we start thinking—but that is also added to our credit. Whatever attempt you make towards your meditation, whatever time you give to your meditation, whether you make any apparent progress or not, is added to your credit. You definitely get its effect and its results.

Before we start learning to run, we have to pass through so many stages. You know that when a child takes birth, it is difficult for the child even to lie down properly. Then he has to learn how to sit, and he has to pass through so many processes, so many failures, before he learns to stand on his own legs. After that, he learns to walk, and so many times he falls. Then, slowly and slowly, he picks himself up and learns to run, and does not fall. This whole process is essential before he can run.

Similarly, all these failures are part of our ultimate success. They should be a source of strength to us, provided we continue with our "failures," we continue giving our time to meditation, and do not become disgusted and leave meditation. We should go on making attempt after attempt—that is what it means.

Great Master used to say, "If you can't bring your success to me, bring your failures." It means, assure me that you have at least been giving your time to meditation. Whether you have achieved any results or not is a different question, but you bring me at least your failures, because that means you have been attempting to meditate, you have been doing your best. And if you haven't noticed any results, that is entirely for Him to see about. We should do our best. Whether we succeed or fail in meditation is a different thing.

333 **Q.** If one is sitting down for a long time but not necessarily concentrating, and a leg falls asleep or feels painful just from sitting for a long time, is this the same thing that happens in the withdrawal of consciousness from the body? Is that the same, or is there a difference?

A. Sister, it can't be the same. It's not so easy to withdraw the consciousness to the eye center. We have to pass through so many stages before we learn to concentrate and be in touch with the Divine Melody within. First, the mind refuses to sit; you have to force the mind to sit, you have to create that habit in the mind to sit. Then if you succeed in that, sleep overpowers you; and then sometimes there is so much uneasiness in the body that you feel like running out of the room.

These are all steps towards progress. You have to pass through all these stages before you can concentrate and be one with the Sound. You can't just say that right from the first day you will be able to concentrate and be one with the Sound. It's a constant struggle with the mind, and every step is a step forward.

334 Q. If a man sits for three hours in meditation and at the end of that time he finds that his mind has not concentrated for a single second, will that time be taken by the Lord as sitting in meditation?

A. If on that day he has been able to achieve one second of concentration, the second day with that fight he will be able to achieve two seconds, the third day he may achieve ten seconds, and the fourth day he may be able to achieve half an hour. But if on the very first day he thinks, "Because I couldn't succeed for even one second, I'm not going to sit tomorrow," he will never be able to achieve anything. So every step is progress forward.

Naturally it will be only a degree of success, but you can't just skip all that and come to complete success at once. You have to pass through those phases. When you try to learn cycling, how much difficulty you have to face! You can't even walk on the road along with the cycle, what to say of riding it, and then you fall along with the cycle. There are so many stages to cross before you're so expert that you can even ride the cycle without hands. You can't ride the cycle without hands the very first day. So you have to practice meditation every day, and ultimately you succeed.

335 Q. Last night I went for a walk by myself, and I was trying to repeat the holy names constantly while walking. Perhaps I was walking and doing simran for about forty minutes. Then I returned to my room and I did bhajan for perhaps twenty minutes. Now would this be an hour of meditation or twenty minutes of meditation? To qualify as the practice of meditation, should I have been in my room with my eyes closed for the whole hour?

A. I said whatever time you devote to your meditation is to your credit in one way or another.

Whatever time you devote to meditation, to some extent, is to your credit. It is saving you from worldly thoughts, it is keeping your mind in the right direction and giving you its effect, and it will be to your credit.

Q. You don't have to sit down then with your eyes closed and close the door of the room?

A. It is comparative; there is a degree of advantage. Naturally the advantage you get while sitting in meditation is much greater, but you can't always sit. You also want to walk, so make the best use of that time also if you can.

336 **Q.** Maharaj Ji, it has been said that a great deal of our supposed meditation is only practicing meditation. At what point can we feel that our efforts are really meditation?

A. Sister, whether you are knocking very softly at the door, whether you are knocking very hard at the door, or whether you are frightened to knock and are only shouting, you are at the door, and you want the door to be opened to you. Even if we are nervous to knock, our intention is that the door should open and we should get admission. All efforts are there. Everybody has a different approach, but everybody who is on the Path wants the door to be opened. When we are sitting in meditation, whether we are knocking or whether we are too nervous to knock, we want the door to be opened. That is why we are giving time to meditation.

337 **Q.** Master, I've heard it said that in the beginning we can do too much meditation, that a long period of meditation would stir up old seeds that you couldn't handle.

A. The problem, brother, is only that sometimes we try to give a very long time to meditation, and when we don't get apparent results from it, we become frustrated and leave meditation altogether. That is why we are always warned that we should try to give that particular time of two to three hours for meditation and not worry much about progress. Then there's no frustration or reaction over the time spent in meditation.

If we enjoy meditation within ourselves, we can give more time to it. It is all right. But the mind shouldn't revolt. Sometimes it's filled with love and devotion; it wants to give a lot of time. At other times it feels blank and absolutely void; it doesn't want to sit at all. That is not right. Meditation should become a habit, a part of our daily routine, and we should be regular and punctual as far as possible. Then we won't feel frustrated.

338 **Q.** Is it ever possible for a disciple to try and meditate too much?

A. I don't know what you mean by too much. "Too much" is comparative. You may call half an hour too much, or you may call four or five hours very little.

Generally we are advised that while continuing

our daily routine, our activities in life, we should try to devote a couple of hours or two and a half hours to meditation. That is the general pattern. But if you enjoy the bliss within and you have more spare time to give, there's no harm in giving more time. It's always to your advantage.

Those people, however, who fight with themselves to give much more time than two and a half hours to begin with, and don't find progress to their satisfaction, often leave giving even half an hour. It should never be that way. If you continue giving the proper time regularly, you will be able to keep to that time. Then slowly and slowly you will go on making progress, and you may be able to devote more and more time as the bliss grows within. That is why we are generally advised to meditate for about one tenth of our time, which is two and a half hours.

This does not mean that from the very day of initiation you must start sitting that long at one stretch, because the mind may rebel. We're not in the habit of sitting still in a room for even ten minutes. Nor are we in the habit of closing ourselves in a room for an hour or so, let alone sitting quietly.

So we are advised, depending upon the individual, that we can start with half an hour and slowly and slowly try to increase our time. You can have two sittings, you can have three sittings, to begin with, and then try to increase your first sitting so that eventually you are giving two hours and thirty minutes at a stretch in one sitting. If you enjoy the bliss within, if you're fortunate enough to be at peace in that bliss within, then naturally you would like to enjoy it more and more; of course, keeping up your other activities in life.

339 **Q.** Will more meditation enable us to make quicker progress?

A. Some people make progress even with a little time. Some people may not be able to make apparent progress even with much more time. It depends upon the individual's load of karmas. We're not conscious of the load of karmas we have collected in past lives and so we do not know how much has to be cleared before we see our progress. For example, you are sitting on one side of a wall and you are boring from this side, trying to make a hole to the other side, but you don't know how thick the wall is. It may be one inch thick, it may be two feet, it may be three feet, or it may be just a little curtain. The thickness of the wall depends upon our karmas. Unless the hole is drilled all the way through, you won't be able to see any light from the other side of the wall. Everybody has an individual thickness of karmas through which he has to pierce with meditation. You can't fix any time limit, that since this person has given four hours a day he should make more progress, or that person has given only half an hour, he should make less progress—because you don't know the thickness of the wall that you have to pierce.

340 **Q.** Master, in the United States I've heard a lot of discussion between disciples about whether or not they should do more than two and a half hours of meditation a day. Some say their worldly work and family obligations are so strong they have enough time to do just their two and a half. Other people say they could do more, and someone said that if you don't do more than two and a half hours a day, that you won't reach the Radiant Form in this life.

A. Brother, generally we are advised to give two and a half hours, because we have to give one tenth of our time. That is the general, normal advice. But if one is fortunate enough, and his circumstances permit him to give more time, naturally he would like to give more time. But if at least this much time is given, it is enough because then automatically you will increase your time when you feel the pull from within, when you experience that bliss within.

When you fall in love with somebody, you automatically want to remain in the company of that person, but before falling in love, you don't plan to spend much time in the company of that person. Similarly, when you fall in love with meditation and you feel peace and bliss within, then whatever little time you can manage, you would at once like to attend to meditation, because you want to be there in that peace, in that bliss. It will increase by itself—you don't have to put forth an effort then at all.

341 Q. Is it possible that although someone is steadfast on the Path, attending to their meditation, that due to their heavy load of karma they're not conscious of any progress whatsoever during their whole lifetime, but then at the time of death they have actually made enough progress to not have to come back, but never to have realized it before that time?

A. Well, rother, if there is a wall ten feet in width and you start making a hole from one side, a man sitting on the other side does not know how deep you have been able to make the hole until the last brick is pierced. Then he knows how much progress you have made. Even if the hole has gone nine feet through the wall, still the man sitting on the other side doesn't know till the last layer is broken. In the same way, with whatever time we give to meditation, we are definitely making progress, but we do not know how thick the wall of karmas are that we have to pierce through. Not a single moment of meditation goes waste. It is taking care of thousands and thousands of karmas which we have been committing in our past lives.

And as far as coming back to this world is concerned, it's not so much your spiritual progress which determines that, but your attachments. If you are not attached to this creation, if you are not attached to people in this world, although you have not made much progress within spiritually, you may not come back to this world at all. On the other hand, even if you have made spiritual progress, but there are certain strong attachments left in you—your mind has made certain grooves which you cannot get rid of—those attachments can definitely pull you back to this creation again. Then when you come back to this world, again you will make progress and get rid of those attachments through meditation, and you can go back Home. Whatever progress you have made does not go to waste when you leave the body. In the next birth you will just pick up from where you left off.

So actually, it is our attachments which are pulling us back to this creation. Meditation is the only way to detach ourselves from all these attachments. With the help of meditation, we are able to detach ourselves from all these bondages in this world by attaching our mind to the Shabd and Nam, to the Light and Sound within, which pulls us to its own level.

342 Q. Are we usually conscious of our strongest attachments, or are they sometimes so subtle that even if we're as honest as possible within ourselves we still don't really know how attached we are to something?

A. There are many types of attachments. Some attachments fade out after some time, and they don't leave any mark on your mind. There are other attachments which go with you right till the end of your life. You can't get rid of them, and even if you try to forget, they remain in your subconscious mind, and they spring up whenever they get the chance.

Suppose a person has a strong desire to become rich, but he has been able intellectually to convince himself, "I don't need so much money. What would I do with it? Why am I bothering about it?" But still the desire to become rich remains in his consciousness, and he can't get rid of the idea. That impression remains on his mind, and at the time of his death, it may be there before him, and it can pull him back to the riches of this world.

This is just a crude way of explaining, but certainly in this way, sometimes attachments which you can't get rid of remain in your subconscious. Our desires are attachments. When you can't fulfill certain desires, slowly and slowly they make a groove on the mind, and after death, they may pull you back to this creation.

343 Q. So is it a good idea, then, to try and go with your desires, and if you want something, to let yourself have it?

A. No. It doesn't mean that by fulfilling a desire you have been able to get rid of that desire. By fulfilling it, you have created karma; for that also you have to pay. Moreover, if you satisfy one desire, the mind will bring up many more. And once you have sown a seed, you may have to come back to the world to reap its fruit.

If there's only one desire and you don't stoop to its level of fulfillment, there's a possibility that you can get rid of it by meditation, that it will fade out in time. But if you have already fulfilled a desire and sown the seed of further karma, then it is not in your hand not to reap the results of that seed. There are many desires that sometimes we feel are very strong in us, but the next moment they just become meaningless.

344 **Q.** Maharaj Ji, how can you become detached if you don't make progress within? I thought that's the only way you can become detached.

A. Of course, by your meditating. Visible results are not there within, but the meditation which you are doing is detaching you from this world. These attachments become meaningless to you when you are meditating. You have a sense of detachment even without any visible progress within.

345 **Q.** Master, if you feel in meditation that you're not making any progress but yet in life you feel that there is a higher power helping you, can you look forward to that, or must you just ignore it?

A. Well, brother, Master's protecting hand is always there, whether you ignore it or accept it. By attending to meditation, even if we don't feel any progress within, we will definitely feel the effect of meditation in our life. Progress we may not see within, but we will feel the effect of meditation in our nature, in our dealings with people, in the way our whole attitude towards life changes. We should not feel much concerned about progress, because progress is always there. The effect of meditation can never be removed, and nobody can escape that effect.

346 Q. Master, why do so many of us come here—I'll speak for myself—why do I come here and why do I struggle with meditation day after day, and yet I feel so empty of love and devotion?

A. Because we analyze ourselves too much, or our ideal seems to be very high, or we want to know that we are in love. We want to be sure that we are in love, so we're always trying to analyze whether we are really in love or not. Without that pull from within, how can anybody come here?

But then it depends upon the seed: whether it has just been sown in the ground, or it has sprouted, or it has taken roots, or it has become a tree. But the seed is the same. Some seeds have become trees, some seeds are still in the ground fighting to come out of the earth; but the seed has to sprout.

347 Q. Why does meditation get harder instead of easier? At first you can do two and a half hours when you start, but it seems to get more and more difficult. Initiates, when new, seem to do better than those who have struggled for a long time. Many satsangis find meditation increasingly difficult.

A. That is what they feel, that it is becoming increasingly difficult, because they become so anxious to achieve what they want to achieve, that when they don't achieve it, they think their meditation is becoming difficult. Actually, it is becoming easier and easier. The very fact that they feel it is becoming difficult is because of the longing, the desire in their heart and their mind to go back to the Lord. And that is His love. More longing and love is coming in them, and they're becoming more anxious and more desperate to go back to Him. They're achieving the result of meditation without their even realizing it. For the devotion, the love, and the earnestness that is coming in us every day to go back to the Father paves our way ahead.

We had faults even before coming to the Path, but now we have become conscious of our faults and they appear magnified, or they have become clearer to us since we are on the Path. This also may make us feel that things are becoming harder. Before, we used to take pride in those very weaknesses; we never thought that they were weaknesses. But now we realize what they are, we become conscious of those weaknesses—not that we are falling, we are coming up, and we will get rid of them, too.

348 Q. Maharaj Ji, I asked a satsangi once about what seemed to be an increase or an intensification of the negative emotions occurring along with increased concentration, and he said that it's more like they have not increased, just your awareness of their existence has become—

A. When you're on the Path and meditating, you don't become worse than before; you become more aware of your weaknesses. I often give an example also: you are in a closed room and it's absolutely dark; a little ray of light comes from the ventilator and suddenly you can see so much in the room. You see dust particles and so many things that are moving about. But until that ray of light came, you were not conscious of all that was in that room. So with meditation, that ray of light comes in us, and those very things of which we used to feel proud, which we blindly thought were achievements, now we feel ashamed of them.

It doesn't mean that we have fallen or we have become worse by meditation. We have just become conscious of those weaknesses. And when you become conscious of them, naturally you are ashamed of them, and that makes you want to get rid of them.

349 Q. Maharaj Ji, some satsangis attend to their meditation regularly and with full time but over the years seem to make very little progress. How can they overcome the discouragement that naturally occurs as a result.

A. You mean, how should they overcome their discouragement? By meditation. When we are discouraged, it means we need more effort in meditation. We shouldn't worry much about progress or anything. We should go on giving our time to meditation, and attend to meditation with an absolutely relaxed mind, without any tension, without any excitement, and progress automatically goes on.

Discouragement can be interpreted in another way, too. When you have been able to build up love and devotion for the Father and you have not been able to meet the Father, you can't call that feeling, discouragement. You are discouraged if you're not satisfied with your love and devotion and you don't want this love and devotion. But you don't want to lose that love and devotion which you have been able to build for the Father, and by meditation, you are able to build up that love and devotion even more within yourself. You feel the separation from the Father, and you are all the time thinking about the Father, and at no cost would you like to get rid of that. So it's not a question of discouragement at all.

A lover is never discouraged! It means there is some deficiency in our love. A lover is never discouraged because he's in love with the Being, and he's concerned only with his love. He's never discouraged that he has not been able to meet the Beloved, if it's real love.

350 Q. Maharaj Ji, we're told that we're supposed to be patient on this Path, but how do you reconcile patience with longing?

A. It is the same question in another way. I think we have a lot of patience. Right from the beginning of the creation we have been separated from the Father. Is that not the height of patience? We have no alternative but to have patience, because nothing is in our hands. If it were in our hands, we wouldn't remain separated from the Father. Guru Nanak says: "If it were in my hands to come back to You, do You think I would keep myself separated from You? I weep and cry in separation because it's not in my hands, it is in Your hands." So when it is in His hands, then the question of impatience doesn't arise. Then all that we need is patience and more patience, because it is not in our hands. We can only put forth an effort and do our best, and then leave everything to Him.

351 Q. There's an emphasis on patience on the Path, and also there seems to be an emphasis on a kind of urgency, that we should really work and get to the eye center. How can we reconcile those two?

A. Urgency means that we should attend to meditation. Patience means we should wait for the results with patience.

352 **Q.** Master, we wait so long to come to the Dera, then when we're here we spend a lot of time waiting to see you, and during the whole time we're waiting in our meditation; and the Master is always waiting at the third eye for us. Why is there all this waiting?

A. Why all this waiting? Because we are separated. We are separated from our focus and we are not at the door of our house. The Master is there at the door of our house, and we are waiting to go to the door. Let us go to the door of the house, then there is no more waiting.

353 **Q.** I read, I believe it was in *Light on Sant Mat,* that you said that the best prayer that a disciple could offer would be to help him to be able to accept whatever came his way as the Will of the Lord. Would a disciple be wrong, then, in praying earnestly to be able to be merged in the Master, or should he try and be more patient and wait?

A. I can tell you one thing: just attend to your meditation. There's no other way, there's no other short cut. By attending to meditation you are automatically progressing towards your destination, and you will become another being and lose your identity. Meditation is the only remedy. There's no other way to lose your identity. When there is so much rust on a knife, the only way to remove it is to rub the knife against the sandstone. Otherwise, the rust won't go, the knife won't shine. Mere talk won't solve your problem; intellectual discussion won't lead you anywhere. The main thing is practice.

The Lord gives us hunger; the more we attend to meditation, the more hungry we become. When we become hungry, He provides us with food. As Christ said, the harvest is ready. The harvest is always ready, but we have to lift our consciousness to that level where we can collect that harvest.[5]

> **Q.** Then it seems like it boils down to just wanting the desire to sit and serve. Is that wrong to ask for that? Just to be able to want to want to sit?

A. Just change your way of life according to the teachings and attend to meditation. That is all that is required. From meditation, love will come, submission will come, humility will come. Everything will come.

LOVE IS HIS GIFT

354 **Q.** Master, we hear sometimes that if the disciple stills the mind, he must see Light inside. What I want to know is, does a disciple who goes into meditation and still doesn't see any Light, require a detached attitude or should he be desirous to go inside?

A. I think we should go on attending to our meditation. When He gives, we will receive. He is more anxious to give than we are anxious to receive, but we should attend to our meditation. He doesn't withhold what we want if we are attending to meditation, because He has created that desire in us to meditate.

He wouldn't create that desire in us to meditate if He were not anxious to give to us. He's anxious to give to us, so we should go on attending to our meditation. That shows He is very desirous to pull us to His own level. Otherwise He wouldn't put that instinct in us to meditate. He wouldn't give us the facilities and opportunities and environments to meditate, if He were not anxious to pull us out of the creation.

Guru Arjan Dev says, "The One who has sent you to this creation, He is calling you. He is calling, 'Come with me. Let's go back to the Father.' " Only they will hear the call who have to go back to the Father. Other people won't hear the call at all. So when He calls, we will hear the call. When we are hearing the call, it means He is calling us. He is anxious to give if He has created that desire in us to meditate, and we should make use of that desire.

355 **Q.** What if you don't get very far in meditation? Then when you die, does that mean you'll go into darkness?

A. Well, if you are in darkness now, then what else can you expect after death? But then, as we discussed, we can always depend upon His grace. If the student is very obedient in the class, and very disciplined, the professor is always anxious to help him, with one excuse or another. If we are not intelligent enough to secure that high standard of marking, let us be at least disciplined and good and obedient so that we can invoke His grace to get through. But the One who has pulled us to the Path, the One who is pushing us on the Path, He doesn't forget us after death.

356 **Q.** This may sound a little silly, but what happens when you give a blessing, not necessarily making something parshad, but a shawl or robe or anything?

A. Just attend to your meditation. That purifies the mind, that does everything. You can't find any short cut by wearing that blessed shawl or using that mat—nothing. Meditation makes everything blessed, and there cannot be a better parshad than the initiation which a disciple gets. That is why Christ said that it's a new birth.[1] Just as a child grows under the care and protection of the parents after birth, similarly the disciple also grows under the care and protection of the Master. That's a new birth for that disciple, and that is real parshad, real grace.

357 Q. Master, Baba Ji wrote in one of his letters that one does not get purified by a hundred years of bhajan so much as by a moment of intense yearning. Does that mean then—

A. Baba Ji means to say that we must attend to our meditation with love and devotion for the Father. There must be love and devotion for the Father or for the Master, which means that we are attending to meditation because our Master wants us to attend to meditation, and we are obeying him because we love him. That type of meditation is required. Mechanical meditation without devotion does not give us much results. But just by attending to meditation, the love will grow, the longing will grow. So that meditation will eventually give us the intense yearning that Baba Ji is talking about.

358 Q. I've read in the books that simran and bhajan doesn't really do too much good unless we have an attitude of submission and love and devotion and faith. On the other hand if we ask Master, "I don't have any of this love and submission, what can I do? My meditation doesn't seem to be producing any results," the only answer usually is simran and bhajan, and so this is kind of a paradox.

A. Is there any alternative to bhajan and simran? Why do you ask for one when you don't see anything except bhajan and simran? Master of course will give you the advice to do bhajan and simran, but you will not follow the advice unless there is something within you that is forcing you to follow the advice. You will take credit that you have followed Master's advice and you are sitting in meditation, but there is something in you which is forcing you to follow the advice and is making you sit in meditation. That part you ignore. You'll feel miserable if you won't give your time to meditation. You will not feel that you are true to yourself if you don't devote time to meditation. There is something within you which you are not conscious of which is forcing you to follow that advice.

Meditation always does good. Sincere effort in meditation will also create that submission, it will create that love.

359 Q. Then we have to do one of two things: either submit to the Master or do bhajan and simran.

A. Eliminating your own self and becoming another being is submission, is surrendering. You have no will of your own then. You have surrendered your will to the Will of the Master. If he says bhajan and simran, then why do you bring in your mind to think otherwise? Automatically bhajan and simran will give you love and devotion. That is submission. And if he advises you to do bhajan and simran, he will also create that atmosphere in you for bhajan and simran, he will also create that pull in you for bhajan and simran, and he will also make you sit for bhajan and simran.

There's no other answer. There's no short cut. Whether the answer to your question is in six pages or in a book or in one line, the answer is the same: bhajan and simran! It depends upon how much time you want to take to understand that answer—whether by reading the whole book or by understanding only one or two words. It depends upon your approach.

360 Q. On this level here, on the earth level, how do we develop love for the Lord?

A. Well, without developing love for the Lord, nobody can reach the third eye. Unless we feel the pull of the Lord from within, we won't even think of reaching the third eye. He creates the desire, He creates the love. He is the One who is pulling us from within. He is instigating us to come to the third eye. He is giving us the facilities, the opportunities, the right atmosphere, and so many good environments, just for us to come to Him, and to create that desire in us to come to the third eye. He is the One who's doing all this drama from within. By our own effort, we will never even think about the Father. The mind is so fond of worldly pleasures and so attached to the senses that it will never think about the Father unless He starts pulling from within.

361 Q. Maharaj Ji, a great many of the Saints who wrote mystical poetry speak about the longing for the Lord in the early parts of their works, it seems, and then later they speak of the realization of the Lord, and they seem to just be on fire with that longing. I was just wondering, how does that, where does that come from? Is that strictly just a gift from the Lord, that longing?

A. It is a gift from the Lord. You can't create it. He creates His own longing, the longing for Himself. I don't think there is any way to create that longing at all. He is the One who created that yearning and longing within the Saints. Meditation strengthens that longing and helps us to rise to the level where we can experience that longing, and ultimately merge into that Being.

362 Q. Does the seed of love grow independently of anything we can do except simran and bhajan?

A. To be very frank, we can't do anything at all. When love comes, it just comes from within. The Lord may have His own ways and means to create that feeling within us, but it comes from within. All that we can do is to attend to meditation and leave it to His grace.

363 Q. Maharaj Ji, I know that the disciple must struggle to learn to develop the proper love for the Master. Can you speak about the nature of the Master's love for the disciple?

A. Master's love for the disciple? The disciple only thinks that he loves the Master. Actually, it is the Master who creates that love in him. We only think that we worship the Father. Actually, He is the One who is pulling us from within to make us worship Him. He is the One who is behind the screen, and the string is absolutely in His hands. He makes us dance in His love and devotion, and we are just puppets. So we take pleasure of course, and pride too, sometimes, that we love the Master, that we love the Father. Actually, He is responsible for it rather than we.

364 Q. Master, if we have no love and we have no devotion and we have no desire to meditate, how do we come to the Master?

A. If we had no devotion, no desire for meditation, we would not have come to the Path at all. The One who has pulled us to the Path will also give us all those things. He has not forgotten us after pulling us to the Path. He is still there within us.

365 Q. When we are attending to meditation, can it be a problem to feel that we are putting in an effort in meditation, in that we are feeding our own ego? In other words, who makes the effort in meditation? Is it really we or is it the Master who is actually doing the meditation?

A. Well, from a higher point of view it is all the Lord's grace that we are attending to meditation. But here, at this level, we feel as though we are putting in effort to achieve our object. He's the One who is pulling us from within. He's the One who is creating that desire in us to meditate. He's the One who is giving us that atmosphere and those circumstances and environments in which we can build our meditation. He worships Himself in us.

So you can say, "I am doing the meditation," provided you are doing it. But when you really do it, then you won't say, "I am doing it." "I" only comes when we don't do it. When we truly meditate, then "I" just disappears. Then we realize His grace, that but for Him how could we ever think or even attend to it. Then there is no "I," there is nothing but gratefulness—everything in gratitude. Then we know our insignificance. The more we attend to our meditation, the nearer we are to the goal, the more we realize our insignificance.

366 Q. Why doesn't the Master just take us up? Why do we have to go through all this meditation?

A. How do you know the Master is not taking you up? Do you think your meditation is taking you up? Nobody's meditation is taking him up to the Father. It's absolutely wrong. It's only the Lord and the Master who are uprooting us from here and taking us to that level. If anybody says, "I can reach back to the Father by my effort, by my meditation," he's wrong.

I try to explain every day that the Lord Himself creates His own love and desire within us. But for that seed of His love and devotion which He sows within us, we would never think about the Father. He sows that seed. Then He gives us those environments, that atmosphere, the circumstances in which our love and devotion in the Father are being strengthened. Then we come to know about the technique and the Path which takes us back to the Father, and we meet the Guide who can lead us back to Him.

Everything the Lord is doing Himself. What are we doing? Leaving all these things to one's own effort, one could never go back to the Father. The question of going back wouldn't ever arise. One could never even think about the Father. So it is not the meditation which is taking us back to the Father. It is the Father Himself, through the Master, who is taking us back to the Father.

You read St. John where Christ says that there was a man who was with God, who came from God, whose name was John the Baptist. First he explains the darkness within, that there is a Light within every one of us, but due to that darkness, we do not comprehend that Light. That is the condition of every one of us. And how do we eliminate that darkness? Christ says there was a man sent by God, and at that time it was John the Baptist. He sent somebody from His level to our level to tell us how to eliminate that veil of darkness and how to see that Light which is within every one of us.[2] Unless that man is sent to our level, unless he tells us how to eliminate that darkness, how can we see that Light? So what have we done?

When you fall in love with somebody, you automatically run after that person. But who makes you fall in love? You say, "I don't know, I have just fallen in love." You never calculate to fall in love. After falling in love, running after the beloved becomes natural. You don't have to put forth an effort to run after the beloved, neither did you have to put forth an effort to fall in love. There's something within you which prompted you to love that person. You found yourself helplessly in love, and now there is something within you which is making you run after the person. What are *you* doing? If you want to take the credit that you are running after the beloved, you are wrong. But for that love, you would never run after the beloved.

So if we are meditating, there is something within us which is urging us to meditate. There is something within us which is giving us that atmosphere, that environment, those circumstances, and creating that yearning, that feeling of separation. As Christ said, blessed are those who mourn for the Father.[3] The Father creates that feeling of separation in us, and when we feel that separation, we long to become one with Him.

Who makes us yearn? It's not our meditation. It is the Father Himself. He uproots us from here and takes us to His own level. Practically, we do nothing. You can take credit that you sit for two hours or three hours, but there is something which makes you sit. It's not you. Left to you, you would never even sit for five minutes. So if you see this from the higher point of view, it's definitely the Father who is pulling us up to His own level. It's not our efforts at all.

367 Q. Maharaj Ji, Dr. Johnson, I think mentioned in *The Path of the Masters* that there might be a Golden Age coming up. Is there any hope?

A. Sister, don't you think this is a Golden Age when we are on the Path, we are meditating, and we are doing our best to go back to the Father and lose our own identity? Isn't this a Golden Age?

REFERENCES

1

Teachings of the Saints

[1] John 6:38.

See also John 5:37—And the Father himself, which hath sent me, hath borne witness of me.

John 12:49—For I have not spoken of myself; but the Father which sent me, he gave me a commandment, what I should say, and what I should speak.

John 14:24—The word which ye hear is not mine, but the Father's which sent me.

[2] Adi Granth, *Rag Suhi*, *M.* 5, p. 749.

[3] *Namdev ki Hindi Padavali*, poem 92.

[4] 2 Cor. 6:16.

[5] 1 Cor. 3:16–17.

[6] Adi Granth, *Rag Suhi*, *M.* 3, p. 754.

[7] Ibid., *Rag Prabhati*, *M.* 3, p. 1346.

[8] John 10:34.

On the value of the human form:

Matt. 6:26—Behold the fowls of the air....—Are ye not much better than they?

Matt. 10:31—Fear ye not therefore, ye are of more value than many sparrows.

Matt. 12:12—How much then is a man better than a sheep?

Gen. 1:26–27—And God said, Let us make man in our image, after our likeness....

So God created man in his own image, in the image of God created he him; male and female created he them.

[9] Soami Ji, *Sar Bachan* (Beas, Punjab: Radha Soami Satsang Beas, 1974), p. 127.

[10] Adi Granth, *Rag Gauri*, *M.* 5, p. 176.

[11] Ibid., *Rag Suhi*, *M.* 3, p. 753.

[12] In the Bible, the Word or Creative Power has also been called the Name. *See for example:*

John 20:31—But these [signs] are written, that ye might believe that Jesus is the Christ, the Son of God; and that believing ye might have life through his name.

John 1:12–13—But as many as received him, to them gave he power to become the sons of God, even to them that believe on his name: Which were born, not of blood, nor of the will of the flesh, nor of the will of man, but of God.

John 3:18—He that believeth on him is not condemned: but he that believeth not is condemned already, because he hath not believed in the name of the only begotten Son of God.

Rev. 22:4—And they shall see his face; and his name shall be in their foreheads.

Ps. 72:17—His name shall endure for ever.

Prov. 18:10—The name of the Lord is a strong tower: the righteous runneth into it, and is safe. (*Or:* is set on high.)

Isa. 56:5—Even unto them will I give in mine house and within my walls a place and a name better than of sons and of daughters: I will give them an everlasting name, that shall not be cut off.

Zech. 14:8–9—And it shall be in that day, that living waters shall go out from Jerusalem.... And the Lord shall be king over all the earth: in that day shall there be one Lord, and his name one.

[13] John 1:1–3.

[14] Soami Ji, *Sar Bachan*, p. 113.

[15] Ibid., p. 151.

[16] Adi Granth, *Rag Majh*, *M.* 5, p. 134.

[17] Gal. 6:7.

[18] John 8:34–35.

[19] Matt. 5:25–26.

Cf. Ps. 142:7—Bring my soul out of prison, that I may praise thy name.

Isa. 42:6–7—I the Lord have called [my servant]... To open the blind eyes, to bring out the prisoners from the prison, and them that sit in darkness out of the prison house.

[20] Matt. 4:17.

[21] John 4:23–24.

[22] Adi Granth, *Rag Basant*, *M.* 4, p. 1179.

[23] Matt. 7:7.

[24] Ibid.

[25] Adi Granth, *Rag Majh*, *M.* 3, p. 124.

[26] Matt. 6:22.

[27] Adi Granth, *Rag Sorath*, Namdev, p. 657.

[28] Soami Ji, *Sar Bachan*, p. 93.

[29] Adi Granth, *Rag Majh*, *M.* 3, p. 124.

[30] Ibid., *Rag Maru*, *M.* 3, p. 1046.

[31] Ibid., *Rag Gond*, M.5, p. 64.

[32] John 14:9, 11.

[33] Adi Granth, *Rag Bharon*, *M.* 5, p. 1141.

[34] John 14:6.

[35] Ibid., 9:5.

[36] Soami Ji, *Sar Bachan*, p. 6.

[37] Adi Granth, *Rag Maru Solhas*, *M.* 5, p. 1076.

[38] John 10:30.

[39] Ibid., 3:3, 5.

[40] Ibid., 3:6–7.

[41] Adi Granth, *Rag Ramkali*, *M.* 1, p. 940.

42 *Adi Granth, Var* of *Rag Bihagara*, *M.* 3, p. 550.

43 1 Cor. 15:31.

44 John 5:25, 28–29.

45 Matt. 11:5.

46 John 5:25.

47 Matt. 13:13.

48 Adi Granth, *Var* of *Rag Majh*, *M.* 2, p. 139.

49 Ibid., *Var* of *Rag Bihagara*, *M.* 3, p. 555.

50 Ibid., *Var* of *Rag Ramkali*, *M.* 3, p. 956.

51 Soami Ji, *Sar Bachan*, pp. 161 and 165.

52 Adi Granth, *Sri Rag*, M. 1, p. 21.

53 Ibid., *Rag Suhi*, *M.* 4, p. 775.

54 Ibid., *Rag Malar*, *M.* 3, p. 1276.

55 Ibid., *Rag Sorath*, *M.* 3, p. 604.

56 *Namdev Gatha*, poem 1365.

57 Adi Granth, *Rag Ramkali*, *M.* 1, p. 940.

58 Guru Amar Das in Adi Granth, *Var* of *Rag Bihagara*, *M.* 3, p. 554.

2

The Divine Design

1 John 1:1–3—In the beginning was the Word, and the Word was with God, and the Word was God.

The same was in the beginning with God.

All things were made by him; and without him was not any thing made that was made.

2 John 14:20—At that day ye shall know that I am in my Father, and ye in me, and I in you.

John 14:23—If a man love me, he will keep my words: and my Father will love him, and we will come unto him, and make our abode with him.

[3] John 10:5—And a stranger will they not follow, but will flee from him: for they know not the voice of strangers.

John 10:27—My sheep hear my voice, and I know them, and they follow me.

[4] John 3:17–18—For God sent not his Son into the world to condemn the world; but that the world through him might be saved.

He that believeth on him is not condemned: but he that believeth not is condemned already, because he hath not believed in the name of the only begotten Son of God.

[5] Matt. 6:30—Wherefore, if God so clothe the grass of the field, which today is, and tomorrow is cast into the oven, shall he not much more clothe you, O ye of little faith?

[6] Matt. 12:46–50—While he yet talked to the people, behold, his mother and his brethren stood without, desiring to speak with him.

Then one said unto him, Behold, thy mother and thy brethren stand without, desiring to speak with thee.

But he answered and said unto him that told him, Who is my mother? and who are my brethren?

And he stretched forth his hand toward his disciples, and said, Behold my mother and my brethren!

For whosoever shall do the will of my Father which is in heaven, the same is my brother, and sister, and mother.

[7] Matt. 12:31–32—Wherefore I say unto you, All manner of sin and blasphemy shall be forgiven unto men: but the blasphemy against the Holy Ghost shall not be forgiven unto men.

And whosoever speaketh a word against the Son of man, it shall be forgiven him: but whosoever speaketh against the Holy Ghost, it shall not be forgiven him, neither in this world, neither in the world to come.

[8] Maharaj Jagat Singh, *Spiritual Bouquet*, quote 35: "One day's negligence in bhajan retards the progress of the journey by one month."

[9] Matt. 12:31–32. *See* Note 7.

[10] John 8:28—Then said Jesus unto them, When ye have lifted up the Son of man, then shall ye know that I am he, and that I do nothing of myself; but as my Father hath taught me, I speak these things.

[11] Matt. 5:4.

3
Creating the Atmosphere

ESSENTIAL PREREQUISITES

[1] Matt. 7:24–27—Therefore whosoever heareth these sayings of mine, and doeth them, I will liken him unto a wise man, which built his house upon a rock:

And the rain descended, and the floods came, and the winds blew, and beat upon that house; and it fell not: for it was founded upon a rock.

And every one that heareth these sayings of mine, and doeth them not, shall be likened unto a foolish man, which built his house upon the sand:

And the rain descended, and the floods came, and the winds blew, and beat upon that house; and it fell and great was the fall of it.

[2] John 8:10-11—When Jesus had lifted up himself, and saw none but the woman, he said unto her, Woman, where are those thine accusers? hath no man condemned thee?

She said, No man, Lord. And Jesus said unto her, Neither do I condemn thee: go, and sin no more.

[3] Matt. 6:22.

[4] Rai Sahib Munshi Ram, *With the Three Masters*, Vol. 1, p. 111.

[5] John. 16:7—Nevertheless I tell you the truth; it is expedient for you that I go away: for if I go not away, the Comforter will not come unto you; but if I depart, I will send him unto you.

[6] John 14:4—And whither I go ye know, and the way ye know.

[7] John 8:28—Then said Jesus unto them, When ye have lifted up the Son of man, then shall ye know that I am he, and that I do nothing of myself; but as my Father hath taught me, I speak these things.

[8] Matt. 12:31-32. *See* Note 7, The Divine Design.

WAY OF LIFE

[1] Baba Jaimal Singh, *Spiritual Letters.*

4
Meditation

CONCENTRATION

[1] Matt. 7:7—Knock, and it shall be opened unto you.

DYING WHILE LIVING

[1] 1 Cor. 15:31.

[2] John 10:18—No man taketh it from me, but I lay it down of myself. I have power to lay it down, and I have power to take it again.

DHYAN—CONTEMPLATION

[1] John 16:7. *See* Note 5, Essential Prerequisites.

[2] John 10:16—And other sheep I have, which are not of this fold: them also I must bring, and they shall hear my voice; and there shall be one fold, and one shepherd.

[3] Matt. 6:22.

[4] Matt. 17:5-6—behold, a bright cloud overshadowed them: and behold a voice out of the cloud, which said, This is my beloved Son, in whom I am well pleased; hear ye him.

And when the disciples heard it, they fell on their face, and were sore afraid.

[5] Exod. 3:2—And the angel of the Lord appeared unto him in flame of fire out of the midst of a bush: and he looked, and,

behold, the bush burned with fire, and the bush was not consumed.

Exod. 19:16, 18—And it came to pass on the third day in the morning, that there were thunders and lightnings, and a thick cloud upon the mount, and the voice of the trumpet exceeding loud.

And mount Sinai was altogether on a smoke, because the Lord descended upon it in fire: and the smoke thereof ascended as the smoke of a furnace, and the whole mount quaked greatly.

BHAJAN—LISTENING TO THE DIVINE SOUND

1 Maharaj Charan Singh, *Divine Light*, Letter 377: "What you say about hearing the bell Sound, loud and clear, on meeting this other man was, in fact, a warning to you from the Master to beware of the pitfall and to tell you that you were doing wrong in entertaining such desires."

2 Maharaj Sawan Singh, *Spiritual Gems*, letter 13: "If the nirat is not developed, no real progress can be made, even if you go on hearing the Sound all your life."

3 Baba Jaimal Singh, *Spiritual Letters*, letter 28: "When you sit in bhajan, whatever Sound you hear in the beginning, like that of the working of a mill or that of a railway engine, or the sound of fire in the oven *(tandoor)*, put your mind and surat (attention) into it.

INNER GUIDANCE

1 Matt. 10:28—And fear not them which kill the body, but are not able to kill the soul.

2 John 10: 4–5, 7–8, 10, 27—And when he putteth forth his own sheep, he goeth before them, and the sheep follow him: for they know his voice.

And a stranger will they not follow, but will flee from him: for they know not the voice of strangers.

Then said Jesus unto them again, Verily, verily, I say unto you, I am the door of the sheep.

All that ever came before me are thieves and robbers: but the sheep did not hear them.

The thief cometh not, but for to steal, and to kill, and to destroy: I am come that they might have life, and that they might have it more abundantly.

My sheep hear my voice, and I know them, and they follow me.

[3] Maharaj Sawan Singh, *Spiritual Gems*, letter 76: "What you have said about seeing the Radiant Form of Master Jesus is quite true. You will meet Him again when you go in, but you are to go much higher up and beyond Him. You should die daily, as you died on the day you saw the vision of Christ."

[4] John 14:2—In my Father's house are many mansions: if it were not so, I would have told you. I go to prepare a place for you.

John 14:20—At that day ye shall know that I am in my Father, and ye in me, and I in you.

THE EFFECT OF MEDITATION

[1] Matt. 5:14, 16—Ye are the light of the world. A city that is set on an hill cannot be hid.

Let your light so shine before men, that they may see your good works, and glorify your Father which is in heaven.

LOVE AND DEVOTION

[1] Matt. 5:4.

[2] Matt. 5:4.

[3] John 16:7. *See* Note 5, Essential Prerequisites.

[4] John 3:17. *See* Note 4, The Divine Design.

DIVINE GRACE

[1] Matt. 7:13–14—Enter ye in at the strait gate: for wide is the gate, and broad is the way, that leadeth to destruction, and many there be which go in thereat:

Because strait is the gate, and narrow is the way, which leadeth unto life, and few there be that find it.

2 Mark 10:17–22—And when he was gone forth into the way, there came one running, and kneeled to him, and asked him, Good Master, what shall I do that I may inherit eternal life?

And Jesus said unto him, Why callest thou me good? there is none good but one, that is, God.

Thou knowest the commandments, Do not commit adultery, Do not kill, Do not steal, Do not bear false witness, Defraud not, Honour thy father and mother.

And he answered and said unto him, Master, all these have I observed from my youth.

Then Jesus beholding him loved him, and said unto him, One thing thou lackest: go thy way, sell whatsoever thou hast, and give to the poor, and thou shalt have treasure in heaven: and come, take up the cross, and follow me.

And he was sad at that saying, and went away grieved: for he had great possessions.

See also Matt. 19:16–22; Luke 18:18–23.

3 Matt. 7:13–14. *See* Note 1.

4 Matt. 19:30—But many that are first shall be last; and the last shall be first.

Matt. 12:31–32. *See* Note 7, The Divine Design.

5 John 4:35—Say not ye, There are yet four months, and then cometh harvest? behold, I say unto you, Lift up your eyes, and look on the fields; for they are white already to harvest.

LOVE IS HIS GIFT

1 John 3:3—Verily, verily, I say unto thee, Except a man be born again, he cannot see the kingdom of God.

2 John 1:5–7—And the light shineth in darkness; and the darkness comprehended it not.

There was a man sent from God, whose name was John.

The same came for a witness, to bear witness of the Light, that all men through him might believe.

3 Matt. 5:4.

GLOSSARY

Adi Granth	Primal scripture. The Sacred scripture compiled chiefly by Guru Arjan, the fifth Guru in the line of succession to Guru Nanak, about the year 1604. The Granth Sahib consists of hymns of devotion to God. It includes devotional verses composed by Kabir, Namdev, Bhikhan, Trilochan, Sain, Ramanand, Farid and some other saints in addition to the hymns by Guru Nanak and Gurus of his line.
Asana	Yogic posture.
Baba Jaimal Singh	The founder of the Radha Soami Colony at Beas. He was born in July, 1839, in the Punjab village Ghoman, and left this world on December 29, 1903. He was a disciple of SOAMI JI MAHARAJ, and appointed MAHARAJ SAWAN SINGH as his successor.
Baba Ji	*See* BABA JAIMAL SINGH.
Bahadur	Brave; hero; champion; *see also* SARDAR BAHADUR JI.
Bhajan	Worship; prayer; listening for or to the Sound; meditation according to the instructions of the Master, including repetition (simran), contemplation (dhyan) and listening to the Sound (dhun).
Brahm	Lord of the second spiritual region; the power that creates and dissolves the phenomenal world.
Bulleh Shah	(1680–1758)—A Muslim Saint of the Punjab, disciple of Shah Inayat; lived and taught mainly at Lahore.
Bunk Nal	The passage between Sahansdal Kanwal and Trikuti, the first and second spiritual regions.
Chakra	Center, ganglion or plexus in the body.

Chaurasi	Eighty-four; the eighty-four lakh (84 hundred thousand) species into which the soul may incarnate; the wheel of transmigration of the soul.
Dadu	(1544–1603)—A saint of Rajputana well known for his boldness in defying the orthodox priests and in teaching Nam, the Word of God. He was born at Ahmedabad, north of Bombay, and taught chiefly at Jaipur and other centres in Rajputana. He was generally known as Dadu Dayal. It is said that the Mughal Emperor Akbar invited him to Fatehpur Sikri in 1584 and listened to his discourses.
Darshan	To gaze lovingly upon something, usually a holy person.
Dera	Camp or colony; here, Dera refers to DERA BABA JAIMAL SINGH, the Radha Soami Colony, which is situated near Beas, on the west bank of the River Beas, in District Amritsar, Punjab.
Dhyan	Contemplation; to visualize the form of the Master during meditation; to behold the Light or the Radiant Form of the Master inside.
Eye Center	The seat or source of attention in the body during the waking state; the disciple collects his attention in the eye center during meditation, and from here he goes to the higher regions of consciousness. Also *see* THIRD EYE.
First Stage	*See* SAHANSDAL KANWAL
Five Holy Names	The names of the rulers of the five spiritual regions. These names are given to the disciple by the Master at the time of initiation, and are used in the practice of simran (repetition).
Great Master	*See* SAWAN SINGH JI MAHARAJ.
Gunas	The three attributes or qualities:
satogum	harmony, purity;

rajogun	activity, action;
tamogun	inertia, darkness.
Guru Nanak	(1469–1539)—He was born at Talwandi near Lahore (now in Pakistan). His parents were KALU, the village accountant, and TRIPTA. Guru Nanak condemned the orthodox creed of the people with great vigour, and laid emphasis on the spiritual aspect of religion, and on love of God and man. He undertook four major tours to propagate his teachings. The following were his successors to the Mastership:
Guru Angad	(1504–1552)—Second in the line of succession.
Guru Amardas	(1479–1574)—Third
Guru Ram Das	(1534–1581)—Fourth
Guru Arjan Dev	(1563–1606)—Fifth
Guru Har Govind	(1595–1644)—Sixth
Guru Har Rai	(1630–1661)—Seventh
Guru Harkishan	(1656–1664)—Eighth
Guru Tegh Bahadur	(1621–1675)—Ninth
Guru Gobind Singh	(1666–1708)—Tenth
Gurumukh	Literally, one whose face is turned towards the Guru or Master; a perfect disciple.
Hafiz	(1325–1390)—One of the greatest of Persian poets and also an enlightened saint. He was born at Shiraz and spent his life there as a court poet. Hafiz is a pen name that means "one who can recite the Koran by heart." His real name was Shams-ud-Din Mohammed.
Hatha Yoga	A system of yoga consisting chiefly of physical postures (*asanas* and *mudras*) which are intended to keep the body fit and to influence mental currents.
Huzur	August presence; a term of respect used to address kings, holy men and high personages.
Huzur Maharaj Ji	*See* SAWAN SINGH JI MAHARAJ
Jagat Singh Ji Maharaj	*See* SARDAR BAHADUR JI.
Ji	Honorific showing respect or endearment.
Jot *or* Joyti	Light or flame; light of the first spiritual region.

Kabir Sahib (1398–1518)—A renowned Saint who lived in Benares, where he preached and practiced Surat Shabd Yoga. He condemned the external rituals and observances of Hindus and Muslims alike.

Kal Time or death; the Negative Power; the name given to the power that controls the physical, astral and causal worlds, which are all perishable. Kal will not let any soul leave his domain until that soul has accounted for the karmic debts incurred in the present as well as in numerous past lives.

Karma Action; the law of cause and effect; this is the universal law of justice under which we must pay for our misdeeds and receive the rewards for our good deeds; it is the law of merciless justice. There are three types of karmas:

pralabdh or *prarabdh*—that portion of our karma from past lives that determines the destiny of our present life;

kriyaman—new karma, which we are creating in our present life; part of this becomes pralabdh karma for future births, and the balance becomes sinchit karma;

sinchit or *sanchit*—our storehouse of karma, made up of kriyaman karma from many past lives; in each life, the balance of the kriyaman karma is placed in our storehouse, to be undergone in future births.

Koran Sacred scripture of the Muslims; contains the teachings of Prophet Mohammed.

Kriyaman *See* Karma.

Kundalini The coiled energy at the base of the spine; when aroused, it gives the practitioner miraculous powers. This practice is detrimental to spiritual progress and is shunned by satsangis.

Light When concentration is achieved in meditation, the disciple sees Light and hears

	Sound. By following the Light and Sound, he is eventually taken back to his Source, which is God. The inner Master takes his form from the Light and Sound. *See also* SHABD.
M.	Abbreviation for *mahala* (palace, mansion), used in the Adi Granth to identify which of the Gurus composed the peom in question. *M.* 1 is Guru Nanak; *M.* 2 is Guru Angad (the second Guru in the "house" of Nanak); *M.* 3 is Guru Amar Das; *M.* 4 is Guru Ram Das; *M.* 5 is Guru Arjan.
Maharaj Ji	A term of great respect used to address Saints and holy men. Maharaj literally means "great king".
Mat	Creed, teachings.
Maya	Illusion; deception; unreality; phenomenal universe; all that which is not eternal; it appears but is not. The veil of Illusion conceals the vision of God from our sight.
Mirabai	Sixteenth-century woman Saint of Rajasthan, well known for her songs of love and devotion.
Muin Ud Din Chishti	(1141–1236)—A renowned saint of medieval times who was born in Seistan, now in South Western Afghanistan. He was the disciple of Khwaja Usman Harwani of Nishapur who appointed him as his Caliph. He moved at an early age to Ajmer in Rajasthan where, it is said, he remained in meditation for seventeen years and then began to teach the practice of the Word. He had a very large following. Sheikh Farid, Nizamuddin Aulia and Amir Khusro belonged to his line.
Muni	A holy man; a sage who has taken vows of asceticism.
Nam	Name, the same as Shabd, Word or Logos; the Energy and creative power of the

	Supreme Creator. Nam, or the Word, is not actually a word but the Infinite Power that emanates continuously from the Supreme Being. By it the universe is sustained. At the same time, this power resides in every human being. *Also see* SHABD.
Namdev	(1270–1350)—Indian saint who was born in Maharashtra. He was a tailor and calico printer by profession. His songs known as *Abhangas* or "Songs Eternal" were collected in a book known as *Gatha*. He spent the later part of his life in the Punjab and died there in the village Ghuman (District Gurdaspur). His Guru's name was Visoba Khechar.
Nanak	*See* GURU NANAK.
Negative Power	*See* KAL.
Nirat	The faculty of the soul which sees the inner Light; the nirat is opened when one begins to see the inner worlds of Light and beauty.
Paltu	(1710–1780)—A famous Indian saint who lived at Ayodhya, U.P. most of his life. Born at Nanga at Nanga Jalalpur, District Faizabad U.P., he was a disciple of Govind Sahib. Noted for his bold and fearless exposition of the path to God-realization, he was burnt alive by the priests and orthodox people who resented his bold teachings.
Parshad	Something which is blessed, usually food.
Pralabdh *or* Prarabdh	*See* Karma.
Prana	Vital force; essence; vital air, the control and regulation of which is the basis of the system known as pranayam.
Pranayam	The yogic practice consisting of breathing in, holding the breath, then breathing out, and ultimately holding the breath at centers in the body for a long time.
Prasad *or* Prashad	*See* PARSHAD.

Radha Soami *or* Radha Swami	Lord of the soul.
Radiant Form	The inner form of the Master which is manifested from the Shabd and seen by the disciple in the inner regions beyond the eye center.
Rag	Musical scale. Almost every composition in the Adi Granth is assigned a particular *rag*, and is always sung to that tune.
Rishi	Sage or seer of ancient times.
Rumi *or* Maulana Rum	(1207–1273)—A well-known Muslim Saint, born at Balkh, Persia (now Afghanistan); he was a disciple of Shams-i-Tabriz, and the author of the *Masnavi*.
Sach Khand	The fifth spiritual region; the true or imperishable region.
Sahansdal Kanwal	The thousand-petalled lotus; a name of the first spiritual region.
Sahab *or* Sahib	Lord; honorable sir; a term of respect.
Sangat	Congregation.
Sanskaras	Impressions on the mind from karmas of past births; tendencies from past lives.
Sant Mat	Teachings of the Saints.
Sardar Bahadur Ji	Maharaj Jagat Singh (July 20, 1884—October 23, 1951) was a devoted disciple of MAHARAJ SAWAN SINGH, who appointed him his successor in 1948. Sardar Bahadur Ji was Satguru of the Radha Soami Satsang Beas from 1948 to 1951.
Saroop *or* Swaroop	Real form.
Satguru	True Master, perfect Master; a Master who has access to the fifth spiritual region, Sach Khand.
Sat Purush	God.
Satsang	Literally, true association; spiritual discourse; congregational meeting for the purpose of seeing the Master or hearing him speak; thinking about the Master and his teachings. Association with a Saint is external satsang,

	and association of the soul with Shabd is internal satsang; the highest form of satsang is to merge with Shabd.
Satsangi	One who has been initiated by a true Master; a disciple or associate of Truth. However, real satsangis are only those who faithfully perform the spiritual practice, follow the instructions of the Master and conduct themselves accordingly in their daily lives.
Sawan Singh Ji Maharaj	Usually referred to as the Great Master, he was the successor of BABA JAIMAL SINGH, and was born in village Jatana, near Mehmansinghwalla, District Ludhiana, Punjab, on July 20, 1858. He departed from this world on April 2, 1948.
Second Stage	*See* Trikuti.
Seva	Service.
Shabd	This is the Power that forms the very core of the teachings of the Masters. It is the spiritual Sound which the disciple, at the time of initiation, is taught to hear. This spiritual Sound, which also manifests as Light, is the Power that guides the disciple back to his Original Home. The inner Master is a manifestation of the Shabd. The Shabd has been called by many names—Nam, Dhun, Anahad Shabd, Bani, Nad, Kalam-i-Ilahi, Word, Logos, Holy Ghost, Audible Life Stream, Sound Current, and Music of the Spheres, to mention a few.
Shams-i-Tabriz *or* Shamas-i-Tabriz	(1206–1248)—Shams-ud-Din Muhammad Tabrizi, better known as Shams-i-Tabriz, a famous Muslim saint of Persia, was born in Tabriz, Iran. He was the Master of Maulana Rum who named his composition after the name of his master—'Diwan-i-Shams-i-Tabriz.' He was assassinated by religious fanatics.
Simran	Repetition of the Names according to the

	technique given by the Master at the time of initiation. *See also* FIVE HOLY NAMES.
Sinchit *or* Sanchit	*See* KARMA.
Soami Ji *or* Swami Ji	Seth Shiv Dayal Singh, the founder of the Radha Soami Faith. He was born at Agra, in August 1818; after seventeen years of deep meditation, he began to teach publicly and initiate, in 1861; he died in 1878.
Sound	*See* SHABD, *also* LIGHT.
Surat	The hearing faculty of the soul; the word is also used to mean soul, consciousness, inner attention.
Surat Shabd Yoga	The union of the soul with the Shabd.
Tamasic	Pertaining to darkness; ignorance; inertia; *see also* GUNAS.
Third Eye	Situated between the two eyebrows, the third eye is the seat or the headquarters of the mind and the soul in the human body. Esoterically, it is a microscopic aperture through which the soul enters the higher Spiritual Regions during deep meditation. Since the nine doors of the body (eyes, ears, nose, mouth, and the two lower apertures) lead outward and downward, while the Third Eye leads inward and upward to the higher worlds, it is also called the Tenth Door or Tenth Gate, and is referred to as the "single eye" in the Bible. (Matt. 6:22). Also see EYE CENTER.
Trikuti	Three prominences; a name for the second spiritual region; the source of the three gunas.
Tulsi Das	(1532–1623)—A famous North Indian saint who was contemporary of Akbar the Great Mughal. He was born at Kasia in U.P. in a very poor family. He was a disciple of Narhari Dass. His epic, *Ram Charit Manas* is even today, the most popular Hindi classic and he is regarded as one of the greatest medieval devotional poets of North India.

Tulsi Sahib	(1764–1845)—Well-known saint from Maharashtra, connected with the ruling family of Peshwas; left home at an early age, came to Uttar Pradesh and settled at Hathras, near Agra. *Ghat Ramayan* and *Ratan Sagar* are the two of his main compositions, besides many other smaller poems. The members of Soami Ji Maharaj's family were his disciples.
Universal Mind	The source of the mind, which is the second spiritual region.
Yoga	To unite; union.

INDEX TO DISCOURSES

PLEASE NOTE: Numbers denote PAGE numbers. Definitions of terms may be found in the Glossary (pp. 315-324).

INDEX TO QUESTIONS AND ANSWERS

PLEASE NOTE: Numbers denote QUESTION numbers. Definitions of terms may be found in the Glossary (pp. 315–324).

Numbers denote QUESTION numbers

Numbers denote QUESTION numbers

Numbers denote QUESTION numbers

Number denote QUESTION numbers

INFORMATION AND BOOKS ARE AVAILABLE FROM:

The Secretary
Radha Soami Satsang Beas
P.O. Dera Baba Jaimal Singh 143204
District Amritsar, Punjab, India

RADHA SOAMI BOOK DEPT.
P. O. Box 242
Gardena, California 90247

CANADA

Dr. J.Khanna, 5550 McMaster Road, Vancouver V6T IJ8, B.C.

Dr.Peter Grayson, 177, Division Street S.Kingsville, Ontario, N9Y IRI, Canada

U.S.A.

Mr. Roland G.de Vries, 10901 Mill Spring Drive, Nevada City, Calif. 95959

Dr. Gene Ivash, 4701 Shadow Lane, Austin, Texas 78731

Mr. Roy E.Ricks, 651 Davis Street, Melrose Park, III.60160

Mr. Henry F. Weekley, 2121 N.Ocean Blvd., Apt. 1108E, Boca Raton, Fla. 33431

MEXICO

Mr. Jorge Angel Santana, Cameta 2821, Jardines Del Bosque Guadalajara, Jalisco

SOUTH AMERICA

Dr. Gonzalo Vargas N.,P.O. Box 2666, Quito, Ecuador

Mr. Leopoldo Luks, Ave. Maracay, Urb. Las Palmas, Qta. Luksenburg, Caracas Venezuela

Mrs. Rajni B. Manglani, c/o Bhagwan's Store, 18 Water Street, Georgetown, Guyana

WEST INDIES

Mr. Thakurdas Chatlani, 2A Gittins Avenue, Maraval, Trinidad

Mr. Sean Finnegan, P.O.Box 2314, Port-au-Prince, Haiti

Mr. Bhagwandas Kessaram, c/o Kiddies Corner, Swan Street, Bridgetown, Barbados

ENGLAND
Mrs. F.E. Wood, c/o Lloyd's Bank, 20 North Street,
Leatherhead, Surrey

SWEDEN
Mr. Lennart Zachen Vintergatan, 15A I, 172 30 Sundbyberg

DENMARK
Ms. Inge Gregersen, Askevenget-15, 2830 Virum

HOLLAND
Mr. Jacob Hofstra Geulwijk 6, 3831 LM Leusden

WEST GERMANY
Mr. Rudolf Walberg, Falkenstr. 18, D-6232 Bad Soden/Taunus

AUSTRIA
Mr. Hansjorg Hammerer, Sezenweingasse 10, A-5020, Salzburg

SWITZERLAND
Mr. Olivier de Coulon, Rue de Centre, CH-1131 Tolochenaz

FRANCE
Count Pierre de Proyart, 7 Quai Voltaire, 75007 Paris

SPAIN
Mr. H.W. Balani, Balani's International, P.O. Box 486, Malaga

PORTUGAL
Mr. Alberto C. Ferreira, R. Machado dos Santos 20, 2775 Parede

GIBRALTAR
Mr. Sunder Mahtani, 5/5, Trafalgar House

ITALY
Mr. Ted Goodman, Via Garigliano 27, Rome 00198

GREECE
Dr. Constantine Siopoulos, Thrakis 7.145 61 Kifissia

CYPRUS
Mr. Hercules Achilleos, Kyriakou Matsi 18,
Pallouriotissa-T.K.9077, Nicosia

LOCAL ADDRESSES

WEST AFRICA

Mr. Krishin Vaswani, Vaan-Ahn Enterprises Ltd.,
P.O.Box 507 Monrovia, Liberia

Mr. Nanik N. Balani, Kewalram (Nig.) Ltd.,
P.O. Box 320, Lagos, Nigeria

Mr. J.O.K. Sekyi, P.O. Box 4615, Accra, Ghana

EAST AFRICA

Mr. Sylvester Kakooza, P.O.Box 31381, Kampala Uganda

Mr. Sohan Singh Bharj, P.O.Box 47036, Nairobi, Kenya

Mr. D.N. Pandit, K.Lands Limited P.O.Box 1000,
Dar-es-Salaam, Tanzania

Mr. David Bowskill, P.O.Box 11012, Chingola, Zambia

Mr. Vernon Lowrie, P.O.Box 690, Harare, Zimbabwe

SOUTH AFRICA

Mr. Sam Busa, P.O.Box 41355, Craighall Transvaal 2024

Mr. R.Attwell, P.O.Box 5702, Durban 4000

MASCARENE ISLANDS

Mr. D.S.Sumboo, 9, Bis Harris Street, Port Louis, Mauritius

ISRAEL

Mrs. H.Mandelbaum, P.O.Box 2815, Tel Aviv-61000

U.A.E.

Mr. Chander Bhatia, Shabnam Trading Corp.
P.O.Box 2296, Dubai

KUWAIT

Mr. & Mrs. Ghassan Alghanem, P.O.Box 25549, 13116, Safat, Kuwait

AFGHANISTAN

Mr. Manak Singh, c/o Manaco, P.O. Box 3163, Kabul

SRI LANKA

Mr. D.H. Jiwat, Geekay Ltd., 33 Bankshall Street, Colombo-11

NEW ZEALAND

Mr. Tony Waddicor, P.O.Box 5331, Wellesley St. P.O.,
Auckland 1

AUSTRALIA
Mrs. Janet Bland, P.O. Box 3, Oaklands Park,
South Australia 5046
Mr. A.J. Walker, 8445, Canning Highway, Melville
Western Australia 6156

INDONESIA
Mr. G.L. Nanwani Yayasan Radha Soami Satsang Beas,
JL.Kelinci Raya No. 32A, Jakarta-Pusat
Mr. Tarachand Chotrani, 51, Dji. Bubutan, P.O.Box 144,
Surabaya

SINGAPORE
Mr. Bhagwan Asnani, 1806 King's Mansion, Singapore-1543

MALAYSIA
Mr. N.Pal, c/o Muhibbah Travel Agency, Sdn.Bhd.,
46 Jalan Tanku Abdul Rahman, Kuala Lumpur01-07

THAILAND
Mr. Harmahinder Singh Sethi, Sawan Textiles Ltd.,
154 Serm Sin Kha, Sampheng, Bangkok-10100

HONG KONG
Mr. S.G. Dasani T.S.T. P.O.Box 96567 Kowloon

PHILIPPINES
Mr. Kay Sham, P.O.Box 2346 MCC, Makati, Metro Manila

JAPAN
Mr. L.H. Parwani, Radha Soami Satsang Beas,
2-18 Nakajimadori 1-Chome, Aotani, Fukiai-ku,
Kobe-651

* * * * * * *

FOR OTHER FOREIGN ORDERS WRITE TO :
Mr. Krishin Babani, Buona Casa Bldg., 2nd floor,
Sir P.M. Road, Fort Bombay-400 001, India

Addresses changed since this book was printed :

BOOKS ON THIS SCIENCE

Soami Ji Maharaj

1. *Sar Bachan*

Baba Jaimal Singh

2. *Spiritual Letters* (to Huzur Maharaj Sawan Singh : 1896-1903)

Huzur Maharaj Sawan Singh

3. *Discourses on Sant Mat*
4. *Philosophy of the Masters (Gurmat Sidhant),* 5 vols. (an encyclopedia on the teachings of the Saints)
5. *My Submission* (introduction to *Philosophy of the Masters)*
6. *Philosophy of the Masters (abridged)*
7. *Tales of the Mystic East* (as narrated in satsangs)
8. *Spiritual Gems* (letters : 1919-1948)
9. *The Dawn of Light* (letters : 1911-1934)

Sardar Bahadur Jagat Singh Maharaj

10. *The Science of the Soul* (discourses and letters : 1948-1951)

Maharaj Charan Singh

11. *Die to Live* (answers to questions on meditation)
12. *Teachings of the Saints* (first Chapter of *Die to Live)*
13. *Divine Light* (discourses and letters : 1959-1964)
14. *The Path* (first part of *Divine Light)*
15. *Light on Saint Matthew*
16. *Light on Sant Mat* (discourses and letters : 1952-1958)
17. *Quest for Light* (letters : 1965-1971)
18. *Light on Saint John*
19. *Spiritual Discourses*
20. *Spiritual Heritage* (from tape-recorded talks)
21. *The Master answers* (to audiences in America : 1964)
22. *Thus Saith the Master* (to audiences in America : 1970)
23. *Truth Eternal* (a discourse)

BOOKS ON THIS SCIENCE

Books about the Masters

1. *Call of the Great Master* – Diwan Daryai Lal Kapur
2. *The Living Master* – Katherine Wason
3. *With a Great Master in India* – Dr. Julian P. Johnson
4. *With the Three Masters,* 3 vols.– from the diary of Rai Sahib Munshi Ram
5. *Heaven on Earth*– Diwan Daryai Lal Kapur

Books on Sant Mat in general

1. *A Soul's Safari*– Netta Pfeifer
2. *In Search of the Way*– Flora E. Wood
3. *Kabir, The Great Mystic*–Isaac A. Ezekiel
4. *Liberation of the Soul*–J. Stanley White, Ph.D.
5. *Message Divine*–Shanti Sethi
6. *Mystic Bible*–Dr. Randolph Stone
7. *Mysticism, The Spiritual Path,* 2 vols. Prof. Lekh Raj Puri
8. *Radha Soami Teachings*–Prof. Lekh Raj Puri
9. *Ringing Radiance*–Sir Colin Garbett
10. *Sant Mat and the Bible*–Narain Das
11. *Sarmad, Jewish Saint of India*–Isaac A.Ezekiel
12. *Teachings of the Gurus*–Prof. Lekh Raj Puri
13. *The Inner Voice*–Colonel C.W. Sanders
14. *The Mystic Philosophy of Sant Mat*—Peter Fripp
15. *The Path of the Masters*–Dr. Julian P. Johnson
16. *Yoga and the Bible*–Joseph Leeming

Mystics of the East Series

1. *Saint Paltu*—Isaac A. Ezekiel
2. *Saint Namdev, His Life and Teachings*–J.R. Puri and V.K. Sethi
3. *Tulsi Sahib, Saint of Hathras*– J.R.Puri and V.K. Sethi
4. *Tukaram, Saint of Maharashtra*–C.Rajwade
5. *Dadu, The Compassionate Mystic*–K.N. Upadhyaya, Ph.D.
6. *Mira, The Divine Lover*–V.K. Sethi
7. *Guru Ravidas, Life and Teachings*–K.N. Upadhyaya, Ph.D.
8. *Guru Nanak, His Mystic Teachings*–J.R. Puri
9. *Kabir, The Weaver of God's Name*–V.K. Sethi
10. *Bhulleh Shah*–J.R. Puri and T.R. Shangari
11. *Dariya Sahib, Saint of Bihar*–K.N. Upadhyaya Ph.D.